E-Commerce

E-Commerce

Grace Silva

Larsen & Keller
www.larsen-keller.com

E-Commerce
Grace Silva
ISBN: 978-1-64172-364-0 (Hardback)

 Larsen & Keller

Published by Larsen and Keller Education,
5 Penn Plaza,
19th Floor,
New York, NY 10001, USA

Cataloging-in-Publication Data

E-commerce / Grace Silva.
   p. cm.
Includes bibliographical references and index.
ISBN 978-1-64172-364-0
1. Electronic commerce. 2. Commerce. 3. Business.
4. Information superhighway. I. Silva, Grace.
HF5548.32 .E36 2020
658.84--dc23

For more information regarding Larsen and Keller Education and its products, please visit the publisher's website www.larsen-keller.com

TABLE OF CONTENTS

PREFACE

It is with great pleasure that I present this book. It has been carefully written after numerous discussions with my peers and other practitioners of the field. I would like to take this opportunity to thank my family and friends who have been extremely supporting at every step in my life.

The utilization of online services and internet to buy and sell products is known as e-commerce and techniques such as supply chain management, electronic data interchange, mobile commerce, electronic funds transfer, inventory management systems and automated data collection systems are used in electronic commerce. Online auctions, online retailing and electronic markets are its three main areas. Classification in e-commerce can take place in two forms. The first classification is based on the types of goods that are sold such as digital content for online consumption, conventional goods and services, and meta-services for facilitating other types of electronic commerce. The second category depends on the nature of the participant such as B2C, B2B, C2C and C2B. E-commerce has a significant impact upon employment, customers, supply chain management and markets. This book outlines the processes and applications of e-commerce in detail. Most of the topics introduced in this book cover new techniques used in this field. It will serve as a valuable source of reference for those interested in this field.

The chapters below are organized to facilitate a comprehensive understanding of the subject:

Chapter – What is E-Commerce?

The buying and selling of goods or services using the internet, and the transfer of money and data to execute these transactions is called e-commerce or electronic commerce. This chapter has been carefully written to provide an easy understanding of the varied facets of e-commerce.

Chapter – E-Commerce Business Models

An e-commerce business model is a set of planned activities designed to result in a profit for an e-commerce enterprise. There are numerous e-commerce business models such as business to business model, consumer to consumer model, business to administration model, etc. This chapter discusses in detail these models related to e-commerce business.

Chapter – Digital Marketing

The marketing of products or services using digital technologies on the internet, through mobile phone apps and other digital mediums is called digital marketing. Some of the techniques involved in digital marketing are content marketing, SEO techniques, inbound marketing, etc. The diverse aspects of these digital marketing techniques have been thoroughly discussed in this chapter.

Chapter – Mobile Commerce

Mobile commerce, also called m-commerce, is an advancement of e-commerce and includes the different monetary transactions which are conducted through mobile devices. This chapter closely examines the key concepts of mobile commerce such as mobile ticketing, mobile banking and mobile marketing to provide an extensive understanding of the subject.

Chapter – Electronic Payment Systems

An electronic payment system or e-payment system is a way of conducting transactions or paying for goods and services through an electronic medium. Some of these electronic payment systems include digital wallet, e-commerce credit card payment system, etc. All these types of electronic payment systems have been carefully analyzed in this chapter.

Chapter – E-Commerce Softwares

E-commerce software refers to the tool which is used to manage the diverse activities in an online store, facilitating the management of inventory, adding or removing products and calculating taxes. This chapter closely examines the key concepts of popular e-commerce software such as Drupal Commerce, NopCommerce and PrestaShop to provide an extensive understanding of the subject.

Grace Silva

What is E-Commerce?

The buying and selling of goods or services using the internet, and the transfer of money and data to execute these transactions is called e-commerce or electronic commerce. This chapter has been carefully written to provide an easy understanding of the varied facets of e-commerce.

E-commerce, also known as electronic commerce or internet commerce, refers to the buying and selling of goods or services using the internet, and the transfer of money and data to execute these transactions. Ecommerce is often used to refer to the sale of physical products online, but it can also describe any kind of commercial transaction that is facilitated through the internet.

Whereas e-business refers to all aspects of operating an online business, ecommerce refers specifically to the transaction of goods and services.

The history of ecommerce begins with the first ever online sale: on the August 11, 1994 a man sold a CD by the band Sting to his friend through his website NetMarket, an American retail platform. This is the first example of a consumer purchasing a product from a business through the World Wide Web or "ecommerce" as we commonly know it today.

Since then, ecommerce has evolved to make products easier to discover and purchase through online retailers and marketplaces. Independent freelancers, small businesses, and large corporations have all benefited from ecommerce, which enables them to sell their goods and services at a scale that was not possible with traditional offline retail.

Types of E-Commerce Models

There are four main types of ecommerce models that can describe almost every transaction that takes place between consumers and businesses.

- Business to Consumer (B2C): When a business sells a good or service to an individual consumer (e.g. You buy a pair of shoes from an online retailer).

- Business to Business (B2B): When a business sells a good or service to another business (e.g. A business sells software-as-a-service for other businesses to use).

- Consumer to Consumer (C2C): When a consumer sells a good or service to another consumer (e.g. You sell your old furniture on eBay to another consumer).

- Consumer to Business (C2B): When a consumer sells their own products or services to a business or organization (e.g. An influencer offers exposure to their online audience in exchange for a fee, or a photographer licenses their photo for a business to use).

Examples of E-commerce:

E-commerce can take on a variety of forms involving different transactional relationships between businesses and consumers, as well as different objects being exchanged as part of these transactions.

- Retail: The sale of a product by a business directly to a customer without any intermediary.

- Wholesale: The sale of products in bulk, often to a retailer that then sells them directly to consumers.

- Dropshipping: The sale of a product, which is manufactured and shipped to the consumer by a third party.

- Crowdfunding: The collection of money from consumers in advance of a product being available in order to raise the startup capital necessary to bring it to market.

- Subscription: The automatic recurring purchase of a product or service on a regular basis until the subscriber chooses to cancel.

- Physical products: Any tangible good that requires inventory to be replenished and orders to be physically shipped to customers as sales are made.

- Digital products: Downloadable digital goods, templates, and courses, or media that must be purchased for consumption or licensed for use.

- Services: A skill or set of skills provided in exchange for compensation. The service provider's time can be purchased for a fee.

Advantages of E-Commerce

E-commerce advantages can be broadly classified in three major categories:

- Advantages to Organizations,

- Advantages to Consumers,

- Advantages to Society.

Advantages to Organizations

- Using e-commerce, organizations can expand their market to national and international markets with minimum capital investment. An organization can easily locate more customers, best suppliers, and suitable business partners across the globe.

- E-commerce helps organizations to reduce the cost to create process, distribute, retrieve and manage the paper based information by digitizing the information.

- E-commerce improves the brand image of the company.

- E-commerce helps organization to provide better customer services.

- E-commerce helps to simplify the business processes and makes them faster and efficient.

- E-commerce reduces the paper work.

- E-commerce increases the productivity of organizations. It supports "pull" type supply management. In "pull" type supply management, a business process starts when a request comes from a customer and it uses just-in-time manufacturing way.

Advantages to Customers

- It provides 24×7 support. Customers can enquire about a product or service and place orders anytime, anywhere from any location.

- E-commerce application provides users with more options and quicker delivery of products.

- E-commerce application provides users with more options to compare and select the cheaper and better options.

- A customer can put review comments about a product and can see what others are buying, or see the review comments of other customers before making a final purchase.

- E-commerce provides options of virtual auctions.

- It provides readily available information. A customer can see the relevant detailed information within seconds, rather than waiting for days or weeks.

- E-commerce increases the competition among organizations and as a result, organizations provides substantial discounts to customers.

Advantages to Society

- Customers need not travel to shop a product, thus less traffic on road and low air pollution.

- E-commerce helps in reducing the cost of products, so less affluent people can also afford the products.

- E-commerce has enabled rural areas to access services and products, which are otherwise not available to them.

- E-commerce helps the government to deliver public services such as healthcare, education, social services at a reduced cost and in an improved manner.

Disadvantages of E-commerce

The disadvantages of e-commerce can be broadly classified into two major categories –

- Technical disadvantages,

- Non-technical disadvantages.

Technical Disadvantages

- There can be lack of system security, reliability or standards owing to poor implementation of e-commerce.

- The software development industry is still evolving and keeps changing rapidly.

- In many countries, network bandwidth might cause an issue.

- Special types of web servers or other software might be required by the vendor, setting the e-commerce environment apart from network servers.

- Sometimes, it becomes difficult to integrate an e-commerce software or website with existing applications or databases.

- There could be software/hardware compatibility issues, as some e-commerce software may be incompatible with some operating system or any other component.

Non-technical Disadvantages

- Initial cost – The cost of creating/building an e-commerce application in-house may be very high. There could be delays in launching an e-commerce application due to mistakes, and lack of experience.

- User resistance – Users may not trust the site being an unknown faceless seller. Such mistrust makes it difficult to convince traditional users to switch from physical stores to online/virtual stores.

- Security/Privacy – It is difficult to ensure the security or privacy on online transactions.

- Lack of touch or feel of products during online shopping is a drawback.

- E-commerce applications are still evolving and changing rapidly.

- Internet access is still not cheaper and is inconvenient to use for many potential customers, for example, those living in remote villages.

E-COMMERCE MARKETING CONCEPTS

Personalization

No matter what you sell, it's essential that your company relates to your potential customers on a personal level. Personalization is the process of tracking what your site visitors look at on (and off) your site so you can get a better understanding of their preferences. Then, once you know their preferences, you can use cookies to each customer an experience on your site that was designed specifically for them.

Personalized website content helps you build relationships with your site's repeat visitors by showing them the perfect message at the perfect time. You can even go so far as to offer special deals to certain individuals who buy specific products on your site. Whatever you choose, it's important that your site has some degree of personalization. Ecommerce shoppers love seeing messages that are tailored to their interests, and it's a great way to move more products.

Product Recommendations

Along with personalization, you can also provide product recommendations. Product recommendations show your potential customers that you pay attention to their wants and needs. It also allows them to get a bigger picture of your inventory and move more products. You can use product recommendations in a number of ways.

First, you can add your own company recommendations. These would most often be products that are similar to something a customer has already bought.

Second, you can highlight user recommendations. These can be items like wish-lists that your customers share with one another. This also requires your site to have the functionality to allow users to share items internally, but it can pay dividends.

Third, you can use recommended products to show customers products that complement what they're currently buying. So if someone's buying a garden hose from your housewares store, you should also show them different hose heads or wall spigots so they're buying a group of products that work together. However, once your customers have those items in their carts, there's no guarantee that they'll buy everything.

Cart Reminders

One of the most frustrating parts of running an ecommerce store is customers who leave your website when they have products in their carts. That's why you need to use cart reminders.

Cart reminders are emails that automatically generate and send whenever someone has a cart of products and leaves your site. The emails can send out a day after the customer leaves, or sometimes as long as a week or month later. Regardless, the point is always the same — to get that customer back to your site and have them finish their transaction.

Shoppers who have accounts with you have already given you their email addresses so you can communicate with them. They've also shown clear interest in the products they added to their cart themselves.

So you're giving them what they want by reminding them about their abandoned cart. And even if they're not able to finish their transaction that same day, they may finish it a week later when your email arrives in their inbox. But carts aren't the only part of ecommerce marketing that you need to add.

Product Social Sharing

Social media marketing is a critical part of any Internet marketing plan. But it's exceptionally important for ecommerce companies.

For every product on your site, you have an opportunity to cause an impact on social media. Someone shopping for your items might find something their friend would like, so it's important that you let them tweet, post, or share about what you have.

Then, the friends of the person who shared your product will see what they posted. That lets them click to your site — at their friend's recommendation — and possibly become a new customer. In other words, social sharing lets your customers market for you. All you have to do is provide the product and the means to share it. But there's still one more marketing concept that you need to implement if you want your ecommerce store to really succeed.

Product Reviews

Did you know that up to 70% of customers check out ratings and reviews before making a purchase? And 63% of customers are more likely to purchase if a site displays product ratings and reviews.

Adding reviews to your ecommerce website provides value to customers and encourages them to buy from your site. Online reviews provide the social proof shoppers are looking for, and they can help your ecommerce store establish trust and credibility with customers.

In addition, new reviews can help keep your site content fresh and improve your chances of earning higher rankings in search engine results.

Be sure to make it easy for customers to leave reviews on your site. You can even offer incentives like coupons, discounts, and sneak previews to encourage customer reviews.

Email Campaigns

Email marketing accounts for over 7% of all ecommerce transactions, so incorporating a strong email strategy can help your ecommerce store attract more customers and earn more revenue.

In addition to sending abandoned cart emails, you can use email marketing to send personalized updates to customers and potential customers. For example, you can send personalized emails on customers' birthdays or other important milestones. Studies show that personalized birthday emails have almost five-times the transaction rate of standard emails.

You can also use email to let customers know about new products and even offer exclusive coupons or promotions to email subscribers. Email marketing is also a great way to connect with customers after they make a purchase and encourage them to review the item.

Responsive Design

Your customers don't just shop on desktops or laptops. They shop on phones, tablets, and other devices that all show your website in different ways.

Responsive design automatically adjusts your website to fit the device that a person is using. So if someone's on your site with their phone and their laptop at the same time, they can still see and read your site perfectly.

That's essential to ecommerce because if your site isn't responsive, you'll lose mobile customers left and right. Mobile customers are becoming more and more common as well — they make up nearly half the market of ecommerce shoppers.

E-PAYMENT SYSTEM

An e-payment system is a way of making transactions or paying for goods and services through an electronic medium, without the use of checks or cash. It's also called an electronic payment system or online payment system.

The electronic payment system has grown increasingly over the last decades due to the growing spread of internet-based banking and shopping. As the world advances more with technology development, we can see the rise of electronic payment systems and payment processing devices. As these increase, improve, and provide ever more secure online payment transactions the percentage of check and cash transactions will decrease.

Electronic Payment Methods

One of the most popular payment forms online are credit and debit cards. Besides them, there are also alternative payment methods, such as bank transfers, electronic wallets, smart cards or bitcoin wallet (bitcoin is the most popular cryptocurrency).

E-payment methods could be classified into two areas, credit payment systems and cash payment systems.

1. Credit Payment System:

- Credit Card — A form of the e-payment system which requires the use of the card issued by a financial institute to the cardholder for making payments online or through an electronic device, without the use of cash.

- E-wallet — A form of prepaid account that stores user's financial data, like debit and credit card information to make an online transaction easier.

- Smart card — A plastic card with a microprocessor that can be loaded with funds to make transactions; also known as a chip card.

2. Cash Payment System:

- Direct debit — A financial transaction in which the account holder instructs the bank to collect a specific amount of money from his account electronically to pay for goods or services.

- E-check — A digital version of an old paper check. It's an electronic transfer of money from a bank account, usually checking account, without the use of the paper check.

- E-cash is a form of an electronic payment system, where a certain amount of money is stored on a client's device and made accessible for online transactions.

- Stored-value card — A card with a certain amount of money that can be used to perform the transaction in the issuer store. A typical example of stored-value cards are gift cards.

Pros and Cons of using an E-payment System

E-payment systems are made to facilitate the acceptance of electronic payments for online transactions. With the growing popularity of online shopping, e-payment systems became a must for online consumers — to make shopping and banking more convenient. It comes with many benefits, such as:

- Reaching more clients from all over the world, which results in more sales.

- More effective and efficient transactions — It's because transactions are made in seconds (with one-click), without wasting customer's time. It comes with speed and simplicity.

- Convenience. Customers can pay for items on an e-commerce website at anytime and anywhere. They just need an internet connected device.

- Lower transaction cost and decreased technology costs.

- Expenses control for customers, as they can always check their virtual account where they can find the transaction history.

- It's easy to add payments to a website, so even a non-technical person may implement it in minutes and start processing online payments.

- Payment gateways and payment providers offer highly effective security and anti-fraud tools to make transactions reliable.

E-BROKERAGE

E-brokerage allows users to buy and sell stocks electronically and obtain information with the help of a website. Almost all e-brokerage houses have simple sign-up and provide users the ability to make them their own financial manager. With the advent of widespread Internet connectivity and smart devices, e-brokerage has seen significant growth.

Two big factors have helped in the growth of e-brokerage, namely Internet access and lower prices. The Internet has allowed users to have ready access to raw data. E-brokerage is capable of offering lower prices than traditional brokerage techniques, as the need for brokers or financial advisers are eliminated in the case of e-brokerage. To attract more customers and retain existing users, most e-brokerage firms provide a number of tools, technical indicators which give real-time information and help in research and decision making.

E-brokerage has many benefits for its users. Users can have more flexibility as well as control over their portfoliios and transactions. One can access their brokerage account at any time, even if trading hours are over. The biggest advantage of e-brokerage is that the commission cost is significantly lower than in case of services of a professional broker. Again, trades are processed quickly in e-brokerage and there are no delays, unlike traditional brokerage methods.

However, there are a few disadvantages associated with e-brokerage. Unlike traditional brokerage, the mentoring relationship between the account holder and professional broker is not there. All financial choices must be made by the user. In essence, the level of service is less than with traditional brokerages.

E-COMMERCE SECURITY

E-commerce security refers to the principles which guide safe electronic transactions, allowing the buying and selling of goods and services through the Internet, but with protocols in place to provide safety for those involved. Successful business online depends on the customers' trust that a company has e-commerce security basics in place.

Privacy

One of the most obvious eCommerce security basics is privacy, which in this situation means not sharing information with unauthorized parties. When you shop online, your personal details or account information should not be accessible to anyone except the seller you have chosen to share it with. Any disclosure of that information by the merchant would be a breach of confidentiality. The business is responsible to provide at least the minimum in encryption, virus protection, and a firewall so that bank details and credit card information remain private.

Integrity

A second concept which is crucial within secure eCommerce is the idea of integrity—that none of the information shared online by the customer will be altered in any way. This principle states that a secure transaction includes unchanged data—that the business is only using exactly what was entered into the Internet site by the buyer. Any tampering with information is breaking the confidence of the buyer in the security of the transaction and the integrity of the company in general.

Authentication

For eCommerce to take place, both seller and buyer have to be who they say they are. A business cannot sell unless it's real, the products are real, and the sale will go through as described online. The buyer must also provide proof of identification so that the merchant can feel secure about the sale. In eCommerce, fraudulent identification and authentication are possible, and many businesses hire an expert to make sure these kinds of eCommerce security basics are in place. Common solutions include technological solutions—customer logins and passwords or additional credit card PINs.

Non-repudiation

Repudiation is denial, and good business depends on both buyers and sellers following through on the part of the transaction which originated with them—not denying those actions. Since eCommerce happens in cyberspace, usually without any live video, it can feel less safe and sure. The legal principle of non-repudiation adds another level of security by confirming that the information which was sent between parties was indeed received and that a purchase or email or signature cannot be denied by the person who completed the transaction.

Customers who don't feel transactions are secure won't buy. Hesitation on the part of the buyer will destroy eCommerce potential. Any breach will cost a business in lost revenues and consumer trust. These eCommerce security basics can guide any business owner regarding safe online transaction protocol.

Payment Security Measures to Deal with Ecommerce

Partner with a Processor who knows Online Payments

Choosing the right payment processor is a prior step for accepting online payments from the customers through credit card. Selection of payment processing partner should be done with utmost care as its experience can help the client to comply with the payment card industry data security standards (PCI DSS).

All you need is an experienced partner who can give you all-time support and maintains the PCI compliance for you by implementing various approaches like a training program, Vulnerability Assessment and full-time customer support. Some processors even reimburse the money for monetary loss in case of fraud event that occurs through a data breach.

Thus it is extremely important to have a partner who had experience and can even understand everything about the payment security and precautions.

Monitored Suspicious Purchasing Activity

You should be aware of the various types of suspicious activities that could be the reason for fraud.

Once a person who logged in to his website and made huge order from the same IP address but used different credit cards. Max was completely unaware of the issue and thus failed to understand the behavior and pattern of the customer indicated that single person is using multiple stolen credit cards to make purchases which lead to serious repercussion.

Large order raises too many doubts and especially the one which was requested for next day Shipping. But this activity alone is not enough to identify a transaction as fraud.

Address Verification System for all Transaction

It is extremely important for store owners to predict and analyze that the person making the purchase is truly a cardholder. Various techniques can be utilized to prevent this fraud. Implementing the address verification system in the eCommerce store is the best way to analyze and verify the fraud.

The system will check if the billing address is correct by verifying it with cardholder's data from the issuing bank. As a result person with a stolen card or card number doesn't have the access to the wrong billing address.

Incorrect billing address may not necessarily mean that the transaction is fraudulent hence it is advisable to take additional security measures to identify the customer.

Encryption Approach

Encryption is a method of converting the original message into encrypted text, which should be too complex to understand and even difficult for a hacker to decode. The main idea of encryption is to ensure security and safety of the data and its transmission.

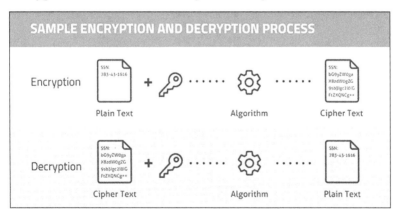

Encryption can be done through various techniques but the choice totally depends on the context and the requirements. Some of the famous techniques in eCommerce are:

- Public key encryption,
- Symmetric key encryption.

Secure Socket Layer

Secure socket layer is the most consistent security model used and developed for eCommerce business, secured through its payment channel.

Through the SSL, transmission of data is encrypted, client and server information is authenticated and message integrity for TCP/IP connections. The protocol is design to prevent tampering of information and forgery while transmitting data over the internet between interacting applications.

Secure Hypertext Transfer Protocol

Secure Hypertext Transfer Protocol (S-HTTP) is an advanced version of normal HTTP internet protocol with enhanced security which ensures secure authentication, public key encryption and digital signatures.

Secure HTTP enabled website makes the transaction more secure by negotiating encryptions schemes used between a server and the clients. It can seamlessly integrate with the HTTP and ensure an optimal end-user security with different defence mechanisms.

Secure Electronic Transaction

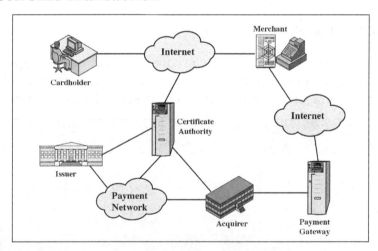

SET is a joint collaboration by MasterCard and VISA which ensures that safety of all parties involved in electronic payments of an eCommerce transaction. It is designed to handle complex and critical functions like:

- Authenticating the cardholders and merchants,
- Confidentiality of information and payment data,
- Define protocols & electronic security service, providers.

Payment Card Industry Compliance

The payment card industry security standard council was formed in the year 2006. It ensures that the companies who deal with the accepting, processing, storing and transmitting credit card information have to maintain a secure environment.

PCI DSS is not a law in itself but a standard made by a collaboration of various branded card company like Visa, Mastercard, JCB, AMEX and Discover. If your company is not PCI compliant has to face some serious consequences like fines, card replacement cost, costly forensic audits and off-course lost to brand image.

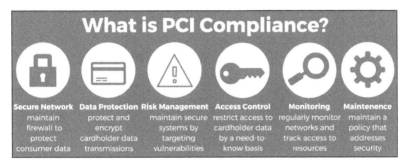

Safe Login Screen

Development of Secure eCommerce website straight away starts from the Login Page. You are half way done if login access to the website is secure. Otherwise, it will be easy for the hackers to infiltrate and get access to sensitive data.

Implementing this safety protocol is moderately easy, but it can efficiently ward off many security threats.

Digital Signature

A digital signature means giving a unique identity to your message. Actually, it is a process of encrypting the message with the private specifically used for verification purpose.

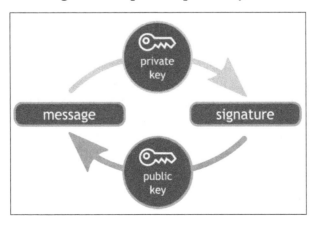

The linkage between data and the signature doesn't allow any alteration and if anyhow data is altered signature is automatically invalidated. Thus digital signature helps to maintain the authority and confidentiality of the data.

ONLINE SHOPPING

Online shopping is the process of researching and purchasing products or services over the Internet. The earliest online stores went into business in 1992, and online retailing took over a significant segment of the retail market during the first decade of the twenty-first century, as ownership of personal computers increased and established retailers began to offer their products over the Internet.

Online Shopping cart.

Electronic commerce is used for both business-to-business (B2B) and business-to-consumer (B2C) transactions. Buying products from an online shop, eshop, e-store, internet shop, webshop, webstore, online store, or virtual store is similar to purchasing from a mail order catalog. Online stores describe products for sale with text, photos, and multimedia files. Typically the customer selects items to be listed on an order form known as a "shopping cart," and pays with a credit card or some form of electronic payment. The products are then shipped to the customer's address, or in the case of digital media products such as music, software, e-books or movies, may be downloaded onto the customer's computer. Online shopping has some advantages over shopping in retail stores, including the ability to easily compare prices from a range of merchants, access to a wide selection of merchandise, and the convenience of not having to drive to a physical store. Online merchants have refined shipping methods and developed incentives such as generous return policies to overcome obstacles like delays in receiving purchases and the inability to try on or sample merchandise before buying. However, online shopping cannot replace the experience of shopping in a retail store or the entertainment value of going to a mall or market.

The idea of online shopping predates the World Wide Web. A technology for real-time transaction processing from a domestic television, based on Videotext, was first demonstrated in 1979 by Michael Aldrich, who designed and installed systems in the UK, including the first Tesco pilot system in 1984. The first business-to-business (B2B) computer network was created by Thomson Holidays in 1981.

In 1990, Tim Berners-Lee created the first World Wide Web server and browser. In 1992, Charles Stack created the first online bookstore, Book Stacks Unlimited, two years before Jeff Bezos started Amazon.com. In 1994, other advances took place, such as online banking and the opening of an online pizza shop by Pizza Hut. During that same year, Netscape introduced SSL encryption (Secure Sockets Layer) of data transferred online, which has become essential for secure online shopping. In 1995, Amazon expanded its online shopping, and in 1996 eBay appeared.

Growth

The majority of the earliest online shoppers were young educated males who were familiar with computer technology, but by 2001 women made up 52.8 percent of the online population. Online shopping had caught the attention of the general public by 1999, and both Internet start-ups and well-known retailers launched Web sites offering their products. During the Christmas shopping season of 1999, when many consumers attempted to do their shopping online for the first time, retailers found themselves unprepared to process and ship their orders efficiently. Online retailers improved their customer service and shipping companies such as FedEx and UPS expanded their operations to accommodate the increasing traffic. By December 2008, many online retailers were able to boost their sales by offering guaranteed overnight delivery to last-minute shoppers on Christmas Eve.

Excitement over the potential of online retailing led to unrealistic business expectations during the "dot.com bubble" of 1999-2001. Start-ups attempted to sell products like groceries and dog food over the Internet without accounting for the prohibitive cost of maintaining warehouses and delivery systems. Companies with established retail stores and vendors of specialty items, however, were able to expand their customer base using the infrastructure they already had in place.

Customers

Online shopping requires access to a computer, and some form of payment such as a bank account and a debit card, credit card, or Paypal account. According to research found, the higher the level of education, income, and occupation of the head of the household, the more favorable the perception of non-store shopping. Increased exposure to technology increases the probability of developing favorable attitudes towards new shopping channels. Online shoppers are most likely to belong to the middle and upper classes, but as the growth of technology has made computers less expensive and available to more people, and increased the ease of connecting to the Internet, the customer base has expanded.

The popularity of online shopping is a global phenomenon. Surveys of Internet users have revealed that 99 percent of South Korean internet users have shopped online, closely followed by 97 percent of internet users in Germany, Japan and the United Kingdom. Ninety-four percent of Internet users in the United States reported that they had purchased something online. Using a credit card to purchase items on the Internet is especially appealing to consumers in emerging markets who cannot easily find or buy items they want in local retail stores.

Merchants

Many successful virtual retailers sell digital products, (including information storage, retrieval, and modification), music, movies, education, communication, software, photography, and financial transactions. Examples of this type of company include: Google, eBay and Paypal. Large numbers of successful marketers, including numerous sellers on eBay, use Drop shipping or affiliate marketing techniques to facilitate transactions of tangible goods without maintaining real inventory. Small items such as books, CDs and jewelry that have a high value-to-weight and can easily fit into a standard mailbox are particularly suitable for virtual stores. The initial success of Amazon, perhaps the longest-enduring dot-com company, was based on selling items that were easy to ship.

High-volume websites, such as Yahoo!, Amazon.com and eBay, offer hosting services for online stores to small retailers. These stores are presented within an integrated navigation framework. Collections of online stores are sometimes known as virtual shopping malls or online marketplaces.

Logistics

Consumers find a product of interest by using a search engine, visiting the Website of the retailer directly, or doing a search across many different vendors using a shopping search engine that offers price and quality comparisons.

Most online retailers use shopping cart software that allows the customer to select multiple items to add to an order and adjust quantities. Once the order is complete, the customer moves through a "checkout" process during which payment and delivery information is collected. Some stores allow consumers to sign up for an online account that keeps payment information and shipping addresses on permanent record so that the checkout process can be automated. The consumer typically sees a confirmation page and is sent an e-mail confirmation once the transaction is complete. Additional emails notify the customer when the order has been shipped and may provide tracking information for the shipment. Less sophisticated stores may simply display a catalog on their Web site and rely on consumers to order by telephone or email.

Payment

Online shoppers commonly use credit card to make payments, however some systems enable users to create accounts and pay by alternative means, such as:

- Debit card,
- Various types of electronic money,
- Cash on delivery,
- Electronic bank check,
- Wire transfer/delivery on payment,
- Postal money order,
- PayPal,
- Google Checkout,
- Amazon Payments,
- Bill Me Later,
- Money bookers,
- Reverse SMS billing to mobile phones,
- Gift cards,
- Direct debit in some countries.

Some merchants are not prepared to ship overseas and will not allow international credit cards and or shipping addresses outside the country in which site does its business. Other sites allow customers from anywhere to send gifts anywhere in the world. The financial part of a transaction may be processed in real time (for example, letting the consumer know immediately that a credit card has been declined), or might be done later as part of the fulfillment process.

Product Delivery

Once a payment has been accepted the goods or services can be delivered in a number of ways:

- Download: This is the method often used for digital media products such as software, music, movies, or images.
- Shipping: The product is shipped to the customer's address.
- Postal service: The merchant uses regular mail services to send the product.

- Drop shipping: The order is passed to the manufacturer or third-party distributor, who ships the item directly to the consumer, bypassing the retailer's physical location to save time, money, and space.

- In-store pickup: The customer orders and pays online, finds a local store using locator software and picks the product up at the closest store. This is the method often used in the bricks and clicks business model.

- If the purchase is an admission ticket or a gift card, the customer may receive a numerical code, or a ticket that can be printed out and presented at the gate. To prevent duplication, the same right of admission cannot be used twice.

- Electronic check-in: A customer purchasing an airline ticket receives only a confirmation email, and checks in at the airport by swiping the same credit card or a passport at a kiosk.

Shopping Cart Systems

- Simple shopping cart systems do not use an online database. The merchant creates an offline database of products, categories, graphics and prices, and then uploads it to an online shopping cart.

- Sophisticated shopping cart software can be bought or rented as a standalone program or as an addition to an enterprise resource planning program. It is usually installed on the company's own Web server and may be integrated into the company's existing supply chain system so that ordering, payment, delivery, accounting and fulfillment can be automated to a large extent.

- A merchant can register and create an online shop on a portal that hosts multiple shops and offers additional services such as credit card processing.

- Open source shopping cart packages include advanced platforms such as Interchange, and off the shelf solutions as Satchmo, osCommerce, Magento, Zen Cart, VirtueMart and PrestaShop. These can be tailored to suit the merchant's needs.

Web Site Design

Customers choose online shopping because of its high level of convenience, and because it offers a broader selection; competitive pricing and greater access to information. For a retailer, a shopping Web site increases sales, increases customer access to its products, and strengthens brand awareness and customer loyalty. Good Web site design is crucial to the success of an online shopping Web site. Many retailers continue to face challenges in creating a satisfactory and appealing online shopping experience for their customers.

Online shopping sites provide detailed product information that is not usually available in a retail store, along with a means of easily comparing the attributes of several similar products. The amount of information and the way in which it is presented directly affects the customer's inclination to buy products and services online. Two important factors that have been found to influence buying behavior are complexity and novelty. "Complexity" refers to the number of different elements or features of a site; a site that presents the same information in several different ways has the potential to induce impulse purchases. Novelty involves adding unexpected, new, or unfamiliar aspects to a site, such as weekly special offers, seasonal products, news articles, and pop-up windows; novelty keeps customers exploring the shopping sites.

User-centered design is very important. The purpose of an online shopping site is to build relationships with customers and make money. The primary focus of the Web site should be satisfying the consumers' expectations, not supporting the organization's culture and brand name. Consumers seek efficiency, good customer service, a sense that the company cares about them, and a consistent experience each time they return to the site. An organization must invest substantial resources to define, design, develop, test, implement, and maintain a shopping Web site. Errors should be corrected as soon as they are discovered. To retain customers, a customer service network must return emails in a timely fashion, notify customers of problems, be honest, and be a good steward of the customers' data. Internet sales cannot be fully automated; a large number of online shoppers contact the company by telephone or email to ask questions before making a purchase, and to resolve problems afterwards.

Web design must allow for the cultural peculiarities and tastes of prospective customers. Design elements that appeal to a Japanese or Chinese customer may have the opposite effect on a German customer. It is important to make the information on a site available in the language of the customers to avoid misunderstandings and increase their confidence in the product. A user's familiarity with the internet also affects behavior on a shopping site. Experienced users focus more on the variables that directly influence the task at hand, while novice users concentrate on locating and understanding the information on a shopping site.

Online Shopping and Retail Shopping

Online shopping offers certain benefits and advantages, but it will never replace the experience of shopping in a retail store. A customer who knows exactly what he or she wants can look it up online, read and compare the information, and purchase from the site that offers the best price or service. A shopper who is uncertain what to look for, or who just enjoys browsing through items on display, will prefer a retail store where the merchandise can be seen, handled and sampled. The decor, music and arrangement of goods in a retail store creates a multi-dimensional shopping environment that cannot be duplicated online. For many people, going shopping at a mall, department store or market is a form of entertainment and a social experience. Many people who are currently unfamiliar with computers and do not feel comfortable using the Internet to shop are not likely to change their habits.

Online stores must describe products for sale with text, photos, and multimedia files, while in a retail store, the actual product and the manufacturer's packaging are available for direct inspection which might involve a test drive, fitting, or other experimentation. In a conventional retail store, clerks are typically available to answer questions. Some items, like clothing and shoes, may need to be tried on before the customer can be certain that they are the right size. Online shopping sites offer size charts, diagrams and multi-sided views to help the customer make a selection. Most offer generous return policies to encourage customers to place an order.

Advantages of Online Shopping

Online stores are available 24 hours a day, and many consumers have Internet access both at work and at home. A visit to a conventional retail store requires travel and must take place during business hours. During the holiday season and on weekends, shoppers in retail stores must contend with crowds and long lines.

Searching or browsing an online catalog can be faster than browsing the aisles of a physical store. One advantage of shopping online is being able to quickly seek out and compare prices for items or services from many different vendors using search engines and online price comparison services. In certain market segments such as books and music, computers and consumer electronics, shoppers find a greater selection online and may be able to locate refurbished or second-hand items at much lower prices.

Collectors and hobbyists can find supplies and rare items online that are rarely available in retail stores, and can use auction sites to sell, trade and research collectibles, antiques and one-of-a-kind pieces. Specialty products such as ethnic foods and wines, outdoor equipment, and sporting goods are also sold at competitive prices online. Online shopping is also an efficient way to buy automobile parts and replacement parts for appliances, since it is difficult for a retail outlet to keep them in stock.

Some online stores provide or link to supplemental product information, such as instructions, safety procedures, demonstrations, manufacturer specifications, advice, or how-to guides. Many shopping sites allow customers to comment or rate their items. There are also dedicated review sites that host user reviews for different products.

Shipping

In most cases, merchandise purchased online must be shipped to the customer. This introduces a significant delay and potential uncertainty about whether or not the item was actually in stock at the time of purchase. Many retailers inform customers how long they can expect to wait before receiving a package and provide a delivery tracking number. Even if a purchase can be made 24 hours a day, the customer must often be at home during normal business hours to accept the delivery.

In the event of a problem with the item, the customer may need to contact the retailer, visit the post office and pay return shipping, and then wait for a replacement or refund.

Shipping costs (if applicable) reduce the price advantage of online merchandise, though depending on the jurisdiction, a lack of sales tax may compensate for this. Online retailers sometimes make a profit by charging a standard shipping fee that exceeds the actual cost of shipping the item.

Bricks and clicks stores offer the ability to buy an item online and pick it up in a nearby store. Orders are filled immediately so that they are ready before the customer has time to arrive at the store. This feature gives retail stores a competitive edge over other online retailers who might offer lower prices but must ship out merchandise, and satisfies customers who want their goods immediately. It also brings online customers onto the store premises where they might buy additional merchandise or seek assistance with a product.

Trends

A large proportion of people that shop online use a search engine to find what they are looking for while others find websites by word of mouth. Many shoppers respond to special offers in emails and advertising, or find a merchant through a price comparison Web site.

Trust is a significant factor in selecting an online merchant. Sixty percent of online shoppers who have a good first experience with a certain Web site return to that website to buy more. An established retailer with a well-known brand is more likely to be trusted than an unknown merchant.

Books and music are the most popular online purchases, followed by clothing and accessories, shoes, videos and DVDs, games, airline tickets and electronic equipment. Cosmetics, nutrition products, and groceries are increasingly being purchased online. About one fourth of travelers buy their airplane tickets online because it is a quick and easy way to compare airline travel and make a purchase.

Many successful purely virtual companies deal with digital products, (including information storage, retrieval, and modification), music, movies, office supplies, education, communication, software, photography, and financial transactions. Examples of this type of company include: Google, eBay and Paypal. Other successful marketers use Drop shipping or affiliate marketing techniques to facilitate transactions of tangible goods without maintaining real inventory. Examples include numerous sellers on eBay.

Bricks-and-mortar retailers often use their online shopping sites to drive sales both online and at their retail stores by posting information about in-store specials online and by offering free add-ons such as batteries or accessories to customers who research products on their Web sites.

Concerns

Fraud and Security Concerns

Online shoppers have a higher risk of being defrauded by a merchant because they are unable to physically examine merchandise before purchasing it. Dishonest sellers occasionally accept payment for an order and never send the merchandise. Most credit card services offer protection against this type of fraud. Merchants also risk losses from purchases made using stolen credit cards, or fraudulent repudiation of online purchases.

Secure Sockets Layer (SSL) encryption prevents credit card numbers from being intercepted in transit between the consumer and the merchant. Identity theft is still a concern for consumers if hackers break into a merchant's web site and steal names, addresses and credit card numbers. Computer security is a major concern for merchants and e-commerce service providers, who deploy countermeasures such as firewalls and anti-virus software to protect their networks.

Phishing, in which consumers are fooled into thinking they are dealing with a reputable retailer, and are manipulated into giving private information to a malicious party, is another danger. Denial of service attacks are a minor risk for merchants, as are server and network outages.

Consumers can protect themselves when using online retailer services by:

- Using known stores, ensuring that there is comprehensive contact information on the website before using the service, and noting if the retailer has enrolled in industry oversight programs such as trust mark or trust seal.

- Ensuring that the retailer has posted a privacy policy stating that it will not share private information with others without consent.

- Ensuring that the vendor address is protected with SSL when entering credit card information. The URL of the credit card information entry screen should start with "HTTPS."

- Using strong passwords, which do not include personal information such as names or birthdates.

- Reading independent consumer reviews of personal experiences with a company or product. These can often be found by typing the company name into a search engine.

- Confirming that special offers in emails or online advertising are genuine by going directly to the merchant's site.

Most companies offer shipping insurance in case a product is lost or damaged; if an item is particularly valuable the customer should confirm that it is insured.

Privacy

Protection of personal information is important to some consumers. Legal jurisdictions have different laws concerning consumer privacy, and different levels of enforcement. Many consumers wish to avoid spam and telemarketing which could result from supplying contact information to an online merchant. Most merchants promise not to use consumer information for these purposes, or provide a mechanism to opt-out of such contacts.

Retail stores also collect consumer information. Some ask for addresses and phone numbers at the cash register, though consumers may refuse to provide it. Larger companies sometimes use the address information encoded on consumers' credit cards to add them to a catalog mailing list.

CONVERSATIONAL COMMERCE

Conversational commerce is a term coined by Uber's Chris Messina in a 2015 piece published on Medium. It refers to the intersection of messaging apps and shopping. Meaning, the trend toward interacting with businesses through messaging and chat apps like Facebook Messenger, WhatsApp, Talk, and WeChat or through voice technology, like Amazon's Echo product, which interfaces with companies through voice commands.

Consumers can chat with company representatives, get customer support, ask questions, get personalized recommendations, read reviews, and click to purchase all from within messaging apps. With conversational commerce, the consumer engages in this interaction with a human representative, chatbot, or a mix of both.

On the business side, companies can use chatbots to automate customer service messages. It's how companies are enabling consumers to buy from them without ever leaving the messaging app they are using. Now companies can send order confirmations in Facebook Messenger, as well as shipping and delivery notifications. Using chatbots, businesses can resolve customer service issues, provide recommendations, create wishlists, and interact with buyers in real-time.

The Market Shift

Consumers are increasingly relying on messaging apps for all forms of communication, whether personal, business, or commerce. Increasingly, consumers are using chat to find and select products and services, and to complete the payment process, all without having to call, email, or even visit a brand's website. Everything is happening within the messaging app.

More than 94 trillion digital messages were sent in 2015, with the bulk being through email. However, instant messaging has just about reached its tipping point, with the total number of instant messages sent overtaking emails by mid-2016.

Means for Consumers

Chat companies are now partnering with brands to make it simpler for customers to buy from them. Facebook Messenger, for example, has partnered with Uber to make it possible for customers to order an Uber driver without leaving the messaging app – the conversation. Amazon's Echo – a voice activated tool – has partnered with Capital One so that the bank's customers can inquire about their balance, make a payment, or check recent transactions, all through Echo.

Not only is conversational commerce simpler for consumers who, thanks to messaging apps, no longer need to toggle back and forth between text conversations and websites to gather information and make purchases, but it's also a step closer to the attention you might get from a sales associate in the store. When ordering from a website, you can read reviews to get a sense of whether a product will work for you, but using chat you can ask for help comparing your options – more like the advice you would receive in-store.

Reducing the steps required, and the number of information sources consumers need to turn to, shortens the distance between prospect and purchase.

ETHICS, SOCIAL AND POLITICAL ISSUES IN E-COMMERCE

Defining the rights of people to express their ideas and the property rights of copyright owners are just two of many ethical, social, and political issues raised by the rapid evolution of e-commerce.

The ethical, social, and political issues raised in e-commerce, provide a framework for organizing the issues, and make recommendations for managers who are given the responsibility of operating e-commerce companies within commonly accepted standards of appropriateness. Understanding in E-commerce Internet and its use in e-commerce have raised pervasive ethical, social and political issues on a scale unprecedented for computer technology.

We live in an "information society," where power and wealth increasingly depend on information and knowledge as central assets. Controversies over information are often in fact disagreements over power, wealth, influence, and other things thought to be valuable. Like other technologies such as steam, electricity, telephones, and television, the Internet and ecommerce can be used to achieve social progress, and for the most part, this has occurred. However, the same technologies can be used to commit crimes, despoil the environment, and threaten cherished social values. Before automobiles, there was very little interstate crime and very little federal jurisdiction over crime. Likewise with the Internet - Before the Internet, there was very little "cyber crime."

Many business firms and individuals are benefiting from the commercial development of the Internet, but this development also exacts a price from individuals, organizations, and societies. These costs and benefits must be carefully considered by those seeking to make ethical and socially responsible decisions in this new environment.

Public Policy Issues in E-commerce

The major ethical, social, and political issues that have developed around e-commerce over the past seven to eight years can be loosely categorized into four major dimensions: information rights, property rights, governance, and public safety and welfare. Some of the ethical, social, and political issues raised in each of these areas include the following:

- Information rights: What rights to their own personal information do individuals have in a public marketplace, or in their private homes, when Internet technology make information collection so pervasive and efficient? What rights do individuals have to access information about business firms and other organizations?

- Property rights: How can traditional intellectual property rights be enforced in an internet world where perfect copies of protected works can be made and easily distributed worldwide in seconds?

- Governance: Should the Internet and e-commerce be subject to public laws? And if so, what law-making bodies have jurisdiction - state, federal, and international?

- Public safety and welfare: What efforts should be undertaken to ensure equitable access to the Internet and ecommerce channels? Should governments be responsible for ensuring that schools and colleges have access to the Internet? Is certain online content and activities – such as pornography and gambling - a threat to public safety and welfare? Should mobile commerce be allowed from moving vehicles?

To illustrate, imagine that at any given moment society and individuals are more or less in an ethical equilibrium brought about by a delicate balancing of individuals, social organizations, and political institutions. Individuals know what is expected of them, social organizations such as business firms know their limits, capabilities, and roles and political institutions provide a supportive framework of market regulation, banking and commercial law that provides sanctions against violators. Now, imagine we drop into the middle of this calm setting a powerful new technology such as the Internet and e-commerce. Suddenly individuals, business firms, and political institutions are confronted by new possibilities of behavior. For instance, individuals discover that they can download perfect digital copies of music tracks, something which, under the old technology of CDs, would have been impossible. This can be done, despite the fact that these music tracks still "belong" as a legal matter to the owners of the copyright - musicians and record label companies.

The introduction of the Internet and e-commerce impacts individuals, societies, and political institutions. These impacts can be classified into four moral dimensions: property rights, information rights, governance, and public safety and welfare Then business firms discover that they can make a business out of aggregating these musical tracks - or creating a mechanism for sharing musical tracks- even though they do not "own" them in the traditional sense. The record companies, courts, and Congress were not prepared at first to cope with the onslaught of online digital copying. Courts and legislative bodies will have to make new laws and reach new judgments about who owns digital copies of copyrighted works and under what conditions such works can be "shared." It may take years to develop new understandings, laws, and acceptable behavior in just this one area of social impact. In the meantime, as an individual and a manager, you will have to decide what you and your firm should do in legal "grey" areas, where there is conflict between ethical principles, but no clear-cutural guidelines. How can you make good decisions in this type of situation?

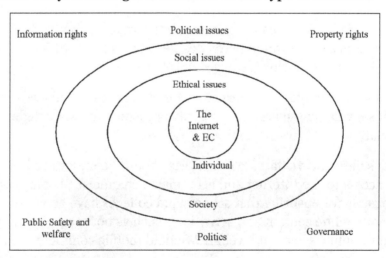

Responsibility Accountability and Liability

Ethics is at the heart of social and political debates about the Internet. Ethics is the study of principles that individuals and organizations can use to determine right and wrong courses of action. It is assumed in ethics that individuals are free moral agents who are in a position to make choices.

Extending ethics from individuals *to* business firms and even entire societies can be difficult, but it is not impossible. As long as there is a decision-making body or individual (such as a Board of Directors or CEO in a business firm or a governmental body in a society), their decisions can be judged against a variety of ethical principles. If you understand some basic ethical principles, your ability *to* reason about larger social and political debates will be improved. In western culture, there are ability and liability principles that all ethical schools of thought share: responsibility, account-liability.

Responsibility means that as free moral agents, individuals, organizations and societies are responsible for the actions they take. Accountability means that individuals, organizations, and societies should be held accountable to others for the consequences of their actions. The third principle liability, extends the concepts of responsibility and accountability to the area of law. Liability is a feature of political systems in which a body of law is in place that permits individuals to recover the damages done to them by other actors, systems, or organizations. Due process is a feature of law-governed societies and refers to a process in which laws are known and understood and there is an ability to appeal to higher authorities to ensure that the laws have been applied correctly.

Analyzing Ethical Dilemmas

Ethical, social, and political controversies usually present themselves as dilemmas. A dilemma is a situation in which there are at least two diametrically opposed actions, each of which supports a desirable outcome. When confronted with a situation that seems to present ethical dilemmas, how can you analyze and reason about the situation? The following is a five step process that should help.

- Identify and describe clearly the facts. Find out who did what to whom, and where, when, and how. In many instances, you will be surprised at the errors in the initially reported facts, and often you will find that simply getting the facts straight helps define the solution. It also helps to get the opposing parties involved in an ethical dilemma to agree on the facts.

- Define the conflict or dilemma and identify the higher order value involved. Ethical, social, and political issues always reference higher values. Otherwise, there would be no debate. The parties to a dispute all claim to be pursuing higher values (e.g., freedom, privacy, protection of property, and the -enterprise system). For example, Double Click and its supporters argue that their tracking of consumer movements on the Web increases market efficiency and the wealth of the entire society. Opponents argue this claimed efficiency comes at the expense of individual privacy, and Double Click should cease its or offer Web users the option of not participating in such tracking.

- Identify the stakeholders. Every ethical, social, and political issue has stake-holders: players in the game who have an interest in the outcome, who have its vested in the situation, and usually who have vocal opinions. Find out the identity of these groups and what they want. This will be useful later when designing a solution.

- Identity the options that you can reasonably take. You may find that none of the options satisfies all the interests involved, but that some options do a better job than others. Sometimes, arriving at a "good" or ethical solution may not, always be a balancing of consequences to stakeholders.

- Identify the potential consequences of your options. Some options may be ethically correct, but disastrous from other points of view. Other options may work in this one instance, but not in other similar instances. Always ask, "what if you choose this option consistently over time?" Once your analysis is complete, you can refer to the following well established ethical principle to help decide the matter.

Privacy and Information Rights

The Internet and the Web provide an ideal environment for invading the personal privacy of millions of users on a scale unprecedented in history. Perhaps no other recent issue has raised as much widespread social and political concern as protecting the privacy of over 160 million Web users in the United States alone.

The major ethical issues related to ecommerce and privacy includes the following:Under what conditions should we invade the privacy of others? What legitimates intruding into others lives through unobtrusive surveillance, market research, or other means?

The major social issues related to e-commerce and privacy concern the development of "exception of privacy" or privacy norms, as well as public attitudes. In what areas of should we as a society encourage people to think they are in "private territory" as opposed to public view? The major political issues related to ecommerce and privacy concern the development of statutes that govern the relations between record keepers and individuals.

Concept of Privacy

Privacy is the moral right of individuals to be left alone, free from surveillance or interference from other individuals or organizations, including the state. Privacy is a girder supporting freedom. Without the privacy required to think, write, plan, and associate independently and without fear, social and political freedom is weakened, and perhaps destroyed. Information privacy is a subset of privacy. The right to information privacy includes both the claim that certain information should not be collected at all by governments or business firms, and the claim of individuals to control over personal of whatever information that is collected about them. Individual control over personal information is at the core of the privacy concept. Due process also plays an important role in defining privacy. The best statement of due process in record keeping is given by the Fair Information Practices doctrine developed in the early 1970s and extended to the online privacy debate in the late 1990s.

References

- What-is-ecommerce, encyclopedia: shopify.in, Retrieved 22 February, 2019

- E-commerce-advantages, e-commerce: tutorialspoint.com, Retrieved 25 March, 2019

- E-commerce-disadvantages, e-commerce: tutorialspoint.com, Retrieved 26 April, 2019

- Basic-ecommerce-marketing-concepts, ecommerce, retail-ecommerce, industries: webfx.com, Retrieved 27 May, 2019

- E-payment-system: securionpay.com, Retrieved 28 June, 2019

- Ecommerce-security-basic, security: cardinalcommerce.com, Retrieved 29 July, 2019

- Ethical-social-and-political-issues-in-ecommerce, e-commerce-concepts-tutorial-7: wisdomjobs.com, Retrieved 30 August, 2019

E-Commerce Business Models

An e-commerce business model is a set of planned activities designed to result in a profit for an e-commerce enterprise. There are numerous e-commerce business models such as business to business model, consumer to consumer model, business to administration model, etc. This chapter discusses in detail these models related to e-commerce business.

BUSINESS-TO-BUSINESS

A website following the Business-to-business (B2B) business model sells its products to an intermediate buyer who then sells the products to the final customer. As an example, a wholesaler places an order from a company's website and after receiving the consignment, it sells the endproduct to the final customer who comes to buy the product at the wholesaler's retail outlet.

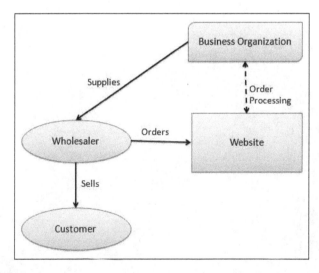

B2B identifies both the seller as well as the buyer as business entities. B2B covers a large number of applications, which enables business to form relationships with their distributors, re-sellers, suppliers, etc. Following are the leading items in B2B e-commerce.

- Electronics,

- Shipping and Warehousing,

- Motor Vehicles,

- Petrochemicals,

- Paper,

- Office products,

- Food,

- Agriculture.

Key Technologies

Following are the key technologies used in B2B e-commerce:

- Electronic Data Interchange (EDI) – EDI is an inter-organizational exchange of business documents in a structured and machine processable format.

- Internet – Internet represents the World Wide Web or the network of networks connecting computers across the world.

- Intranet – Intranet represents a dedicated network of computers within a single organization.

- Extranet – Extranet represents a network where the outside business partners, suppliers, or customers can have a limited access to a portion of enterprise intranet/network.

- Back-end Information System Integration – Back-end information systems are database management systems used to manage the business data.

Architectural Models

Following are the architectural models in B2B e-commerce:

- Supplier Oriented marketplace – In this type of model, a common marketplace provided by supplier is used by both individual customers as well as business users. A supplier offers an e-stores for sales promotion.

- Buyer Oriented marketplace – In this type of model, buyer has his/her own market place or e-market. He invites suppliers to bid on product's catalog. A Buyer company opens a bidding site.

- Intermediary Oriented marketplace – In this type of model, an intermediary company runs a market place where business buyers and sellers can transact with each other.

BUSINESS-TO-CONSUMER

Business-to-consumer (B2C) is an Internet and electronic commerce (e-commerce) model that denotes a financial transaction or online sale between a business and consumer. B2C involves a service or product exchange from a business to a consumer, whereby merchants sell products to consumers. B2C is also known as business-to-customer (B2C).

A business that sells online merchandise to individual consumers is categorized B2C. Experts have suggested that online B2C activities played a vital role in shaping the Internet, despite the dotcom bubble burst in the late 1990s. While many online B2C business websites shut down at that time, an electronic customer surge occurred shortly thereafter, which helped catapult e-commerce activities. Companies took advantage of this by creating electronic storefronts after discovering they could sell larger volumes of merchandise through B2C models.

CONSUMER-TO-CONSUMER

Consumer-to-consumer electronic commerce is a growing area of e-commerce. However, according to Meta analysis of critical themes of e-commerce, C2C e-commerce was only represented in the area of online auctions. C2C transactions generally involve products sold through a classified or auction system. Products sold are often used or second hand. C2C is projected to grow in the future because of its cost effective; this means it minimizes the cost of using third parties. Retailers see it as very important, given the growing use of social media channels by consumers to share their option about specific stock, which often drives increased traffic to stores. C2C is the oldest form of e-commerce we know, used well before internet appeared, although they can and are supported by large websites nowadays. They are a way of helping people to deal directly with each other or to buy more conveniently from companies. The goal of C2C is to enable buyers and sellers to find each other easily. They benefit in two crucial commerce areas. Firstly, they benefit from competition for product and second they can easily find products that are otherwise difficult to locate.

C2C e-commerce differs from a business-to-business model or business-to-consumer model because consumers interact directly with each other. However, a business does operate the online platform on which C2C transaction takes place. Buyer can shop for free, but sellers sometimes have to pay a fee to list their products. Consumers often play an active role in monitoring e-commerce sites for scam and other inappropriate content.

In most cases, C2C e-commerce is helped along by a third party who officiate the transaction to make sure goods are received and payments are made. This offers some protection for consumers taking part in C2C e-commerce, allowing the chance to take advantage of the prices offered by motivated seller.

There are two implementation of C2C e-commerce that is credited with its origin. These are classified and auction.The oldest auction house is Stockholm Auction House which was established in Sweden in 1674. Auction however, has been recorded as far back as 500 B.C. Auction have since been widely used method of liquidating assets, and has evolved into many different variations. The most successful current form of auction is based on the internet with systems such as eBay.

C2C e-commerce has become more famous recently with the advent of the internet. Companies such as Craigslist, eBay, and other classified and auction based sites have allowed for greater interaction between consumers, facilitating the customer to customer model. Newspapers and other similar publications were frequent circulation and therefore were able to be used to facilitate a common need. Some people wanted things; others had things and wanted to sell them. This was the birth of classifieds. C2C has come a long way and will still enjoy the current changes in technologies as they appear.

This is a business model where two individuals or consumers transact or conduct business with each other directly. Generally, an intermediary/third party maybe involved, but the purpose of the intermediary is only to facilitate the transaction and provide a platform for the people to connect to each other. The intermediary would receive a fee or commission, but is not responsible for the product exchange. C2C normally takes the form of an auction where the bidding is done online.

Functionalities of C2C Web Application

- The buyer can purchase products from multiple sellers.

- The same customer can act as both buyer as well as seller.

- The online market place will allow buyer to browse products by using different criteria such as: best seller, most popular product, from your city and many more.

- Different sellers can bid on the products wish list item listed by the buyer, what they are looking for so that the buyer can get different best prices and offers from sellers.

- The social media linking functionalities include, community or forum discussion and blog and other social media website link interface.

- The back end interface includes features for administration to manage buyer and seller accounts, payment settings, gallery setting, etc.

C2C E-commerce Business Model

The C2C model involves transactions between consumers. Here a consumer sells directly to another consumer. eBay and bazee are common examples of online auction websites that provide a consumer to advertise and sell their product online to another consumer. However, it is important that both the seller and the buyer register with the auction site. While the seller needs to pay a fixed fee to the online auction house to sell their products, the buyer can bid without paying any fee. The site brings the buyer and seller together to conduct deals.

Figure shows two customers (customer 1 and customer 2) and a website providing the space for advertisement. Customer 1 places advert on the website about products he wants to sell and customer 2 visits the website to search for products he wants to buy. The transaction between the customers goes on until payment and delivery of product is done.

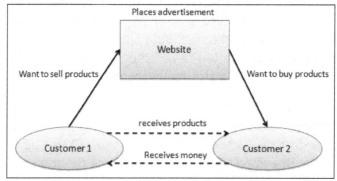

C2C business model.

C2C E-commerce Statistics

C2C e-commerce is facilitated in large part by websites offering free classified advertisement, auctions, forums, and individual pages for start-up entrepreneurs. Etsy, eBay, Craigslist, Taobao, Amazon, and kickstarter all offer functions to enable C2C transactions and interactions. Since its launch in 1995, the online auction and selling website eBay has been one of the leaders of C2C e-commerce and statistics show that it is one of the fastest growing internet companies with its annual net revenue doubling between 2008 and 2013. Recent market data shows that eBay's audience stretches over most over most of the world and drew over 84million USA visitors in the beginning of 2014. The success of eBay makes Alibaba realize that Chinese C2C market is also a big gold mine. Currently the monthly volume of business on eBay website is 60million or so, and increase 20% per month. Though eBay charges commission that is only less than 1/10 of the whole business, and has made no profit, these categories of eBay proves that C2C categories are feasible in China. Alibaba invested a huge amount of money to create Taobao website, at the same time eBay declared that it would add to Chinese eBay more investment and pay 15,000,000 Yuan to buy the remaining share of American eBay in order to put eBay under full control.

Analysys International estimates that the Chinese B2C and C2C online market will reach RMB 2,568 billion ($412 billion) by 2015 with an associated marketing spend of 48.87 billion RMB. Currently Taobao generates 50,000 sales per minutes as China's biggest C2C mall. There are 242 million online shoppers spending $40,000 per seconds. 17% of online shoppers account for 47% of sales. There are 5 million online shoppers and there are 146 million shoppers using mobile connection. The figure below shows the monthly worldwide revenue of Etsy.

During those months, the C2C e-commerce website's sales generated revenue of $14.7 million up from 115.2million U.S dollars in online sales in October 2013.

In 2014, C2C has recorded 105billion dollars market size as compared to 71billion dollars for B2C e-commerce.

C2C market size has experienced tremendous increase from 2004 to date. This increase in market size could be attributed to popularity and patronage C2C has got since its existence.

The figure below shows the e-commerce (C2C, B2C) market size.

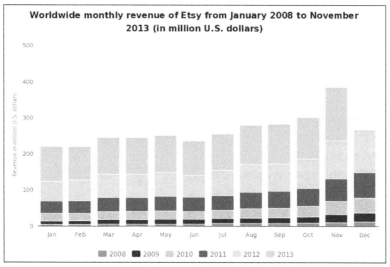

Etsy worldwide monthly revenue.

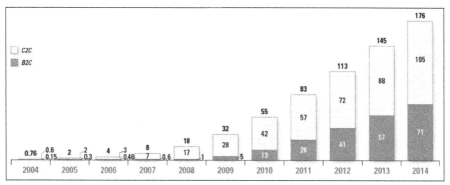

E-commerce (C2C, B2C) market size.

Advantages of C2C E-commerce

- It is always available so that consumers can have access to whenever they feel like shopping.

- There is regular updating of the website.

- Consumers selling products to other consumers benefit from the higher profitability that result from selling directly to one another.

- There is a low transaction cost; sellers can post their goods over the internet at a cheaper rate far better than higher price of renting a space in a store.

- Customer can directly contact sellers and do without an intermediary.

Disadvantages of C2C E-commerce

- Payment made has no guarantee.

- There could be theft as scammers might try to create their website with names of some famous C2C websites such as eBay to attract customers.

- There is lack of controlling quality of the products.

CONSUMER-TO-BUSINESS

C2B ecommerce is also known as consumer-to-business. This change heralds a complete reversal of the traditional model, with those who would normally be end-users creating products and services that are consumed by the businesses and organizations they themselves buy from.

Elance (now operated by Upwork) was the first truly C2B
ecommerce site, which inverted the usual relationship.

Instead of a business advertising a service to someone and waiting for them to take it up, customers now demanded a service for a price that they're happy to pay and waited for a business (or freelancer) to fill the gap. This inversion of the usual way of working is now becoming even more common.

This has come in a large part to the power the Internet has put in the hands of consumers. Customers are now starting to realize the power they wield and are looking to leverage that power for profits. In much the same way as a brand leverages its prestige, consumers can now leverage their influences. It is a new form of currency that has nevertheless proven very effective for both sides.

C2B Examples:

To help you better understand the concept, think Upwork (otherwise known as Elance in the beginning). It was the first business C2B model where consumers can post their services and interested businesses can answer with bid proposals.

Working of C2B Marketing

C2B marketing works because there are three different groups whose relationships are changing. These are broken down as the customer, the business, and the intermediary.

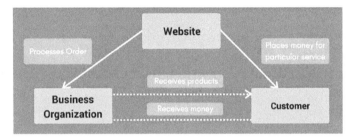

Customers

The customer is an individual who has something to offer. This can be broken down into goods or services.

Top 6 Internet Marketing Specialists Hired This Month

This is how people are promoting their services in Upwork.

For example:

- A webmaster or blogger can offer a service by showcasing the latest product.

- Someone who is active on social media and has thousands of followers or subscribers can share their use of a product to introduce it to new audiences.

- Someone who takes great photographs might sell them as stock photos for businesses.

- People who are willing to answer polls can provide valuable market research data.

- Those with connections can help refer potential hires to the business.

Throughout these examples, there's one key theme, which is a changing nature of the relationship to customers away from being top-down and toward being back-and-forth. Consumers are now no longer a market, they are a network.

Business

In this particular transactional relationship, the business is the for-profit institution that purchases goods or services from individuals. This can be for many reasons, and in both direct or indirect ways.

C2B ecommerce like Amazon affiliates allows the purchase of a product, for which the website owner will receive revenues or commission from a successful sale.

- Companies may need to advertise online and seek exposure from those who can give it to them.

- Advertising agencies who need to buy stock photos to populate their content.

- Companies who need to make a new hire and want to find the best people through referral hiring sites.

- Manufacturers that need feedback on their products to help inform the development of new products.

Intermediary

In C2B ecommerce, the intermediary is *the portal*, or the medium that is used by both businesses and individuals, and connect the two.

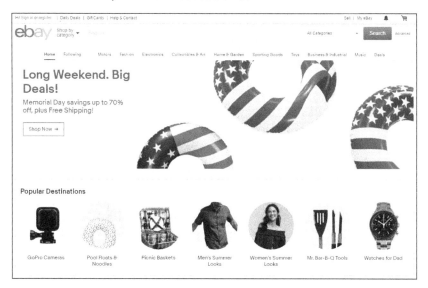

BUSINESS-TO-ADMINISTRATION

Business-to-government (B2G) is a business model that refers to the companies selling products, services or information to governments or government agencies. B2G models provide an opportunity for businesses to bid on government contracts or products that government might buy or need for their firms. This can comprise of public sector companies that propose the bids. B2G bidding is increasingly being executed online through real-time bidding. B2G is also known as public sector marketing.

Types

Types of B2G methods called integrated marketing communications include Web-based communications and public relations and e-marketing. The solicitations given by government are for the businesses that have something to offer to the government. The solicitations can be in the form of reverse auctions where numbers of sellers are competing to get the business.

Requirements

Social networking sites such as LinkedIn, Facebook and Twitter can also be a part of this market, although companies mostly neglect this form of selling. Companies have to provide the documents related to their product and capabilities that they can offer to the government. Business-to-government (B2G) is a type of B2B marketing and includes public sector companies that want to get into public offerings. The government works on a pre-decided price and it is non- negotiable at a later stage.

CONSUMER-TO-ADMINISTRATION

Consumer to Administration or Consumer to Government deals with the communication of consumer directly to the Administration. The e-commerce system helps a consumer to post their feedbacks or request for information about public sectors, which is directly linked with government administration or authorities.

Such as paying electricity bill on government websites, paying taxes, paying health insurance as well. It means the government websites probably done with C2A Model. Basically, C2A E-commerce system builds a strong bond with an instant and easy solution of communication between consumers and government administrations.

References

- E-commerce-b2b-mode, e-commerce: tutorialspoint.com, Retrieved 1 January, 2019

- Business-to-consumer, definition: techopedia.com, Retrieved 2 February, 2019

- What-is-c2b-ecommerce: seopressor.com, Retrieved 3 March, 2019

- Business-to-government, marketing-and-strategy-terms, business-concepts: mbaskool.com, Retrieved 4 April, 2019

- Types-of-e-commerce-with-examples: digitalopment.com, Retrieved 5 May, 2019

Digital Marketing

The marketing of products or services using digital technologies on the internet, through mobile phone apps and other digital mediums is called digital marketing. Some of the techniques involved in digital marketing are content marketing, SEO techniques, inbound marketing, etc. The diverse aspects of these digital marketing techniques have been thoroughly discussed in this chapter.

Digital marketing encompasses all marketing efforts that use an electronic device or the internet. Businesses leverage digital channels such as search engines, social media, email, and other websites to connect with current and prospective customers.

A seasoned inbound marketer might say inbound marketing and digital marketing are virtually the same thing, but there are some minor differences. And conversations with marketers and business owners in the U.S., U.K., Asia, Australia, and New Zealand.

While traditional marketing might exist in print ads, phone communication, or phsycial marketing, digital marketing can occur electronically and online. This means that there are a number of endless possibilities for brands including email, video, social media, or website-based marketing opportunities.

Because digital marketing has so many options and strategies associated with it, you can get creative and experiment with a variety of marketing tactics on a budget. With digital marketing, you can also use tools like analytics dashboards to monitor the success and ROI of your campaigns more than you could with a traditional promotional content - such as a billboard or print ad.

How does a Business define Digital Marketing

Digital marketing is defined by the use of numerous digital tactics and channels to connect with customers where they spend much of their time: online. From the website itself to a business's online branding assets - digital advertising, email marketing, online brochures, and beyond - there's a spectrum of tactics that fall under the umbrella of "digital marketing."

The best digital marketers have a clear picture of how each digital marketing campaign supports their overarching goals. And depending on the goals of their marketing strategy, marketers can support a larger campaign through the free and paid channels at their disposal.

A content marketer, for example, can create a series of blog posts that serve to generate leads from a new ebook the business recently created. The company's social media marketer might then help promote these blog posts through paid and organic posts on the business's social media accounts. Perhaps the email marketer creates an email campaign to send those who download the ebook more information on the company.

Digital Marketing Examples:

- Search Engine Optimization (SEO),

- Content Marketing,

- Social Media Marketing,

- Pay Per Click (PPC),

- Affiliate Marketing,

- Native Advertising,

- Marketing Automation,

- Email Marketing,

- Online PR,

- Inbound Marketing.

Search Engine Optimization

This is the process of optimizing your website to "rank" higher in search engine results pages, thereby increasing the amount of organic (or free) traffic your website receives. The channels that benefit from SEO include websites, blogs, and infographics.

There are a number of ways to approach SEO in order to generate qualified traffic to your website. These include:

- On page SEO: This type of SEO focuses on all of the content that exists "on the page" when looking at a website. By researching keywords for their search volume and intent (or meaning), you can answer questions for readers and rank higher on the search engine results pages (SERPs) those questions produce.

- Off page SEO: This type of SEO focuses on all of the activity that takes place "off the page" when looking to optimize your website. "What activity not on my own website could affect my ranking?" You might ask. The answer is inbound links, also known as backlinks. The number of publishers that link to you, and the relative "authority" of those publishers, affect how highly you rank for the keywords you care about. By networking with other publishers, writing guest posts on these websites (and linking back to your website), and generating external attention, you can earn the backlinks you need to move your website up on all the right SERPs.

- Technical SEO: This type of SEO focuses on the backend of your website, and how your pages are coded. Image compression, structured data, and CSS file optimization are all forms of technical SEO that can increase your website's loading speed - an important ranking factor in the eyes of search engines like Google.

Content Marketing

This term denotes the creation and promotion of content assets for the purpose of generating brand awareness, traffic growth, lead generation, and customers. The channels that can play a part in your content marketing strategy include:

- Blog posts: Writing and publishing articles on a company blog helps you demonstrate your industry expertise and generates organic search traffic for your business. This ultimately gives you more opportunities to convert website visitors into leads for your sales team.

- Ebooks and whitepapers: Ebooks, whitepapers, and similar long-form content helps further educate website visitors. It also allows you to exchange content for a reader's contact information, generating leads for your company and moving people through the buyer's journey.

- Infographics: Sometimes, readers want you to show, not tell. Infographics are a form of visual content that helps website visitors visualize a concept you want to help them learn.

Social Media Marketing

This practice promotes your brand and your content on social media channels to increase brand awareness, drive traffic, and generate leads for your business. The channels you can use in social media marketing include:

- Facebook.
- Twitter.
- LinkedIn.
- Instagram.

- Snapchat.

- Pinterest.

If you're new to social platforms, you can use tools to connect channels like LinkedIn and Facebook in one place. This way, you can easily schedule content for multiple channels at once, and monitor analytics from the platform as well.

On top of connecting social accounts for posting purposes, you can also integrate your social media inboxes into HubSpot, so you can get your direct messages in one place.

Pay Per Click

Pay Per Click (PPC) is a method of driving traffic to your website by paying a publisher every time your ad is clicked. One of the most common types of PPC is Google Ads, which allows you to pay for top slots on Google's search engine results pages at a price "per click" of the links you place. Other channels where you can use PPC include:

- Paid ads on Facebook: Here, users can pay to customize a video, image post, or slideshow, which Facebook will publish to the newsfeeds of people who match your business's audience.

- Twitter Ads campaigns: Here, users can pay to place a series of posts or profile badges to the news feeds of a specific audience, all dedicated to accomplish a specific goal for your business. This goal can be website traffic, more Twitter followers, tweet engagement, or even app downloads.

- Sponsored Messages on LinkedIn: Here, users can pay to send messages directly to specific LinkedIn users based on their industry and background.

Affiliate Marketing

This is a type of performance-based advertising where you receive commission for promoting someone else's products or services on your website. Affiliate marketing channels include:

- Hosting video ads through the YouTube Partner Program.

- Posting affiliate links from your social media accounts.

Native Advertising

Native advertising refers to advertisements that are primarily content-led and featured on a platform alongside other, non-paid content. BuzzFeed-sponsored posts are a good example, but many people also consider social media advertising to be "native" - Facebook advertising and Instagram advertising.

Marketing Automation

Marketing automation refers to the software that serves to automate your basic marketing operations. Many marketing departments can automate repetitive tasks they would otherwise do manually, such as:

- Email newsletters: Email automation doesn't just allow you to automatically send emails to your subscribers. It can also help you shrink and expand your contact list as needed so your newsletters are only going to the people who want to see them in their inboxes.

- Social media post scheduling: If you want to grow your organization's presence on a social network, you need to post frequently. This makes manual posting a bit of an unruly process. Social media scheduling tools push your content to your social media channels for you, so you can spend more time focusing on content strategy.

- Lead-nurturing workflows: Generating leads, and converting those leads into customers, can be a long process. You can automate that process by sending leads specific emails and content once they fit certain criteria, such as when they download and open an ebook.

- Campaign tracking and reporting: Marketing campaigns can include a ton of different people, emails, content, webpages, phone calls, and more. Marketing automation can help you sort everything you work on by the campaign it's serving, and then track the performance of that campaign based on the progress all of these components make over time.

Email Marketing

Companies use email marketing as a way of communicating with their audiences. Email is often used to promote content, discounts and events, as well as to direct people toward the business's website. The types of emails you might send in an email marketing campaign include:

- Blog subscription newsletters.

- Follow-up emails to website visitors who downloaded something.

- Customer welcome emails.

- Holiday promotions to loyalty program members.

- Tips or similar series emails for customer nurturing.

Online PR

Online PR is the practice of securing earned online coverage with digital publications, blogs, and other content-based websites. It's much like traditional PR, but in the online space. The channels you can use to maximize your PR efforts include:

- Reporter outreach via social media: Talking to journalists on Twitter, for example, is a great way to develop a relationship with the press that produces earned media opportunities for your company.

- Engaging online reviews of your company: When someone reviews your company online, whether that review is good or bad, your instinct might be not to touch it. On the contrary, engaging company reviews helps you humanize your brand and deliver powerful messaging that protects your reputation.

- Engaging comments on your personal website or blog: Similar to the way you'd respond to reviews of your company, responding to the people who are reading your content is the best way to generate productive conversation around your industry.

Inbound Marketing

Inbound marketing refers to a marketing methodology wherein you attract, engage, and delight customers at every stage of the buyer's journey. You can use every digital marketing tactic listed above, throughout an inbound marketing strategy, to create a customer experience that works *with* the customer, not *against* them. Here are some classic examples of inbound marketing versus traditional marketing:

- Blogging vs. pop-up ads,

- Video marketing vs. commercial advertising,

- Email contact lists vs. email spam.

Inbound Marketing vs. Digital Marketing

On the surface, the two seem similar: Both occur primarily online, and both focus on creating digital content for people to consume. So what's the difference?

The term "digital marketing" doesn't differentiate between push and pull marketing tactics (or what we might now refer to as 'inbound' and 'outbound' methods). Both can still fall under the umbrella of digital marketing.

Digital outbound tactics aim to put a marketing message directly in front of as many people as possible in the online space - regardless of whether it's relevant or welcomed. For example, the garish banner ads you see at the top of many websites try to push a product or promotion onto people who aren't necessarily ready to receive it.

On the other hand, marketers who employ digital inbound tactics use online content to attract their target customers onto their websites by providing assets that are helpful to them. One of the simplest yet most powerful inbound digital marketing assets is a blog, which allows your website to capitalize on the terms which your ideal customers are searching for.

Ultimately, inbound marketing is a methodology that uses digital marketing assets to attract, engage, and delight customers online. Digital marketing, on the other hand, is simply an umbrella term to describe online marketing tactics of any kind, regardless of whether they're considered inbound or outbound.

Does Digital Marketing work for all Businesses?

Digital marketing can work for any business in any industry. Regardless of what your company sells, digital marketing still involves building out buyer personas to identify your audience's needs, and creating valuable online content. However, that's not to say all businesses should implement a digital marketing strategy in the same way.

B2B Digital Marketing

If your company is business-to-business (B2B), your digital marketing efforts are likely to be centered around online lead generation, with the end goal being for someone to speak to a salesperson. For that reason, the role of your marketing strategy is to attract and convert the highest quality leads for your salespeople via your website and supporting digital channels.

Beyond your website, you'll probably choose to focus your efforts on business-focused channels like LinkedIn where your demographic is spending their time online.

B2C Digital Marketing

If your company is business-to-consumer (B2C), depending on the price point of your products, it's likely that the goal of your digital marketing efforts is to attract people to your website and have them become customers without ever needing to speak to a salesperson.

For that reason, you're probably less likely to focus on 'leads' in their traditional sense, and more likely to focus on building an accelerated buyer's journey, from the moment someone lands on your website, to the moment that they make a purchase. This will often mean your product features in your content higher up in the marketing funnel than it might for a B2B business, and you might need to use stronger calls-to-action (CTAs).

For B2C companies, channels like Instagram and Pinterest can often be more valuable than business-focused platforms LinkedIn.

Role of Digital Marketing to a Company

Unlike most offline marketing efforts, digital marketing allows marketers to see accurate results in real time. If you've ever put an advert in a newspaper, you'll know how difficult it is to estimate how many people actually flipped to that page and paid attention to your ad. There's no surefire way to know if that ad was responsible for any sales at all. On the other hand, with digital marketing, you can measure the ROI of pretty much any aspect of your marketing efforts.

Website Traffic

With digital marketing, you can see the exact number of people who have viewed your website's homepage in real time by using digital analytics software, available in marketing platforms.

You can also see how many pages they visited, what device they were using, and where they came from, amongst other digital analytics data.

This intelligence helps you to prioritize which marketing channels to spend more or less time on, based on the number of people those channels are driving to your website. For example, if only 10% of your traffic is coming from organic search, you know that you probably need to spend some time on SEO to increase that percentage.

With offline marketing, it's very difficult to tell how people are interacting with your brand before they have an interaction with a salesperson or make a purchase. With digital marketing, you can identify trends and patterns in people's behavior before they've reached the final stage in their buyer's journey, meaning you can make more informed decisions about how to attract them to your website right at the top of the marketing funnel.

Content Performance and Lead Generation

Imagine you've created a product brochure and posted it through people's letterboxes - that brochure is a form of content, albeit offline. The problem is that you have no idea how many people opened your brochure or how many people threw it straight into the trash.

Now imagine you had that brochure on your website instead. You can measure exactly how many people viewed the page where it's hosted, and you can collect the contact details of those who download it by using forms. Not only can you measure how many people are engaging with your content, but you're also generating qualified leads when people download it.

Attribution Modeling

An effective digital marketing strategy combined with the right tools and technologies allows you to trace all of your sales back to a customer's first digital touchpoint with your business.

We call this attribution modeling, and it allows you to identify trends in the way people research and buy your product, helping you to make more informed decisions about what parts of your marketing strategy deserve more attention, and what parts of your sales cycle need refining.

Connecting the dots between marketing and sales is hugely important - according to Aberdeen Group, companies with strong sales and marketing alignment achieve a 20% annual growth rate, compared to a 4% decline in revenue for companies with poor alignment. If you can improve your customer's journey through the buying cycle by using digital technologies, then it's likely to reflect positively on your business's bottom line.

Different Types of Digital Content

The kind of content you create depends on your audience's needs at different stages in the buyer's journey. You should start by creating buyer personas (use these free templates, or try makemypersona.com) to identify what your audience's goals and challenges are in relation to your business. On a basic level, your online content should aim to help them meet these goals, and overcome their challenges.

Then, you'll need to think about when they're most likely to be ready to consume this content in relation to what stage they're at in their buyer's journey. We call this content mapping.

With content mapping, the goal is to target content according to:

- The characteristics of the person who will be consuming it (that's where buyer personas come in).

- How close that person is to making a purchase (i.e., their lifecycle stage).

In terms of the format of your content, there are a lot of different things to try. Here are some options we'd recommend using at each stage of the buyer's journey:

Awareness Stage

- Blog posts: Great for increasing your organic traffic when paired with a strong SEO and keyword strategy.

- Infographics: Very shareable, meaning they increase your chances of being found via social media when others share your content.

- Short videos: Again, these are very shareable and can help your brand get found by new audiences by hosting them on platforms like YouTube.

Consideration Stage

- Ebooks: Great for lead generation as they're generally more comprehensive than a blog post or infographic, meaning someone is more likely to exchange their contact information to receive it.

- Research reports: Again, this is a high value content piece which is great for lead generation. Research reports and new data for your industry can also work for the awareness stage though, as they're often picked-up by the media or industry press.

- Webinars: As they're a more detailed, interactive form of video content, webinars are an effective consideration stage content format as they offer more comprehensive content than a blog post or short video.

Decision Stage

- Case studies: Having detailed case studies on your website can be an effective form of content for those who are ready to make a purchasing decision, as it helps you positively influence their decision.

- Testimonials: If case studies aren't a good fit for your business, having short testimonials around your website is a good alternative. For B2C brands, think of testimonials a little more loosely. If you're a clothing brand, these might take the form of photos of how other people styled a shirt or dress, pulled from a branded hashtag where people can contribute.

With digital marketing, it can often feel like you're able to see results much faster than you might with offline marketing due to the fact it's easier to measure ROI. However, it ultimately depends on the scale and effectiveness of your digital marketing strategy.

If you spend time building comprehensive buyer personas to identify the needs of your audience, and you focus on creating quality online content to attract and convert them, then you're likely to see strong results within the first six months.

If paid advertising is part of your digital strategy, then the results come even quicker - but it's recommended to focus on building your organic (or 'free') reach using content, SEO, and social media for long-term, sustainable success.

Budget for Digital Marketing

As with anything, it really depends on what elements of digital marketing you're looking to add to your strategy.

If you're focusing on inbound techniques like SEO, social media, and content creation for a preexisting website, the good news is you don't need very much budget at all. With inbound marketing, the main focus is on creating high quality content that your audience will want to consume, which unless you're planning to outsource the work, the only investment you'll need is your time.

You can get started by hosting a website and creating content. For those on a tight budget, you can get started using WordPress hosted on WP Engine and using a simple them from StudioPress.

With outbound techniques like online advertising and purchasing email lists, there is undoubtedly some expense. What it costs comes down to what kind of visibility you want to receive as a result of the advertising.

For example, to implement PPC using Google AdWords, you'll bid against other companies in your industry to appear at the top of Google's search results for keywords associated with your business. Depending on the competitiveness of the keyword, this can be reasonably affordable, or extremely expensive, which is why it's a good idea to focus building your organic reach, too.

Mobile Marketing into Digital Marketing Strategy

Another key component of digital marketing is mobile marketing. In fact, smartphone usage as a whole accounts for 69% of time spent consuming digital media in the U.S., while desktop-based digital media consumption makes up less than half - and the U.S. still isn't mobile's biggest fan compared to other countries.

This means it's essential to optimize your digital ads, web pages, social media images, and other digital assets for mobile devices. If your company has a mobile app that enables users to engage with your brand or shop your products, your app falls under the digital marketing umbrella too.

Those engaging with your company online via mobile devices need to have the same positive experience as they would on desktop. This means implementing a mobile-friendly or responsive website design to make browsing user-friendly for those on mobile devices. It might also mean reducing the length of your lead generation forms to create a hassle-free experience for people downloading your content on-the-go. As for your social media images, it's important to always have a mobile user in mind when creating them as image dimensions are smaller on mobile devices, meaning text can be cut-off.

There are lots of ways you can optimize your digital marketing assets for mobile users, and when implementing any digital marketing strategy, it's hugely important to consider how the experience will translate on mobile devices. By ensuring this is always front-of-mind, you'll be creating digital experiences that work for your audience, and consequently achieve the results you're hoping for.

INTEGRATED DIGITAL MARKETING

It is important for businesses to realize that integrated digital marketing is not just a fad, but rather an evolution in marketing. Sure, one-off ad campaigns still exist, but they are no longer the touchstone of ROI that they once were. To succeed in today's techonomy, businesses need to adopt sophisticated marketing strategies that would be unrecognizable to Don Draper and Peggy Olson.

Integrated digital marketing requires businesses to synergize their marketing efforts across various media in real-time. Campaigns can no longer be thought of as vaguely measureable units of marketing expenditure. Just like everyone else who is ever-present on the Internet, brands are too. Rather than just creating a presence, brands must be a presence. The best way to achieve this is to understand that integrated digital marketing, and the inbound marketing methodology that underpins it, are not only nice ideas but the axels around which your brand revolves.

Digital Presence Management

A business website is the cornerstone of your brand's online presence. By implementing Responsive Web Design (RWD), consumers will be able to access your website from whatever device they're using now and in the future. While the upfront costs may be more than what your spending at the moment, it will prove cost-efficient result in a lot less headaches in the long-term.

Content Marketing

As the world moves online, content is king. Businesses are using content marketing convey their brand message to key target audience segments. The most important thing to keep in mind when content marketing is that the content you produce must not be salesy. Whatever blogs, videos, or eBooks you create must be sought after and the kind of stuff you might share with someone yourself, not forced upon your target audience.

Targeted Discovery

This element of digital marketing is changing rapidly as mobile device usage and context-based content fragment and redefine search as we know it. The big players on the scene, Google and Facebook are implementing sophisticated ad targeting serves operable over desktop and mobile devices. Further shattering our understanding of traditional SEO, Facebook has introduced a viable social search engine with Graph Search, while Google is expanding its Adwords to automatically include mobile.

Online Engagement

Once you've set up shop on the relevant social media sites, it's important to use each of them in their unique capacities. Rather than just creating a brand presence, you want to *be* a presence. Use the different functions of social media to diversify the way you interact with consumers. Ask questions, take feedback, comment on what others are doing and learn from them.

Social Local Mobile

The beating heart of integrated digital marketing is social, local, mobile (SoLoMo). Now that smart phones have penetrated so deeply into our culture, it is important to be conscious of where buyers are when they reach out to you, and how they're doing it. Are they on a cell phone or a computer? Are they stationary or mobile? When are they most likely to need your brand's service or product? Use SoLoMo to make your business the most convenient option during high-relevance opportunities by enticing buyers with timely deals.

Performance Management

Before you even begin to implement all of these other aspects of your integrated digital marketing strategy, it is important to set up metrics by which you can measure their effectiveness. Although it may be difficult to measure the value of presence, it is important to monitor changes in consumer engagement so that you know what's working and what's not. Use digital marketing analytics data to inform ongoing marketing strategy and real-time interaction.

SEARCH ENGINE OPTIMIZATION

SEO (Search engine optimization) is the process of making a web page easy to find, easy to crawl, and easy to categorize. It is about helping your customers find out your business from among thousand other companies. SEO is an integral part of any digital marketing strategy. It is basically concerned with a holistic move towards driving customers to your business via online platforms. And to do that, one must ensure the website ranks higher in the SERP. To give you an idea on this, let's start with this fact – nearly 14 billion searches online take place every month. The advent of Global economy nearly makes every business have an online presence. Just imagine a fraction of those 14 billion searches happen for your business. To achieve that benchmark, your website must rank higher in the SERP, must perform well in the social media marketing, and the PPC (pay per click) activities must be very well along with other digital marketing tasks.

For any business, advertising is of utmost need. When any business goes online, the advertising works best to garner a huge amount of web traffic. SEO gives an opportunity for a great deal of free advertising.

A proper SEO makes a website rank in the first page of SERP. And the common belief is people generally scan and review the first two pages of the SERP. Nearly, 74% of consumers use search engines to find local business information. Compared to online marketing, such as PPC, social media marketing, email marketing program, SEO provides fairly good ROI. On a daily basis, nearly 80-90% customers check online reviews before finally purchasing any products.

How does SEO Work

Search engine are not humans but the software that crawls the web page content. So, not like humans search engines are text-driven. They complete a number of activities that bring search results – crawling, scanning and storing (or index), courses of action, measuring pertinence, and recovering. The distinction with an excellence count is that you're calculating components of design, rather than actions of an individual. For example, some of the elements that are known to build up a quality score are as follows:

- Website names and URLs,

- Page content,

- Meta tags,

- Characteristics of Link,

- Usability and accessibility,

- Page design.

Steps of SEO Cycle

- Crawling: Every search engine has software, known as Crawler or Spider (in case of Google it is Googlebot), that crawls the webpage content. It is not possible for a crawler to see daily if any new page appeared or any existing page is updated, some crawlers may not visit a webpage for a month or two. In this connection, it should be important to remember what all a search engine can crawl: it cannot crawl image, Flash Movies, JavaScript, Frames, Password protected page, and directories. Therefore, if you have majority of these in your website, it would be better to run a keyword simulator test to see if these are viewable by the spider. Those that are not viewable are not spidered and not indexed or not processed. On the other hand, they will be missing for search engines.

- Indexing: Post-crawling content the Spider stores the indexed page in a giant database from where those can be retrieved upon entering a related search string or keyword. For humans this will not be possible, but for search engine, this is every day's work. Sometimes, the search engines cannot understand the page content. And for that, you need to correctly optimize the page.

- Search work: With every search request, the search engine processes, i.e., it contrasts the key phrases searched with the pages indexed and stored in its record. More than millions of pages have the same search phrases. So, the search engine is an act of measuring the relevancy of all the pages and matches with what it indexed as per the keywords inserted in the SERP.

- Algorithms: A search algorithm is a diagnostic means that takes a puzzle (when there is a search with a particular keyword), sorts through a record that contains cataloged keywords and the URLs that have relevancy with those keywords, estimates some probable answers, and then reverts pages that have the word or phrase that was looked for, either in the body content or in a URL that directs to the page. Three search algorithms are there – On-site, Off-site, and Whole-site algorithms.

  Each type of algorithm definitely looks at different aspects of the webpage, such as Meta tags, title tags, links, keyword density, etc., yet they all are part of a much larger algorithm. That is the reason why same search string generates different results in different search engines having distinct algorithms. And all these search engines (primary, secondary, and targeted) periodically do keep on changing their algorithms, so you must know how to adapt to these changes if you want to stay on the top. This requires sound SEO expertise.

- Retrieving: The end–result will be visible in the search results.

SEO and Digital Marketing

Apparently, it seemed there is no such difference between SEO and digital marketing approaches; both execute the same functions and possess the same skills. Only for marketing needs, different titles are resorted. To understand this, we need to pay a thorough look on these concepts. The below figure will clearly show how SEO is based as a subset of digital marketing.

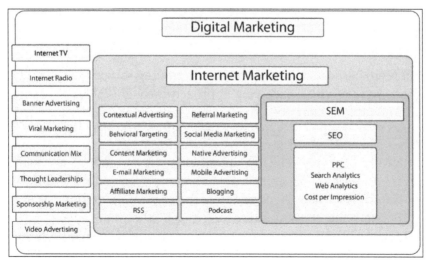

The SEO people are engaged in bringing the organic hits, while the digital marketers aim at total online existence (of a company) that goes beyond SEO. In practice, an SEO consultant generally looks after other areas of digital marketing. And the whole SEO digital marketing service package may be named all under SEO Packages since customers basically comprehend this more easily.

The contemporary trend includes some more services along with optimizing a website and search engine marketing. For example, there are some factors that actually take help of SEO in the sense of selecting the right keywords, such as blogging with SEO content, contextual marketing, behavioral marketing, mobile advertising, Alt-texts in banner advertising, social media marketing, RSS, viral marketing, and video content advertising. And for that a solid digital marketing and SEO strategy should be in place.

Integrated Digital Marketing

And after coming a long way an SEO is called integrated digital marketing by some marketing experts. Let's give some light on this.

More and more, the use of SEO is becoming important for the overall success of digital marketing. And we would get a very good idea if we carefully watch the changing paradigm of SEO over years. In mid 90's when very first SEO came into picture, manual submission, the Meta keywords tag, and keyword stuffing were all usual techniques necessary to rank well in the SERP. Then in 2004, for getting web traffic, anchor text associated link bombing, link buying from automated blog comment spam injectors, and creation of inter-linking websites took place. Then in 2011, the social media marketing and vertical search inclusion became the mainstream methods of conducting SEO. The search engine algorithms get updated time after time for the sake of bringing traffic. The tactics used in 2004 are all outdated now as the new call is something else.

Today, so many new memes totally change the way an SEO consultant once worked though the basic understanding remains the same, such as title tags, H1 tags, and everyone's preferred subject, thanks to Google, links. But many applications that previously were remote to what we used to judge SEO no more are.

- Social Media: Social media marketing is gaining importance because of the increased usage of viral marketing approach through Facebook, LinkedIn, Twitter, Yammer, and Google+. These social networking sites must be in line with the SEO best practices to entirely control SEO potential:

- The more links with a view to ranking higher is not today's approach: The personal reputation has become a crucial aspect. Old school of link building has some improvisations. The common belief of ranking high in the search results is changing – the content strategies are not the main means, but generating the quality inbound links that stay as a much important SEO element to affect the ranking. The concept of 'link' is changing in that respect. The main idea behind the traditional link building to measure all the do-follow links that a website can generate and totally ignore all no-follow links. The practice was to build as many links as possible. That system had drawbacks what some black-hat marketers banked on, and finally Google changed its algorithms, which totally ended the practice of traditional link building practice. This was known as spamming. Even guest-blogging with a sole motive to generate links is also burned down. Guest-blogging really works well if it is to generate new audiences, present yourself as an expert, and engage with your targeted community.

- The implied links factored in: It is called implied linking as there is basically no link to go back to the source site. Brand mentions and online citation must be handled carefully and well-incorporated into the site content; this is done in several forms. In the content, the brand mentions are generally connected to the products or services, and how those are connected to the content is explained. It can be in the comments what is finally implicitly integrated well into the content also. So as long as the brand or website name is used, a brand name or citation is created.

  ○ Better judgement in brand authority: Google does not give that much importance to the former practice of traditional link building. A new brand authority will rule in the form of brand mentions.

  ○ There is no manipulation at all: The Anchor texts and links cannot be manipulated now. The black-hat practice of linking to a site that is totally irrelevant to the source site is replaced by the brand mentions or online citations. Once a brand is flawlessly woven in site content, the implied link should point to sites that must be relevant to the source site.

  ○ Influencing the social signals through brand mentions: Brand mentions or online citation is reckoned as an important factor to leverage the social signals for SEO. The links that got generated through social media are no-follow links that do not affect the SERP rankings. But when any source content is shared, commented, tweeted, or cited socially with or even without these implied links, it must funnel to highest rankings. This entire process of back-linking through social media is called social media optimization.

  ○ Online citation is an important factor for local SEO: Local SEO targets potential customers of the small and medium sized enterprises. Citations are always good for local SEO. Here, the use of name, address, and contact number are taken into consideration by Google for a bigger picture.

- Balance between traditional linking and brand mentions: You should not develop a wrong notion that only brand mentions do exist now-a-days, and the traditional linking has become obsolete. There needs to be a balance between these two. An equal importance must be given. Below is a balanced link building strategy between implied and express links:

- ◦ Just avoid having a higher ratio in the express links to your brand mention to escape the possible danger of getting spammed that can affect your brand.

- ◦ Google likes the practice of visual content that go viral as it is the right way to keep a good ratio of express links to brand mention.

- ◦ Guest-blogging can be used to promote the brand.

- ◦ Link building strategy needs to be as fair and usual as possible.

- ◦ Use every possible avenue to inculcate the brand mentions – social media, guest-blogging, comments, and RSS feeds that can go viral.

- ◦ Last but not the least prepare your website thinking about your target audience – what they deserve. Relevant and valuable content must flow in.

- Social media optimization has a new entrant, video optimization: Today's SEO expert knows how to optimize video content, effectively distribute it, and measure its efficacies in meaningful ways.

- Paid search redefined: A co-optimization plan needs to follow the paid search initiatives with a high degree of group effort with the organic search team for utmost outcomes on both sides of the aisle.

- Use of data: The capability to understand, mine, and use data efficiently to steer strategy and sharing of resources within a restricted budget for highest ROI (return on investment) is another important parameter.

- Miscellaneous factors of modern SEO: The bounce rate, site speed, and very recently, content above the fold are known to be significant factors in the algorithms of the most important search engines. Also, display advertising, including behavioral targeting or retargeted marketing and contextual advertising use the targeted keywords generated in the organic search practices. Most of all, you all need to have a thorough idea on the marketing campaigns and business model, so that you can work in evocative ways.

Create an SEO Strategy

To have a sound SEO system you must have a good SEO strategy in place. Below are some points you need ask yourself while setting SEO strategy:

- Your target market: SEO is not meant to garner as many web traffic as you can to sell your items. Some geographic conditions and the customer demographics are very much important as to where and how you will get your customers. Fine tuning on these parts will make you confident and successful going forward. Google Analytics will help you in your investigations on these factors.

- Concentrate on mobile-friendly approaches: Your website should be able to properly fit into mobile and give equal satisfactions to your customers the way they access your site in their personal computers. One thing is clear, mobile overtakes the desktop. So, be sure to open that lane by checking how your website performs on mobile applications. Test your website URL in Google's Mobile Friendly test for this.

- More options in search engines: Your website should not only perform well in Google, but in every other search engines like Yahoo, MSN, AOL, and DuckDuckGo. Each search engine has different search algorithms that you need to know and accordingly make your website compatible for these searches. Your users may come from any roads.

- Keywords to correspond with your ROI: Spend time on fixing relevant keywords. Focus on Long Tail keyword as those define users' behaviors. Meticulously think about you can frame long tail qualities into your key phrases. The success of keywords should be measured in terms of your ROI (return on investments).

- Clear website and quality content: A user-friendly website, clear navigation, SEO keywords, optimized Meta tags, title tags, and balanced keyword density in the qualitative, relevant, and consistent content are the main aims. Each page should be built around the keyword themes, with unique and non-plagiarised content. There should be no keyword stuffing as well. "Content is a commitment, not a campaign."

- Quality and relevant linking and Social media: You must pay good attention at building quality and relevant links through which you can get a good number of web traffic. And in line with SEO, you need to set up an exhaustive and up-to-date social media platform. You should remember a good number of traffic is generated through social presence of your business.

TYPES OF SEO TECHNIQUES

Spamdexing

In digital marketing and online advertising, spamdexing (also known as search engine spam, search engine poisoning, black-hat search engine optimization (SEO), search spam or web spam) is the deliberate manipulation of search engine indexes. It involves a number of methods, such as link building and repeating unrelated phrases, to manipulate the relevance or prominence of resources indexed, in a manner inconsistent with the purpose of the indexing system.

It could be considered to be a part of search engine optimization, though there are many search engine optimization methods that improve the quality and appearance of the content of web sites and serve content useful to many users. Search engines use a variety of algorithms to determine relevancy ranking. Some of these include determining whether the search term appears in the body text or URL of a web page. Many search engines check for instances of spamdexing and will remove suspect pages from their indexes. Also, search-engine operators can quickly block the results-listing from entire websites that use spamdexing, perhaps alerted by user complaints of false matches. The rise of spamdexing in the mid-1990s made the leading search engines of the time less useful. Using unethical methods to make websites rank higher in search engine results than they otherwise would is commonly referred to in the SEO (search engine optimization) industry as "black-hat SEO". These methods are more focused on breaking the search-engine-promotion rules and guidelines. In addition to this, the perpetrators run the risk of their websites being severely penalized by the Google Panda and Google Penguin search-results ranking algorithms.

Common spamdexing techniques can be classified into two broad classes: content spam (or term spam) and link spam.

Content Spam

These techniques involve altering the logical view that a search engine has over the page's contents. They all aim at variants of the vector space model for information retrieval on text collections.

Keyword Stuffing

Keyword stuffing involves the calculated placement of keywords within a page to raise the keyword count, variety, and density of the page. This is useful to make a page appear to be relevant for a web crawler in a way that makes it more likely to be found. Example: A promoter of a Ponzi scheme wants to attract web surfers to a site where he advertises his scam. He places hidden text appropriate for a fan page of a popular music group on his page, hoping that the page will be listed as a fan site and receive many visits from music lovers. Older versions of indexing programs simply counted how often a keyword appeared, and used that to determine relevance levels. Most modern search engines have the ability to analyze a page for keyword stuffing and determine whether the frequency is consistent with other sites created specifically to attract search engine traffic. Also, large webpages are truncated, so that massive dictionary lists cannot be indexed on a single webpage.

Hidden or Invisible Text

Unrelated hidden text is disguised by making it the same color as the background, using a tiny font size, or hiding it within HTML code such as "no frame" sections, alt attributes, zero-sized DIVs, and "no script" sections. People screening websites for a search-engine company might temporarily or permanently block an entire website for having invisible text on some of its pages. However, hidden text is not always spamdexing: it can also be used to enhance accessibility.

Meta-tag Stuffing

This involves repeating keywords in the meta tags, and using meta keywords that are unrelated to the site's content. This tactic has been ineffective since 2005.

Doorway Pages

"Gateway" or doorway pages are low-quality web pages created with very little content, but are instead stuffed with very similar keywords and phrases. They are designed to rank highly within the search results, but serve no purpose to visitors looking for information. A doorway page will generally have "click here to enter" on the page. In 2006, Google ousted BMW for using "doorway pages" to the company's German site, BMW.de.

Scraper Sites

Scraper sites are created using various programs designed to "scrape" search-engine results pages or other sources of content and create "content" for a website. The specific presentation of content on these sites is unique, but is merely an amalgamation of content taken from other sources, often without permission. Such websites are generally full of advertising (such as pay-per-click ads), or they redirect the user to other sites. It is even feasible for scraper sites to outrank original websites for their own information and organization names.

Article Spinning

Article spinning involves rewriting existing articles, as opposed to merely scraping content from other sites, to avoid penalties imposed by search engines for duplicate content. This process is undertaken by hired writers or automated using a thesaurus database or a neural network.

Machine Translation

Similarly to article spinning, some sites use machine translation to render their content in several languages, with no human editing, resulting in unintelligible texts.

Publishing web pages that contain information that is unrelated to the title is a misleading practice known as deception. Despite being a target for penalties from the leading search engines that rank pages, deception is a common practice in some types of sites, including dictionary and encyclopedia sites.

Link Spam

Link spam is defined as links between pages that are present for reasons other than merit. Link spam takes advantage of link-based ranking algorithms, which gives websites higher rankings the more other highly ranked websites link to it. These techniques also aim at influencing other link-based ranking techniques such as the HITS algorithm. There are many different types of link spam, built for both positive and negative ranking effects on websites.

Link-building Software

A common form of link spam is the use of link-building software to automate the search engine optimization process.

Link Farms

Link farms are tightly-knit networks of websites that link to each other for the sole purpose of gaming the search engine ranking algorithms. These are also known facetiously as mutual admiration societies. Use of links farms has been greatly reduced after Google launched the first Panda Update in February 2011, which introduced significant improvements in its spam-detection algorithm.

Private Blog Networks

Blog networks (PBNs) are a group of authoritative websites used as a source of contextual links that point to the owner's main website to achieve higher search engine ranking. Owners of PBN websites use expired domains or auction domains that have backlinks from high-authority websites. Google targeted and penalized PBN users on several occasions with several massive deindexing campaigns since 2014.

Hidden Links

Putting hyperlinks where visitors will not see them to increase link popularity. Highlighted link text can help rank a webpage higher for matching that phrase.

Sybil Attack

A Sybil attack is the forging of multiple identities for malicious intent, named after the famous multiple personality disorder patient "Sybil". A spammer may create multiple web sites at different domain names that all link to each other, such as fake blogs (known as spam blogs).

Spam Blogs

Spam blogs are blogs created solely for commercial promotion and the passage of link authority to target sites. Often these "splogs" are designed in a misleading manner that will give the effect of a legitimate website but upon close inspection will often be written using spinning software or very poorly written and barely readable content. They are similar in nature to link farms.

Guest Blog Spam

Guest blog spam is the process of placing guest blogs on websites for the sole purpose of gaining a link to another website, or websites. Unfortunately often confused with legitimate forms of guest blogging with other motives than placing links. Made famous by Matt Cutts publicly declaring "war" against this method of link spam.

Buying Expired Domains

Some link spammers utilize expired domain crawler software or monitor DNS records for domains that will expire soon, then buy them when they expire and replace the pages with links to their pages. However, it is possible but not confirmed that Google resets the link data on expired domains. To maintain all previous Google ranking data for the domain, it is advisable that a buyer grabs the domain before it is "dropped". Some of these techniques may be applied for creating a Google bomb — that is, to cooperate with other users to boost the ranking of a particular page for a particular query.

Cookie Stuffing

Cookie stuffing involves placing an affiliate tracking cookie on a website visitor's computer without their knowledge, which will then generate revenue for the person doing the cookie stuffing. This not only generates fraudulent affiliate sales, but also has the potential to overwrite other affiliates' cookies, essentially stealing their legitimately earned commissions.

Using World-writable Pages

Web sites that can be edited by users can be used by spamdexers to insert links to spam sites if the appropriate anti-spam measures are not taken.

Automated spambots can rapidly make the user-editable portion of a site unusable. Programmers have developed a variety of automated spam prevention techniques to block or at least slow down spambots.

Spam in Blogs

Spam in blogs is the placing or solicitation of links randomly on other sites, placing a desired keyword into the hyperlinked text of the inbound link. Guest books, forums, blogs, and any site that accepts visitors' comments are particular targets and are often victims of drive-by spamming where automated software creates nonsense posts with links that are usually irrelevant and unwanted.

Comment Spam

Comment spam is a form of link spam that has arisen in web pages that allow dynamic user editing such as wikis, blogs, and guestbooks. It can be problematic because agents can be written that automatically randomly select a user edited web page.

Wiki Spam

Wiki spam is a form of link spam on wiki pages. The spammer uses the open editability of wiki systems to place links from the wiki site to the spam site. The subject of the spam site is often unrelated to the wiki page where the link is added.

Referrer Log Spamming

Referrer spam takes place when a spam perpetrator or facilitator accesses a web page (the referee), by following a link from another web page (the referrer), so that the referee is given the address of the referrer by the person's Internet browser. Some websites have a referrer log which shows which pages link to that site. By having a robot randomly access many sites enough times, with a message or specific address given as the referrer, that message or Internet address then appears in the referrer log of those sites that have referrer logs. Since some Web search engines base the importance of sites on the number of different sites linking to them, referrer-log spam may increase the search engine rankings of the spammer's sites. Also, site administrators who notice the referrer log entries in their logs may follow the link back to the spammer's referrer page.

Countermeasures

Because of the large amount of spam posted to user-editable webpages, Google proposed a nofollow tag that could be embedded with links. A link-based search engine such as Google's PageRank system, will not use the link to increase the score of the linked website if the link carries a nofollow tag. This ensures that spamming links to user-editable websites will not raise the sites ranking with search engines. Nofollow is used by several major websites, including Wordpress and Blogger.

Other Types

Mirror Websites

A mirror site is the hosting of multiple websites with conceptually similar content but using different URLs. Some search engines give a higher rank to results where the keyword searched for appears in the URL.

URL Redirection

URL redirection is the taking of the user to another page without his or her intervention, e.g., using META refresh tags, Flash, JavaScript, Java or Server side redirects. However, 301 Redirect, or permanent redirect, is not considered as a malicious behavior.

Cloaking

Cloaking refers to any of several means to serve a page to the search-engine spider that is different from that seen by human users. It can be an attempt to mislead search engines regarding the content on a particular web site. Cloaking, however, can also be used to ethically increase accessibility of a site to users with disabilities or provide human users with content that search engines aren't able to process or parse. It is also used to deliver content based on a user's location; Google itself uses IP delivery, a form of cloaking, to deliver results. Another form of cloaking is code swapping, i.e., optimizing a page for top ranking and then swapping another page in its place once a top ranking is achieved. Google refers to these type of redirects as Sneaky Redirects.

Overall Counterplan

By Search Engine Maintainer

Spamdexed pages are sometimes eliminated from search results by the search engine.

By Search Engine User

Users can craft at search keyword, for example, a keyword preceding "-" (minus) will eliminate sites that contains the keyword in their pages or in their domain of URL of the pages from search result. Example, search keyword "naver" will eliminate sites that contains word "naver" in their pages and the pages whose domain of URL contains "naver".

Google Chrome Extension

Google itself launched the Google Chrome extension "Personal Blocklist (by Google)" in 2011 as part of countermeasures against content farming. As of 2018, the extension only works with the PC version of Google Chrome.

White Hat SEO

The term "white hat SEO" refers to SEO tactics that are in line with the terms and conditions of the major search engines, including Google.

White hat SEO is the opposite of Black Hat SEO. Generally, white hat SEO refers to any practice that improves your search rankings on a search engine results page (SERP) while maintaining the integrity of your website and staying within the search engines' terms of service. Examples of white hat SEO include:

- Offering quality content and services.

- Fast site loading times and mobile-friendliness.

- Using descriptive, keyword-rich meta tags.

- Making your site easy to navigate.

Examples of black hat SEO, by contrast, include purchasing links or using deceptive cloaking techniques. Any tactics that are considered deceitful or harmful for consumers would qualify as black hat. Black hat tactics are extremely risky and, as Google's algorithms evolve, less and less likely to work.

Importance of White Hat SEO

Failure to engage only in White Hat SEO practices can get your site banned from Google and other search engines.

As the number one search engine, Google is visited by billions of people per day, and each visit presents the potential for your site to be discovered by a new user.

Google is an undeniably powerful source of traffic to your website, and being banned can result in a drastic drop in website traffic and even business. Consider all the work that goes into your website and then think about what it would be like to be banned from the internet's most commonly used search engine. What's worse, once you're banned from Google, there is no guarantee that they will ever re-list you. A lifetime ban from Google would have tremendous consequences.

CONTENT MARKETING

Content marketing is a form of marketing focused on creating, publishing, and distributing content for a targeted audience online. It is often used by businesses in order to:

- Attract attention and generate leads,

- Expand their customer base,

- Generate or increase online sales,

- Increase brand awareness or credibility,

- Engage an online community of users.

Content marketing attracts prospects and transforms prospects into customers by creating and sharing valuable free content. Content marketing helps companies create sustainable brand loyalty, provides valuable information to consumers, and creates a willingness to purchase products from the company in the future. This relatively new form of marketing does not involve direct sales. Instead, it builds trust and rapport with the audience.

Unlike other forms of online marketing, content marketing relies on anticipating and meeting an existing customer need for information, as opposed to creating demand for a new need. As James O'Brien of Contently wrote on Mashable, "The idea central to content marketing is that a brand must give something valuable to get something valuable in return. Instead of the commercial, be the show. Instead of the banner ad, be the feature story." Content marketing requires continuous delivery of large amounts of content, preferably within a content marketing strategy.

When businesses pursue content marketing, the main focus should be the needs of the prospect or customer. Once a business has identified the customer's need, information can be presented in a variety of formats, including news, video, white papers, e-books, infographics, email newsletters, case studies, podcasts, how-to guides, question and answer articles, photos, blogs, etc. Most of these formats belong to the digital channel.

Digital content marketing is a management process that uses electronic channels to identify, forecast, and satisfy the content requirements of a particular audience. It must be consistently updated and added to in order to influence the behavior of customers.

Implications

The rise of content marketing has turned many traditional businesses into media publishing companies.

- Red Bull, which sells a high-energy beverage, has published YouTube videos, hosted experiences, and sponsored events around extreme sports and activities like mountain biking, BMX, motocross, snowboarding, skateboarding, cliff-diving, freestyle motocross, and Formula 1 racing. Red Bull Media House is a unit of Red Bull that "produces full-length feature films for cinema and downstream channels (DVD, VOD, TV)." The Red Bulletin is an international monthly magazine Red Bull publishes with a focus on men's sports, culture, and lifestyle.

- The personal finance site mint.com used content marketing, specifically their personal finance blog Mint Life, to build an audience for a product they planned to sell. According to entrepreneur Sachin Rekhi, mint.com concentrated on building the audience for MintLife "independent of the eventual mint.com product." Content on the blog included how to guides on paying for college, saving for a house, and getting out of debt. Other popular content included in-depth interview and a series of financial disasters called "Trainwreck Tuesdays." Popularity of the site surged as did demand for the product. "Mint grew quickly enough to sell to Intuit for $170 million after three years in business. By 2013, the tool reached 10 million users, many of whom trusted Mint to handle their sensitive banking information because of the blog's smart, helpful content."

The rise of content marketing has also accelerated the growth of online platforms, such as YouTube, Yelp, LinkedIn, Tumblr, Pinterest, and more.

For example:

- YouTube, a subsidiary of Google, is an online video platform driving (and benefiting from) the surge to content marketing. As of 2016, YouTube had over 1 billion users, representing 1/3 of all internet users and reaching more people 18–34 years of age than any cable provider in the U.S.

- Yelp, an online business directory, has seen 30% year over growth in the number of reviews, ending the second quarter of 2016 with 108 million reviews for over 3 million businesses.

Businesses actively curate their content on these platforms with hopes to expand their reach to new audiences.

Common Metrics

Metrics to determine the success of a content marketing are often tied to the original goals of the campaign. For example, for each of these goals, a content marketer may measure different engagement and conversion metrics which are mention below.

Brand Awareness and Visibility

Businesses focused on expanding their reach to more customers will want to pay attention to the increase in volume of visitors, as well as the quality of those interactions. Traditional measures of volume include number of visitors to a page and number of emails collected, while time spent on page and click-through to other pages/photos are good indicators for engagement.

- Number of visitors to a page.

- Time spent on the page.

- Click-through across pages/photos.

- Number of emails collected.

Brand Health Metrics

Businesses want to measure the impact that their messages have on consumers. Brand health refers to the positive or negative feedback that a company gets. It also measures how important a brand is for consumers. With this companies want to find out if brand reputation influences their customers to make a purchase.

Measures in this part comprise:

- Share of voice (SOV) is the number of times a brand has been talked versus its competitors (conversations). Outside the digital world, SOV stands for the space and frequency a brand advertisement is placed on traditional media.

- Sentiment is when the brand has positive, negative or neutral feedback.

- Brand Influence refers to the number of times a post, comment or tweet is shared on different platforms.

Diversified user Base

For businesses hoping to reach not only more - but also new - types of customers online, they should pay attention to the demographics of new visitors, as evidenced by cookies that can be installed, different sources of traffic, different online behaviors, and different buying habits of online visitors.

- Demographics of visitors,

- Sources of traffic (i.e., SEO, social media, referral, direct),

- Differences in buying patterns and user-behavior of visitors.

Sales

Businesses focused on increasing sales through content marketing should look at traditional e-commerce metrics including click-through-rate from a product-page to check-out and completion rates at the check-out. Altogether, these form a conversion funnel. Moreover, to better understand customers' buying habits, they should look at other engagement metrics like time spent per page, number of product-page visits per user, and re-engagement.

- Conversion through the sales process (the process from sign-up to check-out), including click-through-rates at each stage of the conversion funnel.

- Time spent on the page.

- Re-engagement (i.e., % of returning visitors).

- Click-through across product pages.

Innovation Metrics

Refers to companies that wants to analyze whether their social media campaigns are generating commentary among consumers. This helps them to come up with ways to improve their product and service. This involves "high level of brand engagement and builds brand loyalty".

Examples:

- When a company makes a post through their social media platforms and shares their ideas, consumers can be influenced or motivated to share their opinions.

- Trend spotting refers to the latest consumers' comments about a brand, product or service that must be targeted. Some tools can be provided by Google Trends, Trendsmap (Twitter) and other sites that report what is in everybody's mouths worldwide.

Digital Use

Digital Content Marketing

Digital content marketing, which is a management process, uses digital products through different electronic channels to identify, forecast and satisfy the necessity of the customers. It must be consistently maintained to preserve or change the behavior of customers.

Examples:

- On March 6, 2012, Dollar Shave Club launched their online video campaign. In the first 48 hours of their video debuting on YouTube they had over 12,000 people signing up for the service. The video cost just $4500 to make and as of November 2015 has had more than 21 million views. The video was considered as one of the best viral marketing campaigns of 2012 and won "Best Out-of-Nowhere Video Campaign" at the 2012 AdAge Viral Video Awards.

- The Big Word Project, launched in 2008, aimed to redefine the Oxford English Dictionary by allowing people to submit their website as the definition of their chosen word. The project, created to fund two Masters students' educations, attracted the attention of bloggers worldwide, and was featured on Daring Fireball and Wired Magazine.

Way of Digital Content Marketing

Combination of the Supply Chain and the users' Experience

The supply chain of digital content marketing mainly consists of commercial stakeholders and end-user stakeholders which represent content providers and distributors and customers separately. In this process, distributors manage the interface between the publisher and the consumer, then distributors could identify the content that consumers need through external channels and implement marketing strategies. For instance, Library and document supply agencies as intermediaries can deliver the digital content of e-books, and e-journal articles to the users according to their search results through the electronic channels. Another example is when consumers pay for the acquisition of some MP3 downloads, search engines can be used to identify different music providers and smart agents can be used by consumers to search for multiple music provider sites. In a word, the digital content marketing process needs to be conducted at the business level and service experience level because when consumers are accessing digital content, their own experience depends on the complex network of relationships in the content marketing channels such as websites and videos. The consumers interact directly with distributors in the big supply chain through various digital products which have an important role in meeting the requirements of the consumers. The design and user experience of these channels directly decides the success of digital content marketing.

Interaction with the Consumer through Electronic Service

Electronic services refer to interactive network services. In the electronic service, the interaction between the customer and the organizations mainly through the network technology, such as using E-mail, telephone, online chat windows for communication. Electronic services are different from traditional services and they are not affected by distance restrictions and opening hours. Digital content marketing through electronic service is usually served together with other channels to achieve marketing purposes including face-to-face, postal, and other remote services. Information companies provide different messages and documents to customers who use multiple search engines on different sites and set up access rights for business groups. These are some channels of digital content marketing.

SEARCH ENGINE MARKETING

Search engine marketing (SEM) is a form of Internet marketing that involves the promotion of websites by increasing their visibility in search engine results pages (SERPs) primarily through paid advertising. SEM may incorporate search engine optimization (SEO), which adjusts or rewrites website content and site architecture to achieve a higher ranking in search engine results pages to enhance pay per click (PPC) listings.

Market

In 2007, U.S. advertisers spent US $24.6 billion on search engine marketing. In Q2 2015, Google (73.7%) and the Yahoo/Bing (26.3%) partnership accounted for almost 100% of U.S. search engine spend. As of 2006, SEM was growing much faster than traditional advertising and even other channels of online marketing. Managing search campaigns is either done directly with the SEM vendor or through an SEM tool provider. It may also be self-serve or through an advertising agency. As of October 2016, Google leads the global search engine market with a market share of 89.3%. Bing comes second with a market share of 4.36%, Yahoo comes third with a market share of 3.3%, and Chinese search engine Baidu is fourth globally with a share of about 0.68%.

Methods and Metrics

Search engine marketing uses at least five methods and metrics to optimize websites.

1. Keyword research and analysis involves three "steps": Ensuring the site can be indexed in the search engines, finding the most relevant and popular keywords for the site and its products, and using those keywords on the site in a way that will generate and convert traffic. A follow-on effect of keyword analysis and research is the search perception impact. Search perception impact describes the identified impact of a brand's search results on consumer perception, including title and meta tags, site indexing, and keyword focus. As online searching is often the first step for potential consumers/customers, the search perception impact shapes the brand impression for each individual.

2. Website saturation and popularity or how much presence a website has on search engines, can be analyzed through the number of pages of the site that are indexed by search engines (saturation) and how many backlinks the site has (popularity). It requires pages to contain keywords people are looking for and ensure that they rank high enough in search engine rankings. Most search engines include some form of link popularity in their ranking algorithms. The following are major tools measuring various aspects of saturation and link popularity: Link Popularity, Top 10 Google Analysis, and Marketleap's Link Popularity and Search Engine Saturation.

3. Back end tools, including Web analytic tools and HTML validators, provide data on a website and its visitors and allow the success of a website to be measured. They range from simple traffic counters to tools that work with log files and to more sophisticated tools that are based on page tagging (putting JavaScript or an image on a page to track actions). These tools can deliver conversion-related information. There are three major tools used by EBSCO: (a) log file analyzing tool: WebTrends by NetIQ; (b) tag-based analytic tool - WebSideStory's Hitbox; and (c) transaction-based tool: TeaLeaf RealiTea. Validators check the invisible parts of websites, highlighting potential problems and many usability issues and ensuring websites meet W3C code standards. Try to use more than one HTML validator or spider simulator because each one tests, highlights, and reports on slightly different aspects of your website.

4. Whois tools reveal the owners of various websites and can provide valuable information relating to copyright and trademark issues.

5. Google Mobile-Friendly Website Checker: This test will analyze a URL and report if the page has a mobile-friendly design.

Search engine marketing is a way to create and edit a website so that search engines rank it higher than other pages. It should be also focused on keyword marketing or pay-per-click advertising (PPC). The technology enables advertisers to bid on specific keywords or phrases and ensures ads appear with the results of search engines.

With the development of this system, the price is growing under the high level of competition. Many advertisers prefer to expand their activities, including increasing search engines and adding more keywords. The more advertisers are willing to pay for clicks, the higher the ranking for advertising, which leads to higher traffic. PPC comes at a cost. The higher position is likely to cost $5 for a given keyword, and $4.50 for a third location. A third advertiser earns 10% less than the top advertiser, while reducing traffic by 50%.

Investors must consider their return on investment when engaging in PPC campaigns. Buying traffic via PPC will deliver a positive ROI when the total cost-per-click for a single conversion remains below the profit margin. That way the amount of money spent to generate revenue is below the actual revenue generated. A positive ROI is the outcome.

There are many reasons explaining why advertisers choose the SEM strategy. First, creating a SEM account is easy and can build traffic quickly based on the degree of competition. The shopper who uses the search engine to find information tends to trust and focus on the links showed in the results pages. However, a large number of online sellers do not buy search engine optimization to obtain higher ranking lists of search results, but prefer paid links. A growing number of online publishers are allowing search engines such as Google to crawl content on their pages and place relevant ads on it. From an online seller's point of view, this is an extension of the payment settlement and an additional incentive to invest in paid advertising projects. Therefore, it is virtually impossible for advertisers with limited budgets to maintain the highest rankings in the increasingly competitive search market.

Google's search engine marketing is one of the western world's marketing leaders, while its search engine marketing is its biggest source of profit. Google's search engine providers are clearly ahead of the Yahoo and Bing network. The display of unknown search results is free, while advertisers are willing to pay for each click of the ad in the sponsored search results.

Paid Inclusion

Paid inclusion involves a search engine company charging fees for the inclusion of a website in their results pages. Also known as sponsored listings, paid inclusion products are provided by most search engine companies either in the main results area or as a separately identified advertising area.

The fee structure is both a filter against superfluous submissions and a revenue generator. Typically, the fee covers an annual subscription for one webpage, which will automatically be catalogued on a regular basis. However, some companies are experimenting with non-subscription based fee structures where purchased listings are displayed permanently. A per-click fee may also apply. Each search engine is different. Some sites allow only paid inclusion, although these have had little success. More frequently, many search engines, like Yahoo, mix paid inclusion (per-page and per-click fee) with results from web crawling. Others, like Google, do not let webmasters pay to be in their search engine listing (advertisements are shown separately and labeled as such).

Some detractors of paid inclusion allege that it causes searches to return results based more on the economic standing of the interests of a web site, and less on the relevancy of that site to end-users.

Often the line between pay per click advertising and paid inclusion is debatable. Some have lobbied for any paid listings to be labeled as an advertisement, while defenders insist they are not actually ads since the webmasters do not control the content of the listing, its ranking, or even whether it is shown to any users. Another advantage of paid inclusion is that it allows site owners to specify particular schedules for crawling pages. In the general case, one has no control as to when their page will be crawled or added to a search engine index. Paid inclusion proves to be particularly useful for cases where pages are dynamically generated and frequently modified.

Paid inclusion is a search engine marketing method in itself, but also a tool of search engine optimization, since experts and firms can test out different approaches to improving ranking and see the results often within a couple of days, instead of waiting weeks or months. Knowledge gained this way can be used to optimize other web pages, without paying the search engine company.

Comparison with SEO

SEM is the wider discipline that incorporates SEO. SEM includes both paid search results (using tools like Google Adwords or Bing Ads, formerly known as Microsoft adCenter) and organic search results (SEO). SEM uses paid advertising with AdWords or Bing Ads, pay per click (particularly beneficial for local providers as it enables potential consumers to contact a company directly with one click), article submissions, advertising and making sure SEO has been done. A keyword analysis is performed for both SEO and SEM, but not necessarily at the same time. SEM and SEO both need to be monitored and updated frequently to reflect evolving best practices.

In some contexts, the term SEM is used exclusively to mean pay per click advertising, particularly in the commercial advertising and marketing communities which have a vested interest in this narrow definition. Such usage excludes the wider search marketing community that is engaged in other forms of SEM such as search engine optimization and search retargeting.

Creating the link between SEO and PPC represents an integral part of the SEM concept. Sometimes, especially when separate teams work on SEO and PPC and the efforts are not synced, positive results of aligning their strategies can be lost. The aim of both SEO and PPC is maximizing the visibility in search and thus, their actions to achieve it should be centrally coordinated. Both teams can benefit from setting shared goals and combined metrics, evaluating data together to determine future strategy or discuss which of the tools works better to get the traffic for selected keywords in the national and local search results. Thanks to this, the search visibility can be increased along with optimizing both conversions and costs.

Another part of SEM is social media marketing (SMM). SMM is a type of marketing that involves exploiting social media to influence consumers that one company's products and services are valuable. Some of the latest theoretical advances include search engine marketing management (SEMM). SEMM relates to activities including SEO but focuses on return on investment (ROI) management instead of relevant traffic building (as is the case of mainstream SEO). SEMM also integrates organic SEO, trying to achieve top ranking without using paid means to achieve it, and pay per click SEO. For example, some of the attention is placed on the web page layout design and how content and information is displayed to the website visitor. SEO and SEM are two pillars of one marketing job and they both run side by side to produce much better results than focusing on only one pillar.

Examples:

AdWords is recognized as a web-based advertising utensil since it adopts keywords which can deliver adverts explicitly to web users looking for information in respect to a certain product or service. It is flexible and provides customizable options like Ad Extensions, access to non-search sites, leveraging the display network to help increase brand awareness. The project hinges on cost per click (CPC) pricing where the maximum cost per day for the campaign can be chosen, thus the payment of the service only applies if the advert has been clicked. SEM companies have embarked on AdWords projects as a way to publicize their SEM and SEO services. One of the most successful approaches to the strategy of this project was to focus on making sure that PPC advertising funds were prudently invested. Moreover, SEM companies have described AdWords as a practical tool for increasing a consumer's investment earnings on Internet advertising. The use of conversion tracking and Google Analytics tools was deemed to be practical for presenting to clients the performance of their canvas from click to conversion. AdWords project has enabled SEM companies to train their clients on the utensil and delivers better performance to the canvass. The assistance of AdWord canvass could contribute to the growth of web traffic for a number of its consumer's websites, by as much as 250% in only nine months.

Another way search engine marketing is managed is by contextual advertising. Here marketers place ads on other sites or portals that carry information relevant to their products so that the ads jump into the circle of vision of browsers who are seeking information from those sites. A successful SEM plan is the approach to capture the relationships amongst information searchers, businesses, and search engines. Search engines were not important to some industries in the past, but over the past years the use of search engines for accessing information has become vital to increase business opportunities. The use of SEM strategic tools for businesses such as tourism can attract potential consumers to view their products, but it could also pose various challenges. These challenges could be the competition that companies face amongst their industry and other sources of information that could draw the attention of online consumers. To assist the combat of challenges, the main objective for businesses applying SEM is to improve and maintain their ranking as high as possible on SERPs so that they can gain visibility. Therefore, search engines are adjusting and developing algorithms and the shifting criteria by which web pages are ranked sequentially to combat against search engine misuse and spamming, and to supply the most relevant information to searchers. This could enhance the relationship amongst information searchers, businesses, and search engines by understanding the strategies of marketing to attract business.

Pay-per-click

Pay-per-click (PPC), also known as cost per click (CPC), is an internet advertising model used to drive traffic to websites, in which an advertiser pays a publisher (typically a search engine, website owner, or a network of websites) when the ad is clicked.

Pay-per-click is commonly associated with first-tier search engines (such as Google Ads and Bing Ads). With search engines, advertisers typically bid on keyword phrases relevant to their target market. In contrast, content sites commonly charge a fixed price per click rather than use a bidding system. PPC "display" advertisements, also known as "banner" ads, are shown on web sites with related content that have agreed to show ads and are typically not pay-per-click advertising. Social networks such as Facebook and Twitter have also adopted pay-per-click as one of their advertising models.

However, websites can offer PPC ads. Websites that utilize PPC ads will display an advertisement when a keyword query matches an advertiser's keyword list that has been added in different ad groups, or when a content site displays relevant content. Such advertisements are called sponsored links or sponsored ads, and appear adjacent to, above, or beneath organic results on search engine results pages, or anywhere a web developer chooses on a content site.

The PPC advertising model is open to abuse through click fraud, although Google and others have implemented automated systems to guard against abusive clicks by competitors or corrupt web developers.

Pay-per-click, along with cost per impression and cost per order, are used to assess the cost effectiveness and profitability of internet marketing. Pay-per-click (PPC) has an advantage over cost per impression in that it conveys information about how effective the advertising was. Clicks are a way to measure attention and interest: if the main purpose of an ad is to generate a click, or more specifically drive traffic to a destination, then pay-per-click is the preferred metric. Once a certain number of web impressions are achieved, the quality and placement of the advertisement will affect click through rates and the resulting pay-per-click.

Construction

Cost-per-click (CPC) is calculated by dividing the advertising cost by the number of clicks generated by an advertisement. The basic formula is:

Cost-per-click ($) = Advertising cost ($)/Ads clicked (#)

There are two primary models for determining pay-per-click: flat-rate and bid-based. In both cases, the advertiser must consider the potential value of a click from a given source. This value is based on the type of individual the advertiser is expecting to receive as a visitor to his or her website, and what the advertiser can gain from that visit, usually revenue, both in the short term as well as in the long term. As with other forms of advertising targeting is key, and factors that often play into PPC campaigns include the target's interest (often defined by a search term they have entered into a search engine, or the content of a page that they are browsing), intent (e.g., to purchase or not), location (for geo targeting), and the day and time that they are browsing.

Flat-rate PPC

In the flat-rate model, the advertiser and publisher agree upon a fixed amount that will be paid for each click. In many cases the publisher has a rate card that lists the pay-per-click (PPC) within different areas of their website or network. These various amounts are often related to the content on pages, with content that generally attracts more valuable visitors having a higher PPC than content that attracts less valuable visitors. However, in many cases advertisers can negotiate lower rates, especially when committing to a long-term or high-value contract.

The flat-rate model is particularly common to comparison shopping engines, which typically publish rate cards. However, these rates are sometimes minimal, and advertisers can pay more for greater visibility. These sites are usually neatly compartmentalized into product or service categories, allowing a high degree of targeting by advertisers. In many cases, the entire core content of these sites is paid ads.

Bid-based PPC

The advertiser signs a contract that allows them to compete against other advertisers in a private auction hosted by a publisher or, more commonly, an advertising network. Each advertiser informs the host of the maximum amount that he or she is willing to pay for a given ad spot (often based on a keyword), usually using online tools to do so. The auction plays out in an automated fashion every time a visitor triggers the ad spot.

When the ad spot is part of a search engine results page (SERP), the automated auction takes place whenever a search for the keyword that is being bid upon occurs. All bids for the keyword that target the searcher's Geo-location, the day and time of the search, etc. are then compared and the winner determined. In situations where there are multiple ad spots, a common occurrence on SERPs, there can be multiple winners whose positions on the page are influenced by the amount each has bid. The bid and Quality Score are used to give each advertiser's advert an ad rank. The ad with the highest ad rank shows up first. The predominant three match types for both Google and Bing are Broad, Exact and Phrase Match. Google also offers the Broad Match Modifier type which differs from broad match in that the keyword must contain the actual keyword terms in any order and doesn't include relevant variations of the terms.

In addition to ad spots on SERPs, the major advertising networks allow for contextual ads to be placed on the properties of 3rd-parties with whom they have partnered. These publishers sign up to host ads on behalf of the network. In return, they receive a portion of the ad revenue that the network generates, which can be anywhere from 50% to over 80% of the gross revenue paid by advertisers. These properties are often referred to as a *content network* and the ads on them as *contextual ads* because the ad spots are associated with keywords based on the context of the page on which they are found. In general, ads on content networks have a much lower click-through rate (CTR) and conversion rate (CR) than ads found on SERPs and consequently are less highly valued. Content network properties can include websites, newsletters, and e-mails.

Advertisers pay for each single click they receive, with the actual amount paid based on the amount of bid. It is common practice amongst auction hosts to charge a winning bidder just slightly more (e.g. one penny) than the next highest bidder or the actual amount bid, whichever is lower. This avoids situations where bidders are constantly adjusting their bids by very small amounts to see if they can still win the auction while paying just a little bit less per click.

To maximize success and achieve scale, automated bid management systems can be deployed. These systems can be used directly by the advertiser, though they are more commonly used by advertising agencies that offer PPC bid management as a service. These tools generally allow for bid management at scale, with thousands or even millions of PPC bids controlled by a highly automated system. The system generally sets each bid based on the goal that has been set for it, such as maximize profit, maximize traffic, get the very targeted customer at break even, and so forth. The system is usually tied into the advertiser's website and fed the results of each click, which then allows it to set bids. The effectiveness of these systems is directly related to the quality and quantity of the performance data that they have to work with — low-traffic ads can lead to a scarcity of data problem that renders many bid management tools useless at worst, or inefficient at best.

As a rule, the contextual advertising system (Google AdWords, Yandex.Direct, etc.) uses an auction approach as the advertising payment system.

Search Analytics

Search analytics is the use of search data to investigate particular interactions among Web searchers, the search engine, or the content during searching episodes. The resulting analysis and aggregation of search engine statistics can be used in search engine marketing (SEM) and search engine optimization (SEO). In other words, search analytics helps website owners understand and improve their performance on search engines, for example identifying highly valuable site visitors, or understanding user intent. Search analytics includes search volume trends and analysis, reverse searching, keyword monitoring, search result and advertisement history, advertisement spending statistics, website comparisons, affiliate marketing statistics, multivariate ad testing.

Data Collection

Search analytics data can be collected in several ways. Search engines provide access to their own data with services such as Google Analytics, Google Trends and Google Insights. Third party services must collect their data from ISP's, phoning home software, or from scraping search engines. Getting traffic statistics from ISP's and phone homes provides for broader reporting of web traffic in addition to search analytics. Services that perform keyword monitoring only scrape a limited set of search results depending on their clients' needs. Services providing reverse search however, must scrape a large set of keywords from the search engines, usually in the millions, to find the keywords that everyone is using.

Since search results, especially advertisements, differ depending on where you are searching from, data collection methods have to account for geographic location. Keyword monitors do this more easily since they typically know what location their client is targeting. However, to get an exhaustive reverse search, several locations need to be scraped for the same keyword.

Accuracy

Search analytics accuracy depends on service being used, data collection method, and data freshness. Google releases its own data, but only in an aggregated way and often without assigning absolute values such as number of visitors to its graphs. ISP logs and phone home methods are accurate for the population they sample, so sample size and demographics must be adequate to accurately represent the larger population. Scraping results can be highly accurate, especially when looking at the non-paid, organic search results. Paid results from Google Adwords for example, are often different for the same search depending on the time, geographic location, and history of searches from a particular computer. This means that scraping advertisers can be hit or miss.

Market Conditions

Taking a look at Google Insights to gauge the popularity of these services shows that compared to searches for the term Adwords (Google's popular search ad system), use of search analytics services is still very low, around 1-25% as of Octuber 2009. This could point to a large opportunity for the users and makers of search analytics given that services have existed since 2004 with several new services being started since.

Calculations

- Sessions with Search: The number of sessions that used your site's search function at least once.

- Percentage of sessions that used internal search: Sessions with Search/Total Sessions.

- Total Unique Searches: The total number of times your site search was used. This excludes multiple searches on the same keyword during the same session.

- Results Pageviews/Search: Pageviews of search result pages/Total Unique Searches.

- Search Exits: The number of searches made immediately before leaving the site.

- Percentage of Search Exits: Search Exits/Total Unique Searches.

- Search Refinements: The number of times a user searched again immediately after performing a search.

- Percentage Search Refinements: The percentage of searches that resulted in a search refinement. Calculated as Search Refinements/Pageviews of search result pages.

- Time after Search: The amount of time users spend on your site after performing a search. This is calculated as Sum of all search_duration across all searches/(search_transitions + 1).

- Search Depth: The number of pages viewed after performing a search. This is calculated as Sum of all search_depth across all searches/(search_transitions + 1).

Cost Per Impression

Cost per thousand impressions (CPM) is a term used in traditional advertising media selection, as well as online advertising and marketing related to web traffic. It refers to the cost of traditional advertising or internet marketing or email advertising campaigns, where advertisers pay each time an ad is displayed. CPI is the cost or expense incurred for each potential customer who views the advertisement(s), while CPM refers to the cost or expense incurred for every thousand potential customers who view the advertisement(s). CPM is an initialism for cost per mille.

Cost per impression, along with pay-per-click (PPC) and cost per order, is used to assess the cost-effectiveness and profitability of online advertising. CPI is the closest online advertising strategy to those offered in other media such as television, radio or print, which sell advertising based on estimated viewership, listenership or readership. CPI provides a comparable measure to contrast internet advertising with other media.

Impression versus Pageview

An impression is the display of an ad to a user while viewing a web page. A single web page may contain multiple ads. In such cases, a single pageview would result in one impression for each ad displayed. In order to count the impressions served as accurately as possible and prevent fraud, an ad server may exclude certain non-qualifying activities such as page-refreshes or other user actions from counting as impressions. When advertising rates are described as CPM or CPI, this is the amount paid for every thousand qualifying impressions served at cost.

Web Analytics

Web analytics is the measurement, collection, analysis and reporting of web data for purposes of understanding and optimizing web usage. However, Web analytics is not just a process for measuring web traffic but can be used as a tool for business and market research, and to assess and improve the effectiveness of a website. Web analytics applications can also help companies measure the results of traditional print or broadcast advertising campaigns. It helps one to estimate how traffic to a website changes after the launch of a new advertising campaign. Web analytics provides information about the number of visitors to a website and the number of page views. It helps gauge traffic and popularity trends which is useful for market research.

Basic Steps of the Web Analytics Process

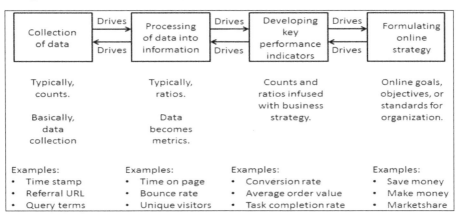

Basic Steps of Web Analytics Process.

Most web analytics processes come down to four essential stages or steps, which are:

- Collection of data: This stage is the collection of the basic, elementary data. Usually, these data are counts of things. The objective of this stage is to gather the data.

- Processing of data into information: This stage usually take counts and make them ratios, although there still may be some counts. The objective of this stage is to take the data and conform it into information, specifically metrics.

- Developing KPI: This stage focuses on using the ratios (and counts) and infusing them with business strategies, referred to as key performance indicators (KPI). Many times, KPIs deal with conversion aspects, but not always. It depends on the organization.

- Formulating online strategy: This stage is concerned with the online goals, objectives, and standards for the organization or business. These strategies are usually related to making money, saving money, or increasing marketshare.

Another essential function developed by the analysts for the optimization of the websites are the experiments:

- Experiments and testings: A/B testing is a controlled experiment with two variants, in online settings, such as web development.

The goal of A/B testing is to identify and suggest changes to web pages that increase or maximize the effect of a statistically tested result of interest.

Each stage impacts or can impact (i.e., drives) the stage preceding or following it. So, sometimes the data that is available for collection impacts the online strategy. Other times, the online strategy affects the data collected.

Web Analytics Technologies

There are at least two categories of web analytics; off-site and on-site web analytics.

- Off-site web analytics refers to web measurement and analysis regardless of whether you own or maintain a website. It includes the measurement of a website's potential audience (opportunity), share of voice (visibility), and buzz (comments) that is happening on the Internet as a whole.

- On-site web analytics, the more common of the two, measure a visitor's behavior once on your website. This includes its drivers and conversions; for example, the degree to which different landing pages are associated with online purchases. On-site web analytics measures the performance of your website in a commercial context. This data is typically compared against key performance indicators for performance and is used to improve a website or marketing campaign's audience response. Google Analytics and Adobe Analytics are the most widely used on-site web analytics service; although new tools are emerging that provide additional layers of information, including heat maps and session replay.

Historically, web analytics has been used to refer to on-site visitor measurement. However, this meaning has become blurred, mainly because vendors are producing tools that span both categories. Many different vendors provide on-site web analytics software and services. There are two main technical ways of collecting the data. The first and traditional method, server log file analysis, reads the logfiles in which the web server records file requests by browsers. The second method, page tagging, uses JavaScript embedded in the webpage to make image requests to a third-party analytics-dedicated server, whenever a webpage is rendered by a web browser or, if desired, when a mouse click occurs. Both collect data that can be processed to produce web traffic reports.

Web Analytics Data Sources

The fundamental goal of web analytics is to collect and analyze data related to web traffic and usage patterns. The data mainly comes from four sources:

1. Direct HTTP request data: It directly comes from HTTP request messages (HTTP request headers).

2. Network level and server generated data associated with HTTP requests: It is not part of an HTTP request, but it is required for successful request transmissions - for example, IP address of a requester.

3. Application level data sent with HTTP requests: It is generated and processed by application level programs (such as JavaScript, PHP, and ASP.Net), including session and referrals. These are usually captured by internal logs rather than public web analytics services.

4. External data: It can be combined with on-site data to help augment the website behavior data described above and interpret web usage. For example, IP addresses are usually associated with Geographic regions and internet service providers, e-mail open and click-through rates, direct mail campaign data, sales and lead history, or other data types as needed.

Web Server Log File Analysis

Web servers record some of their transactions in a log file. It was soon realized that these log files could be read by a program to provide data on the popularity of the website. Thus arose web log analysis software.

In the early 1990s, website statistics consisted primarily of counting the number of client requests (or hits) made to the web server. This was a reasonable method initially, since each website often consisted of a single HTML file. However, with the introduction of images in HTML, and websites that spanned multiple HTML files, this count became less useful. The first true commercial Log Analyzer was released by IPRO in 1994.

Two units of measure were introduced in the mid-1990s to gauge more accurately the amount of human activity on web servers. These were page views and visits (or sessions). A page view was defined as a request made to the web server for a page, as opposed to a graphic, while a visit was defined as a sequence of requests from a uniquely identified client that expired after a certain amount of inactivity, usually 30 minutes. The page views and visits are still commonly displayed metrics, but are now considered rather rudimentary.

The emergence of search engine spiders and robots in the late 1990s, along with web proxies and dynamically assigned IP addresses for large companies and ISPs, made it more difficult to identify unique human visitors to a website. Log analyzers responded by tracking visits by cookies, and by ignoring requests from known spiders.

The extensive use of web caches also presented a problem for log file analysis. If a person revisits a page, the second request will often be retrieved from the browser's cache, and so no request will be received by the web server. This means that the person's path through the site is lost. Caching can be defeated by configuring the web server, but this can result in degraded performance for the visitor and bigger load on the servers.

Page Tagging

Concerns about the accuracy of log file analysis in the presence of caching, and the desire to be able to perform web analytics as an outsourced service, led to the second data collection method, page tagging or 'Web bugs'.

In the mid-1990s, Web counters were commonly seen — these were images included in a web page that showed the number of times the image had been requested, which was an estimate of the number of visits to that page. In the late 1990s, this concept evolved to include a small invisible image instead of a visible one, and by using JavaScript, to pass along with the image request certain information about the page and the visitor. This information can then be processed remotely by a web analytics company, and extensive statistics generated.

The web analytics service also manages the process of assigning a cookie to the user, which can uniquely identify them during their visit and in subsequent visits. Cookie acceptance rates vary significantly between websites and may affect the quality of data collected and reported.

Collecting website data using a third-party data collection server (or even an in-house data collection server) requires an additional DNS lookup by the user's computer to determine the IP address of the collection server. On occasion, delays in completing a successful or failed DNS lookups may result in data not being collected.

With the increasing popularity of Ajax-based solutions, an alternative to the use of an invisible image is to implement a call back to the server from the rendered page. In this case, when the page is rendered on the web browser, a piece of Ajax code would call back to the server and pass information about the client that can then be aggregated by a web analytics company. This is in some ways flawed by browser restrictions on the servers which can be contacted with XmlHttpRequest objects. Also, this method can lead to slightly lower reported traffic levels, since the visitor may stop the page from loading in mid-response before the Ajax call is made.

Logfile Analysis vs. Page Tagging

Both logfile analysis programs and page tagging solutions are readily available to companies that wish to perform web analytics. In some cases, the same web analytics company will offer both approaches. The question then arises of which method a company should choose. There are advantages and disadvantages to each approach.

Advantages of Logfile Analysis

The main advantages of log file analysis over page tagging are as follows:

- The web server normally already produces log files, so the raw data is already available. No changes to the website are required.

- The data is on the company's own servers, and is in a standard, rather than a proprietary format. This makes it easy for a company to switch programs later, use several different programs, and analyze historical data with a new program.

- Logfiles contain information on visits from search engine spiders, which generally are excluded from the analytics tools using JavaScript tagging. Some search engines might not not even execute JavaScript on a page. Although these should not be reported as part of the human activity, it is useful information for search engine optimization.

- Logfiles require no additional DNS lookups or TCP slow starts. Thus there are no external server calls which can slow page load speeds, or result in uncounted page views.

- The web server reliably records every transaction it makes, e.g. serving PDF documents and content generated by scripts, and does not rely on the visitors' browsers cooperating.

Advantages of Page Tagging

The main advantages of page tagging over log file analysis are as follows:

- Counting is activated by opening the page (given that the web client runs the tag scripts), not requesting it from the server. If a page is cached, it will not be counted by server-based log analysis. Cached pages can account for up to one-third of all page views. Not counting cached pages seriously skews many site metrics. It is for this reason server-based log analysis is not considered suitable for analysis of human activity on websites.

- Data is gathered via a component ("tag") in the page, usually written in JavaScript, though Java or Flash can also be used. Ajax can also be used in conjunction with a server-side scripting language (such as PHP) to manipulate and (usually) store it in a database, basically enabling complete control over how the data is represented.

- The script may have access to additional information on the web client or on the user, not sent in the query, such as visitors' screen sizes and the price of the goods they purchased.

- Page tagging can report on events which do not involve a request to the web server, such as interactions within Flash movies, partial form completion, mouse events such as onClick, onMouseOver, onFocus, onBlur etc.

- The page tagging service manages the process of assigning cookies to visitors; with log file analysis, the server has to be configured to do this.

- Page tagging is available to companies who do not have access to their own web servers.

- Lately, page tagging has become a standard in web analytics.

Economic Factors

Logfile analysis is almost always performed in-house. Page tagging can be performed in-house, but it is more often provided as a third-party service. The economic difference between these two models can also be a consideration for a company deciding which to purchase.

- Logfile analysis typically involves a one-off software purchase; however, some vendors are introducing maximum annual page views with additional costs to process additional information. In addition to commercial offerings, several open-source logfile analysis tools are available free of charge.

- For Logfile analysis data must be stored and archived, which often grows large quickly. Although the cost of hardware to do this is minimal, the overhead for an IT department can be considerable.

- For Logfile analysis software need to be maintained, including updates and security patches.

- Complex page tagging vendors charge a monthly fee based on volume i.e. number of page views per month collected.

Which solution is cheaper to implement depends on the amount of technical expertise within the company, the vendor chosen, the amount of activity seen on the websites, the depth and type of information sought, and the number of distinct websites needing statistics.

Regardless of the vendor solution or data collection method employed, the cost of web visitor analysis and interpretation should also be included. That is, the cost of turning raw data into actionable information. This can be from the use of third party consultants, the hiring of an experienced web analyst, or the training of a suitable in-house person. A cost-benefit analysis can then be performed. For example, what revenue increase or cost savings can be gained by analyzing the web visitor data?

Hybrid Methods

Some companies produce solutions that collect data through both log-files and page tagging and can analyze both kinds. By using a hybrid method, they aim to produce more accurate statistics than either method on its own. An early hybrid solution was produced in 1998 by Rufus Evison.

Geolocation of Visitors

With IP geolocation, it is possible to track visitors' locations. Using IP geolocation database or API, visitors can be geolocated to city, region or country level.

IP Intelligence, or Internet Protocol (IP) Intelligence, is a technology that maps the Internet and categorizes IP addresses by parameters such as geographic location (country, region, state, city and postcode), connection type, Internet Service Provider (ISP), proxy information, and more. The first generation of IP Intelligence was referred to as geotargeting or geolocation technology. This information is used by businesses for online audience segmentation in applications such online advertising, behavioral targeting, content localization (or website localization), digital rights management, personalization, online fraud detection, localized search, enhanced analytics, global traffic management, and content distribution.

Click Analytics

Click analytics is a special type of web analytics that gives special attention to clicks. Commonly, click analytics focuses on on-site analytics. An editor of a website uses click analytics to determine the performance of his or her particular site, with regards to where the users of the site are clicking.

Also, click analytics may happen real-time or "unreal"-time, depending on the type of information sought. Typically, front-page editors on high-traffic news media sites will want to monitor their pages in real-time, to optimize the content. Editors, designers or other types of stakeholders may analyze clicks on a wider time frame to help them assess performance of writers, design elements or advertisements etc.

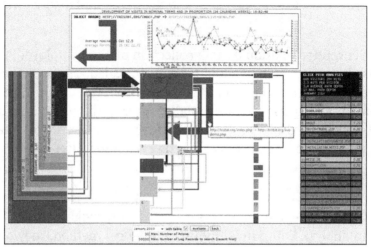

Clickpath Analysis with referring pages on the left and arrows and rectangles differing in thickness and expanse to symbolize movement quantity.

Data about clicks may be gathered in at least two ways. Ideally, a click is "logged" when it occurs, and this method requires some functionality that picks up relevant information when the event occurs. Alternatively, one may institute the assumption that a page view is a result of a click, and therefore log a simulated click that led to that page view.

Customer Lifecycle Analytics

Customer lifecycle analytics is a visitor-centric approach to measuring that falls under the umbrella of lifecycle marketing. Page views, clicks and other events (such as API calls, access to third-party services, etc.) are all tied to an individual visitor instead of being stored as separate data points. Customer lifecycle analytics attempts to connect all the data points into a marketing funnel that can offer insights into visitor behavior and website optimization.

Other Methods of Data Collection

Packet sniffing collects data by sniffing the network traffic passing between the web server and the outside world. Packet sniffing involves no changes to the web pages or web servers. Integrating web analytics into the web server software itself is also possible. Both these methods claim to provide better real-time data than other methods.

On-site Web Analytics

There are no globally agreed definitions within web analytics as the industry bodies have been trying to agree on definitions that are useful and definitive for some time.

The main bodies who have had input in this area have been the IAB (Interactive Advertising Bureau), JICWEBS (The Joint Industry Committee for Web Standards in the UK and Ireland), and DAA (Digital Analytics Association), formally known as the WAA (Web Analytics Association, US). However, many terms are used in consistent ways from one major analytics tool to another, so the following list, based on those conventions can be a useful starting point:

- Bounce Rate - The percentage of visits that are single page visits and without any other interactions (clicks) on that page. In other words, a single click in a particular session is called a bounce.

- Click path - The chronological sequence of page views within a visit or session.

- Hit - A request for a file from the web server. Available only in log analysis. The number of hits received by a website is frequently cited to assert its popularity, but this number is extremely misleading and dramatically overestimates popularity. A single web-page typically consists of multiple (often dozens) of discrete files, each of which is counted as a hit as the page is downloaded, so the number of hits is really an arbitrary number more reflective of the complexity of individual pages on the website than the website's actual popularity. The total number of visits or page views provides a more realistic and accurate assessment of popularity.

- Page view - A request for a file or sometimes an event such as a mouse click, that is defined as a page in the setup of the web analytics tool. An occurrence of the script being run in page tagging. In log analysis, a single page view may generate multiple hits as all the resources required to view the page (images, .js and .css files) are also requested from the web server.

- Visitor/Unique Visitor/Unique User - The uniquely identified client that is generating page views or hits within a defined time period (e.g. day, week or month). A uniquely identified client is usually a combination of a machine (one's desktop computer at work for example) and a browser (Firefox on that machine). The identification is usually via a persistent cookie that has been placed on the computer by the site page code. An older method, used in log file analysis, is the unique combination of the computer's IP address and the User Agent (browser) information provided to the web server by the browser. It is important to understand that the "Visitor" is not the same as the human being sitting at the computer at the time of the visit, since an individual human can use different computers or, on the same computer, can use different browsers, and will be seen as a different visitor in each circumstance. Increasingly, but still somewhat rarely, visitors are uniquely identified by Flash LSO's (Local Shared Object), which are less susceptible to privacy enforcement.

- Visit/Session - A visit or session is defined as a series of page requests or, in the case of tags, image requests from the same uniquely identified client. A unique client is commonly identified by an IP address or a unique ID that is placed in the browser cookie. A visit is considered ended when no requests have been recorded in some number of elapsed minutes. A 30-minute limit ("time out") is used by many analytics tools but can, in some tools (such as Google Analytics), be changed to another number of minutes. Analytics data collectors and analysis tools have no reliable way of knowing if a visitor has looked at other sites between page views; a visit is considered one visit as long as the events (page views, clicks, whatever is being recorded) are 30 minutes or less closer together. Note that a visit can consist of one page view, or thousands. A unique visit's session can also be extended if the time between page loads indicates that a visitor has been viewing the pages continuously.

- Active Time/Engagement Time - Average amount of time that visitors spend actually interacting with content on a web page, based on mouse moves, clicks, hovers and scrolls. Unlike Session Duration and Page View Duration/Time on Page, this metric can accurately measure the length of engagement in the final page view, but it is not available in many analytics tools or data collection methods.

- Average Page Depth/Page Views per Average Session - Page Depth is the approximate "size" of an average visit, calculated by dividing total number of page views by total number of visits.

- Average Page View Duration - Average amount of time that visitors spend on an average page of the site.

- Click - "refers to a single instance of a user following a hyperlink from one page in a site to another".

- Event - A discrete action or class of actions that occurs on a website. A page view is a type of event. Events also encapsulate clicks, form submissions, keypress events, and other client-side user actions.

- Exit Rate/% Exit - A statistic applied to an individual page, not a web site. The percentage of visits seeing a page where that page is the final page viewed in the visit.

- First Visit/First Session - (also called 'Absolute Unique Visitor' in some tools) A visit from a uniquely identified client that has theoretically not made any previous visits. Since the only way of knowing whether the uniquely identified client has been to the site before is the presence of a persistent cookie or via digital fingerprinting that had been received on a previous visit, the First Visit label is not reliable if the site's cookies have been deleted since their previous visit.

- Frequency/Session per Unique - Frequency measures how often visitors come to a website in a given time period. It is calculated by dividing the total number of sessions (or visits) by the total number of unique visitors during a specified time period, such as a month or year. Sometimes it is used interchangeable with the term "loyalty."

- Impression - The most common definition of "Impression" is an instance of an advertisement appearing on a viewed page. Note that an advertisement can be displayed on a viewed page below the area actually displayed on the screen, so most measures of impressions do not necessarily mean an advertisement has been view-able.

- New Visitor - A visitor that has not made any previous visits. This definition creates a certain amount of confusion, and is sometimes substituted with analysis of first visits.

- Page Time Viewed/Page Visibility Time/Page View Duration - The time a single page (or a blog, Ad Banner) is on the screen, measured as the calculated difference between the time of the request for that page and the time of the next recorded request. If there is no next recorded request, then the viewing time of that instance of that page is not included in reports.

- Repeat Visitor - A visitor that has made at least one previous visit. The period between the last and current visit is called visitor recency and is measured in days.

- Return Visitor - A Unique visitor with activity consisting of a visit to a site during a reporting period and where the Unique visitor visited the site prior to the reporting period. The individual is counted only once during the reporting period.

- Session Duration/Visit Duration - Average amount of time that visitors spend on the site each time they visit. It is calculated as the sum total of the duration of all the sessions divided by the total number of sessions. This metric can be complicated by the fact that analytics programs can not measure the length of the final page view.

- Single Page Visit/Singleton - A visit in which only a single page is viewed (this is not a 'bounce').

- Site Overlay is a report technique in which statistics (clicks) or hot spots are superimposed, by physical location, on a visual snapshot of the web page.

Off-site Web Analytics

Off-site web analytics is based on open data analysis, social media exploration, share of voice on web properties. It is usually used to understand how to market a site by identifying the keywords tagged to this site, either from social media or from other websites.

By using HTTP Referer, webpage owners will be able to trace which are the referrer sites that helps bring in traffic to their own site.

Common Sources of Confusion in Web Analytics

Hotel Problem

The hotel problem is generally the first problem encountered by a user of web analytics. The problem is that the unique visitors for each day in a month do not add up to the same total as the unique visitors for that month. This appears to an inexperienced user to be a problem in whatever analytics software they are using. In fact it is a simple property of the metric definitions.

The way to picture the situation is by imagining a hotel. The hotel has two rooms (Room A and Room B).

	Day 01	Day 02	Day 03	Total
Room A	John	John	Mark	2 Unique Users
Room B	Mark	Anne	Anne	2 Unique Users
Total	2	2	2	-

As the table shows, the hotel has two unique users each day over three days. The sum of the totals with respect to the days is therefore six. During the period each room has had two unique users. The sum of the totals with respect to the rooms is therefore four.

Actually only three visitors have been in the hotel over this period. The problem is that a person who stays in a room for two nights will get counted twice if you count them once on each day, but is only counted once if you are looking at the total for the period. Any software for web analytics will sum these correctly for the chosen time period, thus leading to the problem when a user tries to compare the totals.

Web Analytics Methods

Problems with Cookies

Historically, vendors of page-tagging analytics solutions have used third-party cookies sent from the vendor's domain instead of the domain of the website being browsed. Third-party cookies can handle visitors who cross multiple unrelated domains within the company's site, since the cookie is always handled by the vendor's servers.

However, third-party cookies in principle allow tracking an individual user across the sites of different companies, allowing the analytics vendor to collate the user's activity on sites where he provided personal information with his activity on other sites where he thought he was anonymous. Although web analytics companies deny doing this, other companies such as companies supplying banner ads have done so. Privacy concerns about cookies have therefore led a noticeable minority of users to block or delete third-party cookies. In 2005, some reports showed that about 28% of Internet users blocked third-party cookies and 22% deleted them at least once a month. Most vendors of page tagging solutions have now moved to provide at least the option of using first-party cookies (cookies assigned from the client sub-domain).

Another problem is cookie deletion. When web analytics depend on cookies to identify unique visitors, the statistics are dependent on a persistent cookie to hold a unique visitor ID. When users delete cookies, they usually delete both first- and third-party cookies. If this is done between interactions with the site, the user will appear as a first-time visitor at their next interaction point. Without a persistent and unique visitor id, conversions, click-stream analysis, and other metrics dependent on the activities of a unique visitor over time, cannot be accurate.

Cookies are used because IP addresses are not always unique to users and may be shared by large groups or proxies. In some cases, the IP address is combined with the user agent in order to more accurately identify a visitor if cookies are not available. However, this only partially solves the problem because often users behind a proxy server have the same user agent. Other methods of uniquely identifying a user are technically challenging and would limit the trackable audience or would be considered suspicious. Cookies are the selected option because they reach the lowest common denominator without using technologies regarded as spyware.

Secure Analytics Methods

It may be good to be aware that the third-party information gathering is subject to any network limitations and security applied. Service Providers and Private Networks can prevent site visit data from going to third parties. All the methods described have the central problem of being vulnerable to manipulation (both inflation and deflation). This means these methods are imprecise and insecure (in any reasonable model of security). This issue has been addressed in a number of papers, but to-date the solutions suggested in these papers remain theoretical, possibly due to lack of interest from the engineering community, or because of financial gain the current situation provides to the owners of big websites.

SOCIAL MEDIA MARKETING

Social media marketing is the use of social media platforms and websites to promote a product or service. Although the terms e-marketing and digital marketing are still dominant in academia, social media marketing is becoming more popular for both practitioners and researchers. Most social media platforms have built-in data analytics tools, which enable companies to track the progress, success, and engagement of ad campaigns. Companies address a range of stakeholders through social media market-ing, including current and potential customers, current and potential employees, jour-nalists, bloggers, and the general public. On a strategic level, social media marketing includes the management of a marketing campaign, governance, setting the scope (e.g. more active or passive use) and the establishment of a firm's desired social media "cul-ture" and "tone."

When using social media marketing, firms can allow customers and Internet users to post user-generated content (e.g., online comments, product reviews, etc.), also known as "earned media," rather than use marketer-prepared advertising copy.

Platforms

Social Networking Websites

Social networking websites allow individuals, businesses and other organizations to interact with one another and build relationships and communities online. When com-panies join these social channels, consumers can interact with them directly. That in-teraction can be more personal to users than traditional methods of outbound market-ing and advertising. Social networking sites act as word of mouth or more precisely, e-word of mouth. The Internet's ability to reach billions across the globe has given online word of mouth a powerful voice and far reach. The ability to rapidly change buying patterns and product or service acquisition and activity to a growing number of consumers is defined as an influence network. Social networking sites and blogs allow followers to "retweet" or "repost" comments made by others about a product being promoted, which occurs quite frequently on some social media sites. By repeating the message, the user's connections are able to see the message, therefore reaching more people. Because the information about the product is being put out there and is getting repeated, more traffic is brought to the product/company.

Social networking websites are based on building virtual communities that allow con-sumers to express their needs, wants and values online. Social media marketing then connects these consumers and audiences to businesses that share the same needs, wants, and values. Through social networking sites, companies can keep in touch with individual followers. This personal interaction can instill a feeling of loyalty into follow-ers and potential customers. Also, by choosing whom to follow on these sites, products can reach a very narrow target audience. Social networking sites also include much information about what products and services prospective clients might be interested in. Through the use of new semantic analysis technologies, marketers can detect buying signals, such as content shared by people and questions posted online. An understand-ing of buying signals can help sales people target relevant prospects and marketers run micro-targeted campaigns.

In 2014, over 80% of business executives identified social media as an integral part of their business. Business retailers have seen 133% increases in their revenues from social media marketing.

Mobile Phones

More than three billion people in the world are active on the Internet. Over the years, the Internet has continually gained more and more users, jumping from 738 million in 2000 all the way to 3.2 billion in 2015. Roughly 81% of the current population in the United States has some type of social media profile that they engage with frequently. Mobile phone usage is beneficial for social media marketing because of their web browsing capabilities which allow individuals immediate access to social networking sites. Mobile phones have altered the path-to-purchase process by allowing consumers to easily obtain pricing and product information in real time. They have also allowed companies to constantly remind and update their followers. Many companies are now putting QR (Quick Response) codes along with products for individuals to access the company website or online services with their smart phones. Retailers use QR codes to facilitate consumer interaction with brands by linking the code to brand websites, promotions, product information, and any other mobile-enabled content. In addition, Real-time bidding use in the mobile advertising industry is high and rising due to its value for on-the-go web browsing. In 2012, Nexage, a provider of real time bidding in mobile advertising reported a 37% increase in revenue each month. Adfonic, another mobile advertisement publishing platform, reported an increase of 22 billion ad requests that same year.

Mobile devices have become increasingly popular, where 5.7 billion people are using them worldwide. This has played a role in the way consumers interact with media and has many further implications for TV ratings, advertising, mobile commerce, and more. Mobile media consumption such as mobile audio streaming or mobile video are on the rise. In the United States, more than 100 million users are projected to access online video content via mobile device. Mobile video revenue consists of pay-per-view downloads, advertising and subscriptions. As of 2013, worldwide mobile phone Internet user penetration was 73.4%. In 2017, figures suggest that more than 90% of Internet users will access online content through their phones.

Strategies

Passive Approach

Social media can be a useful source of market information and a way to hear customer perspectives. Blogs, content communities, and forums are platforms where individuals share their reviews and recommendations of brands, products, and services. Businesses are able to tap and analyze the customer voices and feedback generated in social media for marketing purposes; in this sense the social media is a relatively inexpensive source of market intelligence which can be used by marketers and managers to track and respond to consumer-identified problems and detect market opportunities. For example, the Internet erupted with videos and pictures of iPhone 6 "bend test" which showed that the coveted phone could be bent by hand pressure. The so-called "bend gate" controversy created confusion amongst customers who had waited months for the launch of the latest rendition of the iPhone. However, Apple promptly issued a statement saying that the problem was extremely rare and that the company had taken several steps to make the mobile device's case stronger and robust. Unlike traditional market research methods such as surveys, focus groups, and data mining which are time-consuming and costly, and which take weeks or even months to analyze, marketers can use social media to obtain 'live' or "real time" information about consumer behavior and viewpoints on a company's brand or products. This can be useful in the highly dynamic, competitive, fast-paced and global marketplace of the 2010s.

Active Approach

Social media can be used not only as public relations and direct marketing tools but also as communication channels targeting very specific audiences with social media influencers and social media personalities and as effective customer engagement tools. Technologies predating social media, such as broadcast TV and newspapers can also provide advertisers with a fairly targeted audience, given that an ad placed during a sports game broadcast or in the sports section of a newspaper is likely to be read by sports fans. However, social media websites can target niche markets even more precisely. Using digital tools such as Google Adsense, advertisers can target their ads to very specific demographics, such as people who are interested in social entrepreneurship, political activism associated with a particular political party, or video gaming. Google Adsense does this by looking for keywords in social media user's online posts and comments. It would be hard for a TV station or paper-based newspaper to provide ads that are this targeted (though not impossible, as can be seen with "special issue" sections on niche issues, which newspapers can use to sell targeted ads).

Social networks are, in many cases, viewed as a great tool for avoiding costly market research. They are known for providing a short, fast, and direct way to reach an audience through a person who is widely known. For example, an athlete who gets endorsed by a sporting goods company also brings their support base of millions of people who are interested in what they do or how they play and now they want to be a part of this athlete through their endorsements with that particular company. At one point consumers would visit stores to view their products with famous athletes, but now you can view a famous athlete's, such as Cristiano Ronaldo, latest apparel online with the click of a button. He advertises them to you directly through his Twitter, Instagram, and FaceBook accounts.

Facebook and LinkedIn are leading social media platforms where users can hyper-target their ads. Hypertargeting not only uses public profile information but also information users submit but hide from others. There are several examples of firms initiating some form of online dialog with the public to foster relations with customers. According to Constantinides, Lorenzo and Gómez Borja "Business executives like Jonathan Swartz, President and CEO of Sun Microsystems, Steve Jobs CEO of Apple Computers, and McDonalds Vice President Bob Langert post regularly in their CEO blogs, encouraging customers to interact and freely express their feelings, ideas, suggestions or remarks about their postings, the company or its products". Using customer influencers (for example popular bloggers) can be a very efficient and cost-effective method to launch new products or services.

Engagement

Engagement with the social web means that customers and stakeholders are active participants rather than passive viewers. An example of these are consumer advocacy groups and groups that criticize companies (e.g., lobby groups or advocacy organizations). Social media use in a business or political context allows all consumers/citizens to express and share an opinion about a company's products, services, business practices, or a government's actions. Each participating customer, non-customer, or citizen who is participating online via social media becomes a part of the marketing department (or a challenge to the marketing effort). Whereas as other customers read their positive or negative comments or reviews. Getting consumers, potential consumers or citizens to be engaged online is fundamental to successful social media marketing. With the advent of social media marketing, it has become increasingly important to gain customer interest in products and services. This can eventually be translated into buying behavior, or voting and donating behavior in a political context. New online marketing concepts of engagement and loyalty have emerged which aim to build customer participation and brand reputation.

Engagement in social media for the purpose of a social media strategy is divided into two parts. The first is proactive, regular posting of new online content. This can be seen through digital photos, digital videos, text, and conversations. It is also represented through sharing of content and information from others via weblinks. The second part is reactive conversations with social media users responding to those who reach out to your social media profiles through commenting or messaging. Traditional media such as TV news shows are limited to one-way interaction with customers or 'push and tell' where only specific information is given to the customer with few or limited mechanisms to obtain customer feedback. Traditional media such as physical newspapers, do give readers the option of sending a letter to the editor. Though, this is a relatively slow process, as the editorial board has to review the letter and decide if it is appropriate for publication. On the other hand, social media is participative and open. Participants are able to instantly share their views on brands, products, and services. Traditional media gave control of message to the marketer, whereas social media shifts the balance to the consumer or citizen.

Campaigns

Local Businesses

Small businesses also use social networking sites as a promotional technique. Businesses can follow individuals social networking site uses in the local area and advertise specials and deals. These can be exclusive and in the form of "get a free drink with a copy of this tweet". This type of message encourages other locals to follow the business on the sites in order to obtain the promotional deal. In the process, the business is getting seen and promoting itself (brand visibility).

Small businesses also use social networking sites to develop their own market research on new products and services. By encouraging their customers to give feedback on new product ideas, businesses can gain valuable insights on whether a product may be accepted by their target market enough to merit full production, or not. In addition, customers will feel the company has engaged them in the process of co-creation—the process in which the business uses customer feedback to create or modify a product or service the filling a need of the target market. Such feedback can present in various forms, such as surveys, contests, polls, etc.

Social networking sites such as LinkedIn, also provide an opportunity for small businesses to find candidates to fill staff positions. Of course, review sites, such as Yelp, also help small businesses to build their reputation beyond just brand visibility. Positive customer peer reviews help to influence new prospects to purchase goods and services more than company advertising.

Purposes and Tactics

One of the main purposes of employing social media in marketing is as a communications tool that makes the companies accessible to those interested in their product and makes them visible to those who have no knowledge of their products. These companies use social media to create buzz, and learn from and target customers. It's the only form of marketing that can finger consumers at each and every stage of the consumer decision journey. Marketing through social media has other benefits as well. Of the top 10 factors that correlate with a strong Google organic search, seven are social media dependent. This means that if brands are less or non-active on social media, they tend to show up less on Google searches. While platforms such as Twitter, Facebook, and Google+ have a larger number of monthly users, the visual media sharing based mobile platforms, however, garner a higher interaction rate in comparison and have registered the fastest growth and have changed the ways in which consumers engage with brand content. Instagram has an interaction rate of 1.46% with an average of 130 million users monthly as opposed to Twitter which has a 0.03% interaction rate with an average of 210 million monthly users. Unlike traditional media that are often cost-prohibitive to many companies, a social media strategy does not require astronomical budgeting.

To this end, companies make use of platforms such as Facebook, Twitter, YouTube, and Instagram to reach audiences much wider than through the use of traditional print/ TV/radio advertisements alone at a fraction of the cost, as most social networking sites can be used at little or no cost (however, some websites charge companies for premium services). This has changed the ways that companies approach to interact with customers, as a substantial percentage of consumer interactions are now being carried out over online platforms with much higher visibility. Customers can now post reviews of products and services, rate customer service, and ask questions or voice concerns directly to companies through social media platforms. According to Measuring Success, over 80% of consumers use the web to research products and services. Thus social media marketing is also used by businesses in order to build relationships of trust with consumers. To this aim, companies may also hire personnel to specifically handle these social media interactions, who usually report under the title of Online community managers. Handling these interactions in a satisfactory manner can result in an increase of consumer trust. To both this aim and to fix the public's perception of a company, 3 steps are taken in order to address consumer concerns, identifying the extent of the social chatter, engaging the influencers to help, and developing a proportional response.

Twitter

Twitter allows companies to promote their products in short messages known as tweets limited to 140 characters which appear on followers' Home timelines. Tweets can contain text, hashtag, photo, video, animated GIF, emoji, or links to the product's website and other social media profiles, etc. Twitter is also used by companies to provide customer service. Some companies make support available 24/7 and answer promptly, thus improving brand loyalty and appreciation.

Facebook

Facebook pages are far more detailed than Twitter accounts. They allow a product to provide videos, photos, longer descriptions, and testimonials where followers can comment on the product pages for others to see. Facebook can link back to the product's Twitter page, as well as send out event reminders. As of May 2015, 93% of businesses marketers use Facebook to promote their brand. A study from 2011 attributed 84% of "engagement" or clicks and likes that link back to Facebook advertising. By 2014, Facebook had restricted the content published from business and brand pages. Adjustments in Facebook algorithms have reduced the audience for non-paying business pages (that have at least 500,000 "Likes") from 16% in 2012 down to 2% in February 2014.

LinkedIn

LinkedIn, a professional business-related networking site, allows companies to create professional profiles for themselves as well as their business to network and meet others. Through the use of widgets, members can promote their various social networking activities, such as Twitter stream or blog entries of their product pages, onto their Linke-dIn profile page. LinkedIn provides its members the opportunity to generate sales leads and business partners. Members can use "Company Pages" similar to Facebook pages to create an area that will allow business owners to promote their products or services and be able to interact with their customers. Due to spread of spam mail sent to job seeker, leading companies prefer to use LinkedIn for employee's recruitment instead using different a job portal. Additionally, companies have voiced a preference for the amount of information that can be gleaned from a LinkedIn profile versus a limited email.

WhatsApp

WhatsApp was founded by Jan Koum and Brian Acton. WhatsApp joined Facebook in 2014, but continues to operate as a separate app with a laser focus on building a mes-saging service that works fast and reliably anywhere in the world. WhatsApp started as an alternative to SMS. WhatsApp now supports sending and receiving a variety of media including text, photos, videos, documents, and location, as well as voice calls. WhatsApp messages and calls are secured with end-to-end encryption, meaning that no third party including WhatsApp can read or listen to them. WhatsApp has a cus-tomer base of 1 billion people in over 180 countries. It is used to send personalised promotional messages to individual customers. It has plenty of advantages over SMS that includes ability to track how Message Broadcast Performs using blue tick option in WhatsApp. It allows sending messages to Do Not Disturb (DND) customers. WhatsApp is also used to send a series of bulk messages to their targeted customers using broad-cast option. Companies started using this to a large extent because it is a cost effective promotional option and quick to spread a message. Still, WhatsApp doesn't allow busi-nesses to place ads in their app.

Yelp

Yelp consists of a comprehensive online index of business profiles. Businesses are searchable by location, similar to Yellow Pages. The website is operational in seven dif-ferent countries, including the United States and Canada. Business account holders are allowed to create, share, and edit business profiles. They may post information such as the business location, contact information, pictures, and service information. The web-site further allows individuals to write, post reviews about businesses, and rate them on a five-point scale. Messaging and talk features are further made available for general members of the website, serving to guide thoughts and opinions.

Instagram

In May 2014, Instagram had over 200 million users. The user engagement rate of Ins-tagram was 15 times higher than of Facebook and 25 times higher than that of Twitter. According to Scott Galloway latest studies estimate that 93% of prestige brands have an active presence on Instagram and include it in their marketing mix. When it comes to brands and businesses, Instagram's goal is to help companies to reach their respective audiences through captivating imagery in a rich, visual environment. Moreover, Instagram provides a platform where user and company can communicate publicly and directly, making itself an ideal platform for companies to connect with their current and potential customers.

Many brands are now heavily using this mobile app to boost their marketing strategy. Instagram can be used to gain the necessary momentum needed to capture the attention of the market segment that has an interest in the product offering or services. As Instagram is supported by Apple and android system, it can be easily accessed by smartphone users. Moreover, it can be accessed by the Internet as well. Thus, the marketers see it as a potential platform to expand their brands exposure to the public, especially the younger target group. On top of this, marketers do not only use social media for traditional Internet advertising, but they also encourage users to create attention for a certain brand. This generally creates an opportunity for greater brand exposure. Furthermore, marketers are also using the platform to drive social shopping and inspire people to collect and share pictures of their favorite products. Many big names have already jumped on board: Starbucks, MTV, Nike, Marc Jacobs, and Red Bull are a few examples of multinationals that adopted the mobile photo app early. Fashion blogger Danielle Bernstein on Instagram, collaborated with Harper's Bazaar to do a piece on how brands are using Instagram to market their products, and how bloggers make money from it. Bernstein, who currently has one and a half million followers on Instagram, and whose "outfit of the day" photos on Snapchat get tens of thousands of screenshots, explained that for a lot of her sponsored posts, she must feature the brand in a certain number of posts, and often cannot wear a competitor's product in the same picture. According to Harper's Bazaar, industry estimates say that brands are spending more than $1 billion per year on consumer-generated advertising. Founder of Instagram Kevin Systrom even went to Paris Fashion week, going to couture shows and meeting with designers to learn more about how style bloggers, editors, and designers are currently dominating much of the content on his application.

Instagram has proven itself a powerful platform for marketers to reach their customers and prospects through sharing pictures and brief messages. According to a study by Simply Measured, 71% of the world's largest brands are now using Instagram as a marketing channel. For companies, Instagram can be used as a tool to connect and communicate with current and potential customers. The company can present a more personal picture of their brand, and by doing so the company conveys a better and true picture of itself. The idea of Instagram pictures lies on on-the-go, a sense that the event is happening right now, and that adds another layer to the personal and accurate picture of the company. In fact, Thomas Rankin, co-founder and CEO of the program Dash Hudson, stated that when he approves a blogger's Instagram post before it is posted on the behalf of a brand his company represents, his only negative feedback is if it looks too posed. "It's not an editorial photo," he explained, "We're not trying to be a magazine. We're trying to create a moment." Another option Instagram provides the opportunity for companies to reflect a true picture of the brandfrom the perspective of the customers, for instance, using the user-generated contents thought the hashtags encouragement. Other than the filters and hashtags functions, the Instagram's 15 second videos and the recently added ability to send private messages between users have opened new opportunities for brands to connect with customers in a new extent, further promoting effective marketing on Instagram.

Snapchat

Snapchat is a popular messaging and picture exchanging application that was created in 2011 by three students at Stanford University named Evan Spiegel, Bobby Murphy, and Reggie Brown. The application was first developed to allow users to message back and forth and to also send photographs that are only available from 1–10 seconds until they are no longer available. The app was an instant hit with social media members and today there are up to 158 million people using snapchat every single day. It is also estimated that Snapchat users are opening the application approximately 18 times per day, which means users are on the app for about 25–30 minutes per day.

YouTube

YouTube is another popular avenue. Advertisements are done in a way to suit the target audience. The type of language used in the commercials and the ideas used to promote the product reflect the audience's style and taste. Also, the ads on this platform are usually in sync with the content of the video requested, this is another advantage YouTube brings for advertisers. Certain ads are presented with certain videos since the content is relevant. Promotional opportunities such as sponsoring a video is also possible on YouTube, "for example, a user who searches for a YouTube video on dog training may be presented with a sponsored video from a dog toy company in results along with other videos." YouTube also enable publishers to earn money through its YouTube Partner Program. Companies can pay YouTube for a special "channel" which promotes the companies products or services.

Social Bookmarking Sites

Websites such as Delicious, Digg, Slashdot, Diigo, Stumbleupon, and Reddit are popular social bookmarking sites used in social media promotion. Each of these sites is dedicated to the collection, curation, and organization of links to other websites that users deem to be of good quality. This process is "crowdsourced", allowing amateur social media network members to sort and prioritize links by relevance and general category. Due to the large user bases of these websites, any link from one of them to another, the smaller website may in a flash crowd, a sudden surge of interest in the target website. In addition to user-generated promotion, these sites also offer advertisements within individual user communities and categories. Because ads can be placed in designated communities with a very specific target audience and demographic, they have far greater potential for traffic generation than ads selected simply through cookie and browser history. Additionally, some of these websites have also implemented measures to make ads more relevant to users by allowing users to vote on which ones will be shown on pages they frequent. The ability to redirect large volumes of web traffic and target specific, relevant audiences makes social bookmarking sites a valuable asset for social media marketers.

Blogs

Platforms like LinkedIn create an environment for companies and clients to connect online. Companies that recognize the need for information, originality and accessibility employ blogs to make their products popular and unique and ultimately reach out to consumers who are privy to social media. Studies show that consumers view coverage in the media or from bloggers as being more neutral and credible than print advertisements, which are not thought of as free or independent. Blogs allow a product or company to provide longer descriptions of products or services, can include testimonials and can link to and from other social network and blog pages. Blogs can be updated frequently and are promotional techniques for keeping customers, and also for acquiring followers and subscribers who can then be directed to social network pages. Online communities can enable a business to reach the clients of other businesses using the platform. To allow firms to measure their standing in the corporate world, sites enable employees to place evaluations of their companies. Some businesses opt out of integrating social media platforms into their traditional marketing regimen. There are also specific corporate standards that apply when interacting online. To maintain an advantage in a business-consumer relationship, businesses have to be aware of four key assets that consumers maintain: information, involvement, community, and control.

Tumblr

Blogging website Tumblr first launched ad products on May 29, 2012. Rather than relying on simple banner ads, Tumblr requires advertisers to create a Tumblr blog so the content of those blogs can be featured on the site. In one year, four native ad formats were created on web and mobile, and had more than 100 brands advertising on Tumblr with 500 cumulative sponsored posts.

Ad Formats

- Sponsored mobile post – Advertisements (Advertisers' blog posts) will show up on user's Dashboard when the user is on a mobile device such as smartphones and tablets, allowing them to like, reblog, and share the sponsored post.

- Sponsored web post – "Largest in-stream ad unit on the web" that catches the users' attention when looking at their Dashboard through their computer or laptop. It also allows the viewers to like, reblog, and share it.

- Sponsored radar – Radar picks up exceptional posts from the whole Tumblr community based on their originality and creativity. It is placed on the right side next to the Dashboard, and it typically earns 120 million daily impressions. Sponsored radar allows advertisers to place their posts there to have an opportunity to earn new followers, reblogs, and likes.

- Sponsored spotlight – Spotlight is a directory of some of the popular blogs throughout the community and a place where users can find new blogs to follow. Advertisers can choose one category out of fifty categories that they can have their blog listed on there.

These posts can be one or more of the following: images, photo sets, animated GIFs, video, audio, and text posts. For the users to differentiate the promoted posts to the regular users' posts, the promoted posts have a dollar symbol on the corner. On May 6, 2014, Tumblr announced customization and theming on mobile apps for brands to advertise.

Advertising Campaigns

- Disney/Pixar's Monsters University: Created a Tumblr account, MUGrumblr, saying that the account is maintained by a 'Monstropolis transplant' and 'self-diagnosed coffee addict' who is currently a sophomore at Monsters University. A "student" from Monsters University uploaded memes, animated GIFs, and Instagram-like photos that are related to the sequel movie.

- Apple's iPhone 5c: Created a Tumblr page, labeling it "Every color has a story" with the website name: "ISee5c". As soon as you visit the website, the page is covered with different colors representing the iPhone 5c phone colors and case colors. When you click on one of the colored section, a 15-second video plays a song and "showcases the dots featured on the rear of the iPhone 5c official cases and on the iOS 7 dynamic wallpapers", concluding with words that are related to the video's theme.

Marketing Techniques

Social media marketing involves the use of social networks, consumer's online brand-related activities (COBRA) and electronic word of mouth (eWOM) to successfully advertise online. Social networks such as Facebook and Twitter provide advertisers with information about the likes and dislikes of their consumers. This technique is crucial, as it provides the businesses with a "target audience". With social networks, information relevant to the user's likes is available to businesses; who then advertise accordingly. Activities such as uploading a picture of your "new Converse sneakers to Facebook" is an example of a COBRA. Electronic recommendations and appraisals are a convenient manner to have a product promoted via "consumer-to-consumer interactions. An example of eWOM would be an online hotel review; the hotel company can have two possible outcomes based on their service. A good service would result in a positive review which gets the hotel free advertising via social media. However, a poor service will result in a negative consumer review which can potentially harm the company's reputation.

Social networking sites such as Facebook, Instagram, Twitter, MySpace etc. have all influenced the buzz of word of mouth marketing. In 1999, Misner said that word-of mouth marketing is, "the world's most effective, yet least understood marketing strategy". Through the influence of opinion leaders, the increased online "buzz" of "word-of-mouth" marketing that a product, service or companies are experiencing is due to the rise in use of social media and smartphones. Businesses and marketers have noticed that, "a persons behavior is influenced by many small groups". These small groups rotate around social networking accounts that are run by influential people (opinion leaders or "thought leaders") who have followers of groups. The types of groups (followers) are called: reference groups (people who know each other either face-to-face or have an indirect influence on a persons attitude or behavior); membership groups (a person has a direct influence on a person's attitude or behavior); and aspirational groups (groups which an individual wishes to belong to).

Marketers target influential people on social media who are recognised as being opinion leaders and opinion-formers to send messages to their target audiences and amplify the impact of their message. A social media post by an opinion leader can have a much greater impact (via the forwarding of the post or "liking" of the post) than a social media post by a regular user. Marketers have come to the understanding that "consumers are more prone to believe in other individuals" who they trust. OL's and OF's can also send their own messages about products and services they choose. The reason the opinion leader or formers have such a strong following base is because their opinion is valued or trusted. They can review products and services for their followings, which can be positive or negative towards the brand. OL's and OF's are people who have a social status and because of their personality, beliefs, values etc. have the potential to influence other people. They usually have a large number of followers otherwise known as their reference, membership or aspirational group. By having an OL or OF support a brands product by posting a photo, video or written recommendation on a blog, the following may be influenced and because they trust the OL/OF a high chance of the brand selling more products or creating a following base. Having an OL/OF helps spread word of mouth talk amongst reference groups and memberships groups e.g. family, friends, work-friends etc. The adjusted communication model shows the use of using opinion leaders and opinion formers. The sender/source gives the message to many, many OL's/OF's who pass the message on along with their personal opinion, the receiver (followers/groups) form their own opinion and send their personal message to their group (friends, family etc).

The platform of social media is another channel or site that business' and brands must seek to influence the content. In contrast with pre-Internet marketing, such as

TV ads and newspaper ads, in which the marketer controlled all aspects of the ad, with social media, users are free to post comments right below an online ad or an online post by a company about its product. Companies are increasing using their social media strategy as part of their traditional marketing effort using magazines, newspapers, radio advertisements, television advertisements. Since in the 2010s, media consumers are often using multiple platforms at the same time (e.g., surfing the Internet on a tablet while watching a streaming TV show), marketing content needs to be consistent across all platforms, whether traditional or new media. Heath wrote about the extent of attention businesses should give to their social media sites. It is about finding a balance between frequently posting but not over posting. There is a lot more attention to be paid towards social media sites because people need updates to gain brand recognition. Therefore, a lot more content is need and this can often be unplanned content.

Planned content begins with the creative/marketing team generating their ideas, once they have completed their ideas they send them off for approval. There is two general ways of doing so. The first is where each sector approves the plan one after another, editor, brand, followed by the legal team. Sectors may differ depending on the size and philosophy of the business. The second is where each sector is given 24 hours (or such designated time) to sign off or disapprove. If no action is given within the 24-hour period the original plan is implemented. Planned content is often noticeable to customers and is un-original or lacks excitement but is also a safer option to avoid unnecessary backlash from the public. Both routes for planned content are time consuming as in the above; the first way to approval takes 72 hours to be approved. Although the second route can be significantly shorter it also holds more risk particularly in the legal department.

Unplanned content is an 'in the moment' idea, "a spontaneous, tactical reaction." The content could be trending and not have the time to take the planned content route. The unplanned content is posted sporadically and is not calendar/date/time arranged. Issues with unplanned content revolve around legal issues and whether the message being sent out represents the business/brand accordingly. If a company sends out a Tweet or Facebook message too hurriedly, the company may unintentionally use insensitive language or messaging that could alienate some consumers. For example, celebrity chef Paula Deen was criticized after she made a social media post commenting about HIV-AIDS and South Africa; her message was deemed to be offensive by many observers. The main difference between planned and unplanned is the time to approve the content. Unplanned content must still be approved by marketing managers, but in a much more rapid manner e.g. 1–2 hours or less. Sectors may miss errors because of being hurried. When using unplanned content Brito says, "be prepared to be reactive and respond to issues when they arise." Brito writes about having a, "crisis escalation plan", because, "It will happen". The plan involves breaking down the issue into topics and classifying the issue into groups. Colour coding the potential risk "identify and flag potential risks" also helps to organise an issue. The problem can then be handled by the correct team and dissolved more effectively rather than any person at hand trying to solve the situation.

Implications on Traditional Advertising

Minimizing Use

Traditional advertising techniques include print and television advertising. The Internet has already overtaken television as the largest advertising market. Web sites often include the banner or pop-up ads. Social networking sites don't always have ads. In exchange, products have entire pages and are able to interact with users. Television commercials often end with a spokesperson asking viewers to check out the product website for more information. While briefly popular, print ads included QR codes on them. These QR codes can be scanned by cell phones and computers, sending viewers to the product website. Advertising is beginning to move viewers from the traditional outlets to the electronic ones.

While traditional media, like newspapers and television advertising, are largely overshadowed by the rise of social media marketing, there is still a place for traditional marketing. For example, with newspapers, readership over the years has shown a decline. However, readership with newspapers is still fiercely loyal to print-only media. 51% of newspaper readers only read the newspaper in its print form, making well-placed ads valuable.

Leaks

The Internet and social networking leaks are one of the issues facing traditional advertising. Video and print ads are often leaked to the world via the Internet earlier than they are scheduled to premiere. Social networking sites allow those leaks to go viral, and be seen by many users more quickly. The time difference is also a problem facing traditional advertisers. When social events occur and are broadcast on television, there is often a time delay between airings on the east coast and west coast of the United States. Social networking sites have become a hub of comment and interaction concerning the event. This allows individuals watching the event on the west coast (time-delayed) to know the outcome before it airs. The 2011 Grammy Awards highlighted this problem. Viewers on the west coast learned who won different awards based on comments made on social networking sites by individuals watching live on the east coast. Since viewers knew who won already, many tuned out and ratings were lower. All the advertisement and promotion put into the event was lost because viewers didn't have a reason to watch.

Mishaps

Social media marketing provides organizations with a way to connect with their customers. However, organizations must protect their information as well as closely watch comments and concerns on the social media they use. A flash poll done on 1225 IT executives from 33 countries revealed that social media mishaps caused organizations a combined $4.3 million in damages in 2010. The top three social media incidents an organization faced during the previous year included employees sharing too much information in public forums, loss or exposure of confidential information, and increased exposure to litigation. Due to the viral nature of the Internet, a mistake by a single employee has in some cases shown to result in devastating consequences for organizations. An example of a social media mishap includes designer Kenneth Cole's Twitter mishap in 2011. When Kenneth Cole tweeted, "Millions are in uproar in #Cairo. Rumor has they heard our new spring collection is now available online at [Kenneth Cole's website]". This reference to the 2011 Egyptian revolution drew an objection from the public; it was widely objected to on the Internet. Kenneth Cole realized his mistake shortly after and responded with a statement apologizing for the tweet.

In 2012, during Hurricane Sandy, Gap sent out a tweet to its followers telling them to stay safe but encouraged them to shop online and offered free shipping. The tweet was deemed insensitive, and Gap eventually took it down and apologized. Numerous additional online marketing mishap examples exist. Examples include a YouTube video of a Domino's Pizza employee violating health code standards, which went viral on the Internet and later resulted in felony charges against two employees. A Twitter hashtag posted by McDonald's in 2012 attracting attention due to numerous complaints and negative events customers experienced at the chain store; and a 2011 tweet posted by a Chrysler Group employee that no one in Detroit knows how to drive. When the Link REIT opened a Facebook page to recommend old-style restaurants, the page was flooded by furious comments criticizing the REIT for having forced a lot of restaurants and stores to shut down. It had to terminate its campaign early amid further deterioration of its corporate image.

In 2018, Max Factor, MAC and other beauty brands were forced to rush to disassociate themselves from Kuwaiti beauty blogger and Instagram 'influencer' Sondos Alqattan after she criticised government moves to improve conditions for domestic workers.

Ethics

The code of ethics that is affiliated with traditional marketing can also be applied to social media. However, with social media being so personal and international, there is another list of complications and challenges that come along with being ethical online. With the invention of social media, the marketer no longer has to focus solely on the basic demographics and psychographics given from television and magazines, but now they can see what consumers like to hear from advertisers, how they engage online, and what their needs and wants are. The general concept of being ethical while marking on social network sites is to be honest with the intentions of the campaign, avoid false advertising, be aware of user privacy conditions (which means not using consumers' private information for gain), respect the dignity of persons in the shared online community, and claim responsibility for any mistakes or mishaps that are results of your marketing campaign. Most social network marketers use websites like Facebook and MySpace to try to drive traffic to another website. While it is ethical to use social networking websites to spread a message to people who are genuinely interested, many people game the system with auto-friend adding programs and spam messages and bulletins. Social networking websites are becoming wise to these practices, however, are effectively weeding out and banning offenders.

In addition, social media platforms have become extremely aware of their users and collect information about their viewers to connect with them in various ways. Social-networking website Facebook Inc. is quietly working on a new advertising system that would let marketers target users with ads based on the massive amounts of information people reveal on the site about themselves. This may be an unethical or ethical feature to some individuals. Some people may react negatively because they believe it is an invasion of privacy. On the other hand, some individuals may enjoy this feature because their social network recognizes their interests and sends them particular advertisements pertaining to those interests. Consumers like to network with people who have interests and desires that are similar to their own. Individuals who agree to have their social media profile public, should be aware that advertisers have the ability to take information that interests them to be able to send them information and advertisements to boost their sales. Managers invest in social media to foster relationships and interact with customers. This is an ethical way for managers to send messages about their advertisements and products to their consumers.

Since social media marketing first came to be, strategists and markets have been getting smarter and more careful with the way they go about collecting information and distributing advertisements. With the presence of data collecting companies, there is no longer a need to target specific audiences. This can be seen as a large ethical gray area. For many users, this is a breach of privacy, but there are no laws that prevent these companies from using the information provided on their websites. Companies like Equifax Inc., TransUnion Corp, and LexisNexis Group thrive on collecting and sharing personal information of social media users. In 2012, Facebook purchased information from 70 million households from a third party company called Datalogix. Facebook later revealed that they purchased the information in order to create a more efficient advertising service.

Facebook had an estimated 144.27 million views in 2016, approximately 12.9 million per month. Despite this high volume of traffic, very little has been done to protect the millions of users who log on to Facebook and other social media platforms each month. President Barack Obama tried to work with the Federal Trade Commission (FTC) to attempt to regulate data mining. He proposed the Privacy Bill of Rights, which would protect the average user from having their private information downloaded and shared with third party companies. The proposed laws would give the consumer more control over what information companies can collect.

Metrics

Web Site Reports

This involves tracking the volume of visits, leads, and customers to a website from the individual social channel. Google Analytics is a free tool that shows the behavior and other information, such as demographics and device type used, of website visitors from social networks. This and other commercial offers can aid marketers in choosing the most effective social networks and social media marketing activities.

Return on Investment Data

The end goal of any marketing effort is to generate sales. Although social media is a useful marketing tool, it is often difficult to quantify to what extent it is contributing to profit. ROI can be measured by comparing marketing analytic value to contact database or CRM and connect marketing efforts directly to sales activity.

Customer Response Rates

Several customers are turning towards social media to express their appreciation or frustration with brands, product or services. Therefore, marketers can measure the frequency of which customers are discussing their brand and judge how effective their SMM strategies are. In recent studies, 72% of people surveyed expressed that they expected a response to their complaints on Twitter within an hour.

Social Media Marketing in Sport

There has been an increase in social media marketing in sport, as sports teams and clubs recognise the importance of keeping a rapport with their fans and other audiences through social media. Sports personalities such as Cristiano Ronaldo have 40.7 million followers on Twitter and 49.6 million on Instagram, creating opportunities for endorsements.

AFFILIATE MARKETING

Affiliate marketing is a type of performance-based marketing in which a business rewards one or more affiliates for each visitor or customer brought by the affiliate's own marketing efforts.'

Structure

The industry has four core players:

- The merchant (also known as 'retailer' or 'brand').

- The network (that contains offers for the affiliate to choose from and also takes care of the payments).

- The publisher (also known as 'the affiliate').

- The customer.

The market has grown in complexity, resulting in the emergence of a secondary tier of players, including affiliate management agencies, super-affiliates, and specialized third party vendors.

Affiliate marketing overlaps with other Internet marketing methods to some degree, because affiliates often use regular advertising methods. Those methods include organic search engine optimization (SEO), paid search engine marketing (PPC – Pay Per Click), e-mail marketing, content marketing, and (in some sense) display advertising. On the other hand, affiliates sometimes use less orthodox techniques, such as publishing reviews of products or services offered by a partner.

Affiliate marketing is commonly confused with referral marketing, as both forms of marketing use third parties to drive sales to the retailer. The two forms of marketing are differentiated, however, in how they drive sales, where affiliate marketing relies purely on financial motivations, while referral marketing relies more on trust and personal relationships.

Affiliate marketing is frequently overlooked by advertisers. While search engines, e-mail, and web site syndication capture much of the attention of online retailers, affiliate marketing carries a much lower profile. Still, affiliates continue to play a significant role in e-retailers' marketing strategies.

Web 2.0

Websites and services based on Web 2.0 concepts—blogging and interactive online communities, for example — have impacted the affiliate marketing world as well. These platforms allow improved communication between merchants and affiliates. Web 2.0 platforms have also opened affiliate marketing channels to personal bloggers, writers, and independent website owners. Contextual ads allow publishers with lower levels of web traffic to place affiliate ads on websites.

Forms of new media have also diversified how companies, brands, and ad networks serve ads to visitors. For instance, YouTube allows video-makers to embed advertisements through Google's affiliate network. New developments have made it more difficult for unscrupulous affiliates to make money. Emerging black sheep are detected and made known to the affiliate marketing community with much greater speed and efficiency.

Compensation Methods

Predominant Compensation Methods

Eighty percent of affiliate programs today use revenue sharing or pay per sale (PPS) as a compensation method, nineteen percent use cost per action (CPA), and the remaining programs use other methods such as cost per click (CPC) or cost per mille (CPM, cost per estimated 1000 views).

Diminished Compensation Methods

Within more mature markets, less than one percent of traditional affiliate marketing programs today use cost per click and cost per mille. However, these compensation methods are used heavily in display advertising and paid search.

Cost per mille requires only that the publisher make the advertising available on his or her website and display it to the page visitors in order to receive a commission. Pay per click requires one additional step in the conversion process to generate revenue for the publisher. A visitor must not only be made aware of the advertisement but must also click on the advertisement to visit the advertiser's website.

Cost per click was more common in the early days of affiliate marketing but has diminished in use over time due to click fraud issues very similar to the click fraud issues modern search engines are facing today. Contextual advertising programs are not considered in the statistic pertaining to the diminished use of cost per click, as it is uncertain if contextual advertising can be considered affiliate marketing.

While these models have diminished in mature e-commerce and online advertising markets they are still prevalent in some more nascent industries. China is one example where Affiliate Marketing does not overtly resemble the same model in the West. With many affiliates being paid a flat "Cost Per Day" with some networks offering Cost Per Click or CPM.

Performance or Affiliate Marketing

In the case of cost per mille/click, the publisher is not concerned about whether a visitor is a member of the audience that the advertiser tries to attract and is able to convert, because at this point the publisher has already earned his commission. This leaves the greater, and in case of cost per mille, the full risk and loss (if the visitor cannot be converted) to the advertiser.

Cost per action/sale methods require that referred visitors do more than visit the advertiser's website before the affiliate receives a commission. The advertiser must convert that visitor first. It is in the best interest of the affiliate to send the most closely targeted traffic to the advertiser as possible to increase the chance of a conversion. The risk and loss are shared between the affiliate and the advertiser.

Affiliate marketing is also called "performance marketing", in reference to how sales employees are typically being compensated. Such employees are typically paid a commission for each sale they close, and sometimes are paid performance incentives for exceeding objectives. Affiliates are not employed by the advertiser whose products or services they promote, but the compensation models applied to affiliate marketing are very similar to the ones used for people in the advertisers' internal sales department.

The phrase, "Affiliates are an extended sales force for your business", which is often used to explain affiliate marketing, is not completely accurate. The primary difference between the two is that affiliate marketers provide little if any influence on a possible prospect in the conversion process once that prospect is directed to the advertiser's website. The sales team of the advertiser, however, does have the control and influence up to the point where the prospect either: a) signs the contract, or b) completes the purchase.

Multi-tier Programs

Some advertisers offer multi-tier programs that distribute commission into a hierarchical referral network of sign-ups and sub-partners. In practical terms, publisher "A" signs up to the program with an advertiser and gets rewarded for the agreed activity conducted by a referred visitor. If publisher "A" attracts publishers "B" and "C" to sign up for the same program using his sign-up code, all future activities performed by publishers "B" and "C" will result in additional commission (at a lower rate) for publisher "A".

Two-tier programs exist in the minority of affiliate programs; most are simply one-tier. Referral programs beyond two-tier resemble multi-level marketing (MLM) or network marketing but are different: Multi-level marketing (MLM) or network marketing associations tend to have more complex commission requirements/qualifications than standard affiliate programs.

Advantages for Merchants

Merchants favor affiliate marketing because in most cases it uses a "pay for performance" model, meaning that the merchant does not incur a marketing expense unless results are accrued (excluding any initial setup cost).

Implementation Options

Some merchants run their own (in-house) affiliate programs using dedicated software, while others use third-party intermediaries to track traffic or sales that are referred from affiliates. There are two different types of affiliate management methods used by merchants: standalone software or hosted services, typically called affiliate networks.

Payouts to affiliates or publishers can be made by the networks on behalf of the merchant, by the network, consolidated across all merchants where the publisher has a relationship with and earned commissions or directly by the merchant itself.

Affiliate Management and Program Management Outsourcing

Uncontrolled affiliate programs aid rogue affiliates, who use spamming, trademark infringement, false advertising, cookie stuffing, typosquatting, and other unethical methods that have given affiliate marketing a negative reputation.

Some merchants are using outsourced (affiliate) program management (OPM) companies, which are themselves often run by affiliate managers and network program managers. OPM companies perform affiliate program management for the merchants as a service, similar to the role an advertising agencies serves in offline marketing.

Types of Affiliate Websites

Affiliate websites are often categorized by merchants (advertisers) and affiliate networks. There are currently no industry-wide standards for the categorization. The following types of websites are generic, yet are commonly understood and used by affiliate marketers.

- Search affiliates that utilize pay per click search engines to promote the advertisers' offers (i.e., search arbitrage).

- Price comparison service websites and directories.

- Loyalty websites, typically characterized by providing a reward or incentive system for purchases via points, miles and cash back.

- Cause Related Marketing sites that offer charitable donations.

- Coupon and rebate websites that focus on sales promotions.

- Content and niche market websites, including product review sites.

- Personal websites.

- Weblogs and websites syndication feeds.

- E-mail marketing list affiliates (i.e., owners of large opt-in mail lists that typically employ e-mail drip marketing) and newsletter list affiliates, which are typically more content-heavy.

- Registration path or co-registration affiliates who include offers from other merchants during the registration process on their own website.

- Shopping directories that list merchants by categories without providing coupons, price comparisons, or other features based on information that changes frequently, thus requiring continual updates.

- Cost per action networks (i.e., top-tier affiliates) that expose offers from the advertiser with which they are affiliated with their own network of affiliates.

- Websites using adbars (e.g. AdSense) to display context-sensitive advertising for products on the site.

- Virtual currency that offers advertising views in exchange for a handout of virtual currency in a game or other virtual platform.

- File-Sharing: Web sites that host directories of music, movies, games and other software. Users upload content to file-hosting sites and then post descriptions of the material and their download links on directory sites. Uploaders are paid by the file-hosting sites based on the number of times their files are downloaded. The file-hosting sites sell premium download access to the files to the general public. The websites that host the directory services sell advertising and do not host the files themselves.

- Video sharing websites: YouTube videos are often utilized by affiliates to do affiliate marketing. A person would create a video and place a link to the affiliate product they are promoting in the video itself and within the description.

Publisher Recruitment

Affiliate networks that already have several advertisers typically also have a large pool of publishers. These publishers could be potentially recruited, and there is also an increased chance that publishers in the network apply to the program on their own, without the need for recruitment efforts by the advertiser.

Relevant websites that attract the same target audiences as the advertiser but without competing with it are potential affiliate partners as well. Vendors or existing customers can also become recruits if doing so makes sense and does not violate any laws or regulations (such as with pyramid schemes).

Almost any website could be recruited as an affiliate publisher, but high traffic websites are more likely interested in (for their sake) low-risk cost per mille or medium-risk cost per click deals rather than higher-risk cost per action or revenue share deals.

Locating Affiliate Programs

There are three primary ways to locate affiliate programs for a target website:

- Affiliate program directories,

- Large affiliate networks that provide the platform for dozens or even hundreds of advertisers,

- The target website itself. (Websites that offer an affiliate program often have a link titled "affiliate program", "affiliates", "referral program", or "webmasters" — usually in the footer or "About" section of the website.)

If the above locations do not yield information pertaining to affiliates, it may be the case that there exists a non-public affiliate program. Utilizing one of the common website correlation methods may provide clues about the affiliate network. The most definitive method for finding this information is to contact the website owner directly if a contact method can be located.

Issues

Since the emergence of affiliate marketing, there has been little control over affiliate activity. Unscrupulous affiliates have used spam, false advertising, forced clicks (to get tracking cookies set on users' computers), adware, and other methods to drive traffic to their sponsors. Although many affiliate programs have terms of service that contain rules against spam, this marketing method has historically proven to attract abuse from spammers.

E-mail Spam

In the infancy of affiliate marketing, many Internet users held negative opinions due to the tendency of affiliates to use spam to promote the programs in which they were enrolled. As affiliate marketing matured, many affiliate merchants have refined their terms and conditions to prohibit affiliates from spamming.

Malicious Browser Extensions

A browser extension is a plug-in that extends the functionality of a web browser. Some extensions are authored using web technologies such as HTML, JavaScript, and CSS. Most modern web browsers have a whole slew of third-party extensions available for download. In recent years, there has been a constant rise in the number of malicious browser extensions flooding the web. Malicious browser extensions will often appear to be legitimate as they seem to originate from vendor websites and come with glowing customer reviews. In the case of affiliate marketing, these malicious extensions are often used to redirect a user's browser to send fake clicks to websites that are supposedly part of legitimate affiliate marketing programs. Typically, users are completely unaware this is happening other than their browser performance slowing down. Websites end up paying for fake traffic number, and users are unwitting participants in these ad schemes.

Search Engine Spam

As search engines have become more prominent, some affiliate marketers have shifted from sending e-mail spam to creating automatically generated web pages that often contain product data feeds provided by merchants. The goal of such web pages is to manipulate the relevancy or prominence of resources indexed by a search engine, also known as spamdexing. Each page can be targeted to a different niche market through the use of specific keywords, with the result being a skewed form of search engine optimization.

Spam is the biggest threat to organic search engines, whose goal is to provide quality search results for keywords or phrases entered by their users. Google's PageRank algorithm update ("BigDaddy") in February 2006 — the final stage of Google's major update ("Jagger") that began in mid-summer 2005 — specifically targeted spamdexing with great success. This update thus enabled Google to remove a large amount of mostly computer-generated duplicate content from its index.

Websites consisting mostly of affiliate links have previously held a negative reputation for underdelivering quality content. In 2005 there were active changes made by Google, where certain websites were labeled as "thin affiliates". Such websites were either removed from Google's index or were relocated within the results page (i.e., moved from the top-most results to a lower position). To avoid this categorization, affiliate marketer webmasters must create quality content on their websites that distinguishes their work from the work of spammers or banner farms, which only contain links leading to merchant sites.

Some commentators originally suggested that affiliate links work best in the context of the information contained within the website itself. For instance, if a website contains information pertaining to publishing a website, an affiliate link leading to a merchant's internet service provider (ISP) within that website's content would be appropriate. If a website contains information pertaining to sports, an affiliate link leading to a sporting goods website may work well within the context of the articles and information about sports. The goal, in this case, is to publish quality information on the website and provide context-oriented links to related merchant's websites.

However, more recent examples exist of "thin" affiliate sites that are using the affiliate marketing model to create value for Consumers by offering them a service. These thin content service Affiliates fall into three categories:

- Price comparison.
- Cause-related marketing.
- Time-saving.

Consumer Countermeasures

The implementation of affiliate marketing on the internet relies heavily on various techniques built into the design of many web-pages and websites, and the use of calls to external domains to track user actions (click tracking, Ad Sense) and to serve up content (advertising) to the user. Most of this activity adds time and is generally a nuisance to the casual web-surfer and is seen as visual clutter. Various countermeasures have evolved over time to prevent or eliminate the appearance of advertising when a web-page is rendered. Third party programs (Ad-Aware, Adblock Plus, Spybot, pop-up blockers, etc.) and particularly, the use of a comprehensive HOSTS file can effectively eliminate the visual clutter and the extra time and bandwidth needed to render many web pages. The use of specific entries in the HOSTS file to block these well-known and persistent marketing and click-tracking domains can also aid in reducing a system's exposure to malware by preventing the content of infected advertising or tracking servers to reach a user's web-browser.

Adware

Although it differs from spyware, adware often uses the same methods and technologies. Merchants initially were uninformed about adware, what impact it had, and how it could damage their brands. Affiliate marketers became aware of the issue much more quickly, especially because they noticed that adware often overwrites tracking cookies, thus resulting in a decline of commissions. Affiliates not employing adware felt that it was stealing commission from them. Adware often has no valuable purpose and rarely provides any useful content to the user, who is typically unaware that such software is installed on his/her computer.

Affiliates discussed the issues in Internet forums and began to organize their efforts. They believed that the best way to address the problem was to discourage merchants from advertising via adware. Merchants that were either indifferent to or supportive of adware were exposed by affiliates, thus damaging those merchants' reputations and tarnishing their affiliate marketing efforts. Many affiliates either terminated the use of such merchants or switched to a competitor's affiliate program. Eventually, affiliate networks were also forced by merchants and affiliates to take a stand and ban certain adware publishers from their network. The result was Code of Conduct by Commission Junction/beFree and Performics, LinkShare's Anti-Predatory Advertising Addendum, and ShareASale's complete ban of software applications as a medium for affiliates to promote advertiser offers. Regardless of the progress made, adware continues to be an issue, as demonstrated by the class action lawsuit against ValueClick and its daughter company Commission Junction filed on April 20, 2007.

Trademark Bidding

Affiliates were among the earliest adopters of pay per click advertising when the first pay-per-click search engines emerged during the end of the 1990s. Later in 2000 Google launched its pay per click service, Google AdWords, which is responsible for the widespread use and acceptance of pay per click as an advertising channel. An increasing number of merchants engaged in pay per click advertising, either directly or via a search marketing agency, and realized that this space was already occupied by their affiliates. Although this situation alone created advertising channel conflicts and debates between advertisers and affiliates, the largest issue concerned affiliates bidding on advertisers names, brands, and trademarks. Several advertisers began to adjust their affiliate program terms to prohibit their affiliates from bidding on those type of keywords. Some advertisers, however, did and still do embrace this behavior, going so far as to allow, or even encourage, affiliates to bid on any term, including the advertiser's trademarks.

Compensation Disclosure

Bloggers and other publishers may not be aware of disclosure guidelines set forth by the FTC. Guidelines affect celebrity endorsements, advertising language, and blogger compensation.

Lack of Industry Standards

Certification and Training

Affiliate marketing currently lacks industry standards for training and certification. There are some training courses and seminars that result in certifications. However, the acceptance of such certifications is mostly due to the reputation of the individual or company issuing the certification. Affiliate marketing is not commonly taught in universities, and only a few college instructors work with Internet marketers to introduce the subject to students majoring in marketing.

Education occurs most often in "real life" by becoming involved and learning the details as time progresses. Although there are several books on the topic, some so-called "how-to" or "silver bullet" books instruct readers to manipulate holes in the Google algorithm, which can quickly become out of date, or suggest strategies no longer endorsed or permitted by advertisers.

Outsourced Program Management companies typically combine formal and informal training, providing much of their training through group collaboration and brainstorming. Such companies also try to send each marketing employee to the industry conference of their choice.

Other training resources used include online forums, weblogs, podcasts, video seminars, and specialty websites.

Code of Conduct

A code of conduct was released by affiliate networks Commission Junction/beFree and Performics in December 2002 to guide practices and adherence to ethical standards for online advertising.

Marketing Term

Members of the marketing industry are recommending that "affiliate marketing" be substituted with an alternative name. Affiliate marketing is often confused with either network marketing or multi-level marketing. *Performance marketing* is a common alternative, but other recommendations have been made as well.

Sales Tax Vulnerability

In April 2008, the State of New York inserted an item in the state budget asserting sales tax jurisdiction over Amazon.com sales to residents of New York, based on the existence of affiliate links from New York–based websites to Amazon. The state asserts that even one such affiliate constitutes Amazon having a business presence in the state, and is sufficient to allow New York to tax all Amazon sales to state residents. Amazon challenged the amendment and lost at the trial level in January 2009. The case is currently making its way through the New York appeals courts.

Cookie Stuffing

Cookie stuffing involves placing an affiliate tracking cookie on a website visitor's computer without their knowledge, which will then generate revenue for the person doing the cookie stuffing. This not only generates fraudulent affiliate sales but also has the potential to overwrite other affiliates' cookies, essentially stealing their legitimately earned commissions.

Click to Reveal

Many voucher code web sites use a click-to-reveal format, which requires the web site user to click to reveal the voucher code. The action of clicking places the cookie on the website visitor's computer. In the United Kingdom, the IAB Affiliate Council under chair Matt Bailey announced regulations that stated that "Affiliates must not use a mechanism whereby users are encouraged to click to interact with content where it is unclear or confusing what the outcome will be."

COST PER ACTION

Cost per acquisition (CPA), also known as cost per action, pay per acquisition (PPA) is an online advertising pricing model where the advertiser pays for a specified acquisition – for example a sale, click, or form submit (e.g., contact request, newsletter sign up, registration).

Direct response advertisers often consider CPA the optimal way to buy online advertising, as an advertiser only pays for the ad when the desired acquisition has occurred. The desired *acquisition* to be performed is determined by the advertiser. In affiliate marketing, this means that advertisers only pay the affiliates for leads that result in a desired action such as a sale. This removes the risk for the advertiser because they know in advance that they will not have to pay for bad referrals, and it encourages the affiliate to send good referrals.

Radio and TV stations also sometimes offer unsold inventory on a cost per acquisition basis, but this form of advertising is most often referred to as "per inquiry". Although less common, print media will also sometimes be sold on a CPA basis.

Cost Per Acquisition

CPA is sometimes referred to as "cost per acquisition" or "cost per action", which has to do with the fact that many CPA offers by advertisers are about acquiring something (typically new customers by making sales).

Formula to Calculate Cost Per Acquisition

Cost per acquisition (CPA) is calculated as: cost divided by the number of acquisitions. So for example, if one spends £150 on a campaign and gets 10 "acquisitions" this would give a cost per acquisition of £15.

Pay Per Lead

Pay per lead (PPL) is a form of cost per acquisition, with the "acquisition" in this case being the delivery of a lead. Online and Offline advertising payment model in which fees are charged based solely on the delivery of leads.

In a pay per lead agreement, the advertiser only pays for leads delivered under the terms of the agreement. No payment is made for leads that don't meet the agreed-upon criteria.

Leads may be delivered by phone under the pay per call model. Conversely, leads may be delivered electronically, such as by email, SMS or a ping/post of the data directly to a database. The information delivered may consist of as little as an email address, or it may involve a detailed profile including multiple contact points and the answers to qualification questions.

There are numerous risks associated with any Pay Per Lead campaign, including the potential for fraudulent activity by incentive marketing partners. Some fraudulent leads are easy to spot. Nonetheless, it is advisable to make a regular audit of the results.

Differences between CPA and CPL Advertising

In cost per lead campaigns, advertisers pay for an interested lead (hence, cost per lead) — i.e. the contact information of a person interested in the advertiser's product or service. CPL campaigns are suitable for brand marketers and direct response marketers looking to engage consumers at multiple touch points — by building a newsletter list, community site, reward program or member acquisition program.

In CPA campaigns, the advertiser typically pays for a completed sale involving a credit card transaction.

There are other important differentiators:

- CPA and affiliate marketing campaigns are publisher-centric. Advertisers cede control over where their brand will appear, as publishers browse offers and pick which to run on their websites. Advertisers generally do not know where their offer is running.

- CPL campaigns are usually high volume and light-weight. In CPL campaigns, consumers submit only basic contact information. The transaction can be as simple as an email address. On the other hand, CPA campaigns are usually low volume and complex. Typically, a consumer has to submit a credit card and other detailed information.

PPC and CPC Campaigns

Pay per click (PPC) and cost per click (CPC) are both forms of CPA (cost per action) with the action being a click. PPC is generally used to refer to paid search marketing such as Google's AdSense or Google Ads. The advertiser pays each time someone clicks on their text or display ad.

When advertising in the Google platform, CPC bidding means that an advertiser pays for each click of an ad placed and that, in ad campaign, he can set a price cap as a maximum CPC bid. Here, the CPC pricing is also sometimes referred to as PPC. In the Facebook social networking platform, the term pertains to the average cost for each link click and it serves as a metric in online advertising for benchmarking online ad efficiency and performance. CPC in the Amazon Marketing Service (AMS) follows the same model, although it is reported that this platform charge lower CPCs compared to other advertising platforms with Google charging the highest.

Also, pay per download (PPD) is another form of CPA where the user completes an action to download a digital content such as apps, digital media, and other files. The actions can include completing surveys or answering quiz in order to generate revenue from a third-party advertiser.

Tracking CPA Campaigns

With payment of CPA campaigns being on an "action" being delivered, accurate tracking is of prime importance to media owners.

This is a complex subject in itself, however if usually performed in three main ways:

- Cookie tracking – When a media owner drives a click a cookie is dropped on the prospect's computer which is linked back to the media owner when the "action" is performed.

- Telephone tracking – Unique telephone numbers are used per instance of a campaign. So media owner XYZ would have their own unique phone number for an offer and when this number is called any resulting "actions" are allocated to media owner XYZ. Often payouts are based on a length of call (commonly 90 seconds) – if a call goes over 90 seconds it is viewed that there is a genuine interest and a "lead" is paid for.

- Promotional codes – Promotional or voucher codes are commonly used for tracking retail campaigns. The prospect is asked to use a code at the checkout to qualify for an offer. The code can then be matched back to the media owner who drove the sale.

Effective Cost Per Action

A related term, effective cost per action (eCPA), is used to measure the effectiveness of advertising inventory purchased (by the advertiser) via a cost per click, cost per impression, or cost per thousand basis.

In other words, the eCPA tells the advertiser what they would have paid if they had purchased the advertising inventory on a cost per action basis (instead of a cost per click, cost per impression, or cost per mille/thousand basis).

If the advertiser is purchasing inventory with a CPA *target*, instead of paying per action at a fixed rate, the goal of the effective CPA (eCPA) should always be below the maximum CPA. As described by Yang's Law, eCPA<CPA. This fundamental view of what the performance of conversion-based campaign should be is served as the baseline for many buy-side platform optimization algorithms.

NATIVE ADVERTISING

Native advertising is a type of advertising that matches the form and function of the platform upon which it appears. In many cases it functions like an advertorial, and manifests as a video, article or editorial. The word "native" refers to this coherence of the content with the other media that appear on the platform.

These ads reduce a consumers' ad recognition by blending the ad into the native content of the platform, using somewhat ambiguous language such as like "sponsored" or "branded" content. They can be difficult to properly identify due to their ambiguous nature.

Product placement (embedded marketing) is a precursor to native advertising. The latter places the product within the content, whereas in native marketing, which is legally permissible in the US to the extent that there is sufficient disclosure, the product and content are merged.

Forms

Despite the ambiguity surrounding native advertising's invention, many experts do consider the Hallmark Hall of Fame, a series which first aired in 1951 and still runs today, as among the earliest instances of the technique. According to Lin Grensing-Pophal, "The award-winning series is arguably one of the earliest examples of 'native' advertising—advertising that is secondary to the message being delivered, but impactful through its association with valued content."

Contemporary formats for native advertising now include promoted videos, images, articles, commentary, music, and other various forms of media. A majority of these methods for delivering the native strategy have been relegated to an online presence, where it is most commonly employed as publisher-produced brand content, a similar concept to the traditional advertorial. Alternative examples of modern technique include search advertising, when ads appear alongside search results that qualify as native to the search experience. Popular examples include, Twitter's promoted Tweets, Facebook's promoted stories, and Tumblr's promoted posts. The most traditionally influenced form of native marketing manifests as the placement of sponsor-funded content alongside editorial content, or showing "other content you might be interested in" which is sponsored by a marketer alongside editorial recommendations.

Most recently, controversy has arisen as to whether Content marketing is a form of native marketing, or if they are inherently separate ideologies and styles, with native market strategists claiming that they utilize content marketing techniques, and some content market strategists claiming to not be a form of native marketing.

Sponsored Content

In most recent years of the millennium, the most notable form of native advertising has been sponsored content. The production of sponsored content involves inclusion of a third party along with a management company or a brand company's personal relations and promotional activities team in reaching out to aforementioned considerably popular third party content producers on social media, often independent, deemed "influencers" in an attempt to promote a product. Often quoted as the predecessor to traditional endorsed and contract advertising; which would instead be featuring celebrities, sponsored content has indubitably become more and more popular on social media platforms in recent years likely due to their cost-effectiveness, time efficiency, as well as the ability to receive instant feedback on the marketability of a product or service.

A technique often used in traditional sponsored advertising is direct and indirect product placement (embedded marketing). Instead of embedded marketing's technique of placing the product within the content, in native marketing, the product and content are merged, and in sponsored content the product, content and active promotion occurs simultaneously across a number of platforms.

Unlike traditional forms of Native Advertising, Sponsored content alludes to requirement of and desire for transparency and thrives on the concept of preexisting and built up trust between consumer and content producer rather than creating a masked net impression, which is a reasonable consumer's understanding of an advertisement. The underlying motives of sponsored content, however, is similar to that of native advertising- which is to inhibit a consumers' ad recognition by blending the ad into the native content of the platform, making many consumers unaware they are looking at an ad to begin with. The sponsored content on social media, like any other type of native advertising, can be difficult to be properly identified by the Federal Trade Commission because of their rather ambiguous nature. Native advertising frequently bypasses this net impression standard, which makes them problematic.

Categories of Sponsored Content

Sponsored Videos

Sponsored videos involve the content producer/influencer including or mentioning the service/product for a particular amount of time within their video. This type of sponsorship is evident across all genres and levels of production regarding video content. There is a history of trouble between content producers and their transparency of sponsors regarding endorsement guidelines set by the Federal Trades Commission. Most sponsored videos include a brief or a contract and can vary from client to client and affects the nature of promotion of the product as well as specific requirements such as length of the promotion period. Notable companies involved in this trade include audible, squarespace, Crunchyroll and vanity planet.

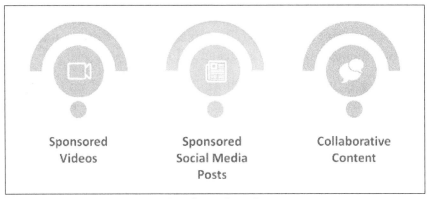

Categories of Spondsored content.

Sponsored Social Media Posts

Sponsored social media posts usually consist of the content producer/influencer including or mentioning the service/product for a particular amount of time within a single or series of social media posts. Most sponsored posts include a brief or a contract and can vary from client to client. Notable companies involved in this trade include fit-tea, sugar bear hair and various diet meal planning services and watch brands.

Collaborative Content

Collaborative content has become more prominent on video platforms and social media in recent years. Content producers/influencers are usually contacted by companies for their creative input and voice in the makings of a product or provided with a discount code to gain a percentage of the profits after consumers incorporate the code as a part their purchase. Collaborative content may also include a brief or a contract and can vary from client to client. However, there is a degree of flexibility as the finished product is supposedly a representation of the content producer. Notable companies involved in this trade include pixi, colourpop and MAC cosmetics.

Advertising Disclosure

As it is the nature of disguised advertising to blend with its surroundings, a clear disclosure is deemed necessary when employing native marketing strategy in order to protect the consumer from being deceived, and to assist audiences in distinguishing between sponsored and regular content. According to the Federal Trade Commission, means of disclosure include visual cues, labels, and other techniques. The most common practices of these are recognizable by understated labels, such as "Advertisement", "Ad", "Promoted", "Sponsored", "Featured Partner", or "Suggested Post" in subtitles, corners, or the bottoms of ads. A widespread tendency in such measures is to mention the brand name of the sponsor, as in "Promoted by [brand]", "Sponsored by [brand]", or "Presented by [brand]". These can vary drastically due to the publisher's choice of disclosure language (i.e. wording used to identify native advertising placement).

In 2009, the Federal Trade Commission released their Endorsement Guideline specifically to increase consumer awareness of endorsements and testimonials in advertising given the rise in popularity of social media and blogging.

The American Society of Magazine Editors (ASME) released updated guidelines in 2015 reaffirming the need of publishers to distinguish editorial and advertising content. The ASME approach recommends both labels to disclose commercial sponsorship and in-content visual evidence to help the user distinguish native advertising from editorial.

A study published by University of California researchers found that even labeled native advertising deceived about a quarter of survey research subjects. In the study,

27% of respondents thought that journalists or editors wrote an advertorial for diet pills, despite the presence of the "Sponsored Content" label. Because the Federal Trade Commission can bring cases concerning practices that mislead a substantial minority of consumers, the authors conclude that many native advertising campaigns are probably deceptive under federal law. The authors also explain two theories of why native advertising is deceptive. First, the schema theory suggests that advertorials mislead by causing consumers not to trigger their innate skepticism to advertising. Second, advertorials also cause source-based misleadingness problems by imbuing advertising material with the authority normally assigned to editorial content. Recognition percentages remain low even as native advertising has expanded in pervasiveness. An academic report has shown that only 17% of participants could identify native advertising and even if readers were primed, that number only increased to 27%. Moreover, when readers learned about covert advertising, their perceptions of the publications declined.

Categories of Online Ads

The Interactive Advertising Bureau (IAB), the primary organization responsible for developing ad industry standards and conducting business research, published a report in 2013, detailing six different categories for differentiating types of native advertisements.

1. In-feed Ad Units: As the name denotes, In-feed ads are units located within the website's normal content feed, meaning they appear as if the content may have been written by or in partnership with the publisher's team to match the surrounding stories. A category that rose to popularity through sites like Upworthy and Buzzfeed's sponsored articles due to its effectiveness, In-feed has also been the source of controversy for native marketing, as it is here the distinction between native and content marketing is typically asserted.

2. Search Ads: Appearing in the list of search results, these are generally found above or below the organic search results or in favorable position, having been sold to advertisers with a guarantee for optimal placement on the search engine page. They usually possess an identical appearance as other results on the page with the exception of disclosure aspects.

3. Recommendation Widgets: Although these ads are part of the content of the site, these do not tend to appear in like manner to the content of the editorial feed. Typically delivered through a widget, recommendation ads are generally recognizable by words which imply external reference, suggestions, and tangentially related topics. "You might also like"; "You might like"; "Elsewhere from around the web"; "From around the web"; "You may have missed", or "Recommended for you" typically characterize these units.

4. Promoted Listings: Usually featured on websites that are not content based,

such as e-commerce sites, promoted listings are presented in identical fashion with the products or services offered on the given site. Similarly justified as search ads, sponsored products are considered native to the experience in much the same way as search ads.

5. In-Ad (IAB Standard): An In-Ad fits in a standard IAB container found outside the feed, containing "contextually relevant content within the ad, links to an offsite page, has been sold with a guaranteed placement, and is measured on brand metrics such as interaction and brand lift."

6. Custom/Can't be Contained: This category is left for the odd ends and ads that do not conform to any of the other content categories.

Digital Platforms

Native advertising platforms are classified into two categories, commonly referred to as "open" and "closed" platforms, but hybrid options are also utilized with some frequency.

Closed platforms are formats created by brands for the purpose of promoting their own content intrinsically on their websites. Advertisements seen on these platforms will not be seen on others, as these ad types are generated for its sole use, and structured around exhibiting ad units within the confines of the website's specific agendas. Namely, advertisements distributed on closed platforms originate from the platform's brand itself. Popular examples include Promoted Tweets on Twitter, Sponsored Stories on Facebook, and TrueView Video Ads on YouTube.

Open platforms are defined by the promotion of the same piece of branded content across multiple platforms ubiquitously, but through some variation of native ad formats. Unlike closed platforms, the content itself lives outside any given website that it appears on, and is usually distributed across multiple sites by a third party company, meaning that the advertisements appearing on open platforms namely are placed there by an advertiser.

Hybrid platforms allow the content publishing platforms to install a private marketplace where advertisers have the option to bid on the inventory of ad space either through direct sales or programmatic auction through what is known as Real-Time Bidding (RTB). Therefore, advertisements distributed on hybrid platforms are placed there by the platform itself, the space having been sold to an open platform advertiser.

MARKETING AUTOMATION

Marketing automation refers to software platforms and technologies designed for marketing departments and organizations to more effectively market on multiple channels online (such as email, social media, websites, etc.) and automate repetitive tasks.

Marketing departments, consultants and part-time marketing employees benefit by specifying criteria and outcomes for tasks and processes which are then interpreted, stored and executed by software, which increases efficiency and reduces human error. Originally focused on email marketing automation, marketing automation refers to a broad range of automation and analytic tools for marketing especially inbound marketing. Marketing Automation platforms are used as a hosted or web-based solution, and no software installation is required by a customer.

The use of a marketing automation platform is to streamline sales and marketing organizations by replacing high-touch, repetitive manual processes with automated solutions.

Marketing automation is a platform that marketers use to plan, coordinate, manage and measure all of their marketing campaigns, both online and offline. It is often used along with lifecycle marketing strategy to closely manage and nurture generated leads, aiming to convert leads into customers.

Marketing Automation is a subset of customer relationship management (CRM) or customer experience management (CXM) that focuses on the definition, segmentation, scheduling and tracking of marketing campaigns. The use of marketing automation makes processes that would otherwise have been performed manually much more efficient and makes new processes possible. Marketing Automation can be defined as a process where technology is used to automate several repetitive tasks that are undertaken on a regular basis in a marketing campaign. A tool that allows an individual to design, execute and automate a time-bound marketing workflow can be called a Marketing Automation platform.

Marketing Automation platforms allow marketers to automate and simplify client communication by managing complex omni-channel marketing strategies from a single tool. Marketing Automation assist greatly in areas like Lead Generation, Segmentation, Lead nurturing and lead scoring, Relationship marketing, Cross-sell and upsell, Retention, Marketing ROI measurement.

There are three categories of marketing automation software:

Marketing Intelligence

Uses tracking codes in social media, email and webpages to track the behavior of anyone interested in a product or service to gain a measure of intent. It can record which social media group or thread they followed, which link was clicked on in an email or which search term was used to access a website. Multiple link analysis can then track buyer behavior - following links and multiple threads related to product A but not B will show an interest only in A. This allows more accurately targeted response and the development of a nurturing program specifically targeted towards their interest and vertical market. This allows businesses to more efficiently and effectively reach target consumers who show, through their internet history behavior, that they will be interested in the company's products. Due to its interactive nature this has been described as Marketing Automation 2.0.

Marketing Automation has a focus on moving leads from the top of the marketing funnel through to becoming sales-ready leads at the bottom of the funnel. Prospects are scored, based on their activities, and receive targeted content and messaging, thus nurturing them from first interest through to sale. Commonly used in business-to-business (B2B), business-to-government (B2G), or longer sales cycle business-to-consumer (B2C) sales cycles, Marketing Automation involves multiple areas of marketing and is really the marriage of email marketing technology coupled with a structured sales process.

Advanced Workflow Automation

Encompasses automation of internal marketing processes. These include budgeting and planning, workflow and approvals, the marketing calendar, internal collaboration, digital asset creation and management and essentially everything that supports the operational efficiency of the internal marketing function. Typically these systems require a CRM or COM administrator to set up a complex series of rules to trigger action items for internal sales and marketing professionals to manually process (designing files, sending letters, sending email campaigns). This type of system increases marketer's ability to deliver relevant content to relevant individuals at relevant times. Limitations may apply, based on the human resource capacity of an organisation and their level of commitment to the tasks as they are assigned.

Effects of GDPR on Marketing Automation

As of 25th May 2018, the General Data Protection Regulation came into effect, this has had a large impact on the way marketing teams and organisations can manage their consumer data. Any organisation using marketing automation tracking is required to ask consent of from the consumer as well as provide transparency on how the data will be processed.

Functionality

In order to effectively aid marketers in fully understanding customers and subsequently developing a strategic marketing plan, marketing automation tools (MAT) are designed to perform eight key tasks:

- Development and analysis of marketing campaigns and customers.

- Management of marketing campaigns.

- Appropriate customer data organization and storage.

- Moving contacts from leads to customers.

- Lead Scoring.

- Integration of multiple touchpoints such as email and social media.

- Lead management.

- Campaign performance analytics (i.e. open rate or click-through rates on emails, conversion rates on landing pages).

EMAIL MARKETING

Email marketing is the act of sending a commercial message, typically to a group of people, using email. In its broadest sense, every email sent to a potential or current customer could be considered email marketing. It usually involves using email to send advertisements, request business, or solicit sales or donations, and is meant to build loyalty, trust, or brand awareness. Marketing emails can be sent to a purchased lead list or a current customer database. The term usually refers to sending email messages with the purpose of enhancing a merchant's relationship with current or previous customers, encouraging customer loyalty and repeat business, acquiring new customers or convincing current customers to purchase something immediately, and sharing third-party ads.

Email marketing has evolved rapidly alongside the technological growth of the 21st century. Prior to this growth, when emails were novelties to the majority of customers, email marketing was not as effective. In 1978, Gary Thuerk of Digital Equipment Corporation (DEC) sent out the first mass email to approximately 400 potential clients via the Advanced Research Projects Agency Network (ARPANET). He claims that this resulted in $13 million worth of sales in DEC products, and highlighted the potential of marketing through mass emails.

However, as email marketing developed as an effective means of direct communication, in the 1990s, users increasingly began referring to it as "spam", and began blocking out content from emails with filters and blocking programs. In order to effectively communicate a message through email, marketers had to develop a way of pushing content through to the end user, without being cut out by automatic filters and spam removing software.

Historically, it has been difficult to measure the effectiveness of marketing campaigns because target markets cannot be adequately defined. Email marketing carries the benefit of allowing marketers to identify returns on investment and measure and improve efficiency. Email marketing allows marketers to see feedback from users in real time, and to monitor how effective their campaign is in achieving market penetration, revealing a communication channel's scope. At the same time, however, it also means that the more personal nature of certain advertising methods, such as television advertisements, cannot be captured.

Types

Transactional Emails

Transactional emails are usually triggered based on a customer's action with a company. To be qualified as transactional or relationship messages, these communications' primary purpose must be "to facilitate, complete, or confirm a commercial transaction that the recipient has previously agreed to enter into with the sender" along with a few other narrow definitions of transactional messaging. Triggered transactional messages include dropped basket messages, password reset emails, purchase or order confirmation emails, order status emails, reorder emails, and email receipts.

The primary purpose of a transactional email is to convey information regarding the action that triggered it. But, due to their high open rates (51.3% compared to 36.6% for email newsletters), transactional emails are an opportunity to introduce or extend the email relationship with customers or subscribers; to anticipate and answer questions; or to cross-sell or up-sell products or services.

Many email newsletter software vendors offer transactional email support, which gives companies the ability to include promotional messages within the body of transactional emails. There are also software vendors that offer specialized transactional email marketing services, which include providing targeted and personalized transactional email messages and running specific marketing campaigns (such as customer referral programs).

Direct Emails

Direct email involves sending an email solely to communicate a promotional message (for example, a special offer or a product catalog). Companies usually collect a list of customer or prospect email addresses to send direct promotional messages to, or they rent a list of email addresses from service companies.

Comparison to Traditional Mail

There are both advantages and disadvantages to using email marketing in comparison to traditional advertising mail.

Advantages

Email marketing is popular with companies for several reasons:

- Email marketing is significantly cheaper and faster than traditional mail, mainly because with email, most of the cost falls on the recipient.

- Businesses and organizations who send a high volume of emails can use an ESP (email service provider) to gather information about the behavior of the recipients. The insights provided by consumer response to email marketing help businesses and organizations understand and make use of consumer behavior.

- Almost half of American Internet users check or send email on a typical day, with emails delivered between 1 am and 5 am local time outperforming those sent at other times in open and click rates.

Disadvantages

- As of mid-2016 email deliverability is still an issue for legitimate marketers. According to the report, legitimate email servers averaged a delivery rate of 73% in the U.S.; six percent were filtered as spam, and 22% were missing. This lags behind other countries: Australia delivers at 90%, Canada at 89%, Britain at 88%, France at 84%, Germany at 80% and Brazil at 79%.

- Additionally, consumers receive on average about 90 emails per day.

- Companies considering the use of an email marketing program must make sure that their program does not violate spam laws such as the United States' Controlling the Assault of Non-Solicited Pornography and Marketing Act (CAN-SPAM), the European Privacy and Electronic Communications Regulations 2003, or their Internet service provider's acceptable use policy.

Opt-in Email Advertising

Opt-in email advertising, or permission marketing, is advertising via email whereby the recipient of the advertisement has consented to receive it.

A common example of permission marketing is a newsletter sent to an advertising firm's customers. Such newsletters inform customers of upcoming events or promotions, or new products. In this type of advertising, a company that wants to send a newsletter to their customers may ask them at the point of purchase if they would like to receive the newsletter.

With a foundation of opted-in contact information stored in their database, marketers can send out promotional materials automatically using autoresponders — known as drip marketing. They can also segment their promotions to specific market segments.

INBOUND MARKETING

Inbound marketing is a marketing methodology that is designed to draw visitors and potential customers in, rather than outwardly pushing a brand, product or service onto prospects in the hope of lead generation or customers.

In terms of digital marketing, this means using a combination of marketing channels – most commonly content marketing, search engine optimization SEO, and social media – in creative ways to attract people's attention. The aim of a successful inbound marketing campaign is to increase reach and drive quality traffic, engagement and conversions using 'earned' and 'owned' media.

Inbound marketing software provider HubSpot coined the phrase 'inbound marketing' back in 2006. HubSpot defines inbound marketing as the process of attracting, converting, closing and delighting customers. Through using various types of content at different stages of the buying cycle, the 'inbound methodology' is "the best way to turn strangers into customers and promoters of your business."

Inbound Marketing vs. Outbound Marketing

The clue to understanding the differences between inbound and outbound marketing is in the name. Inbound marketing focuses on drawing potential customers in, while outbound marketing is about outwardly pushing a business's offering. Inbound marketing is about earning attention, while outbound typically involves buying it.

Inbound Marketing: Owned and Earned Media

Inbound marketing uses owned and earned media to engage potential customers in creative ways.

- Owned media are those channels that a business has control over. For example, your website, blog, brand social media profiles, product landing pages and YouTube channel. You can choose what to publish, how to publish it, and when.

- Earned media is the coverage you earn as a result your hard work. Offline, this includes traditional coverage in newspapers and magazines. Online, it's things such as coverage on news sites often gained through digital PR, but also mentions on social media, use of a campaign hashtag, conversations in online forums, and online reviews. You have less control over earned media, but it should be a reward for the work you've put into your inbound marketing campaign.

Outbound Marketing: Paid Media

On the other hand, outbound marketing is more readily associated with paid media. This could be traditional offline advertising, PPC and display advertising, or paid emails.

Paid media also encompasses social media advertising, for example Facebook advertising or Twitter promoted posts.

Although typically associated with outbound marketing, it's worth noting that social media advertising is often an effective way to boost the performance of inbound marketing campaigns. Advertising on Facebook, for example, allows you to promote your content and campaign to your target audience, no matter how niche it might be.

Benefits of Inbound Marketing

Reach the Right Audience in the Right Place to Generate Quality Traffic

By focusing your inbound marketing strategy on reaching the right audiences in the right places, you can attract your target customers in order to meet your digital marketing objectives. This is instead of spending money attracting traffic from people who are unlikely to ever convert.

Increase Trust

Inbound marketing is all about giving potential customers the information they are looking for – even if they don't know it – in a creative and engaging way. It's not about pushing unwanted sales at every opportunity. By using inbound marketing as a way to present your brand as a useful and reliable resource, the hope is they'll come to you when the time to purchase does arise.

Protect from Over-reliance on One Channel

By pursuing quality traffic from a variety of sources – organic search, social media referrals, referrals from other websites talking about your amazing work – you reduce the reliance on one channel alone, and therefore the associated risk.

Considerations

Measurement

Measuring the impact of inbound marketing in a way that demonstrates understandable ROI has always been a tricky one. The key is to be clear from the beginning.

It may be that you can't track the number of leads generated as a direct result of your campaign, but you can track how many downloads your resource has had, the average duration people watched your video for, how many new social media followers you gained etc.

When you're planning your campaign, be clear about what it is you're trying to achieve and measure that appropriately and honestly. That way, everyone's expectations are set – and therefore, are more likely to be met.

Long-term Strategy

Successful inbound marketing campaigns don't happen overnight. They take time to plan, implement and refine. It can be labor-intensive too – you might need content creators, designers, developers, outreach specialists, social media marketers and a campaign manager to even get the thing off the ground. That said, if you put your time and effort into the right evergreen campaign, you should have something that continues to provide value for the foreseeable future.

Examples of Inbound Marketing:

- Content hubs offering how-to video guides, blogs, case studies, webinars, white papers and related product information.

- User-generated content and social media marketing campaigns, such as photography competitions or review collation.

- Interactive online content pieces created in partnership with related business to increase digital PR and promotional opportunities.

References

- Pulizzi, Joe; Barrett, Newt (February 2010). ""Get Content Get Customers"-Turn Prospects into Buyers with Content Marketing". NSB Management Review. 2 (2): 98–100. Retrieved 29 October 2018

- What-is-digital-marketing, marketing: hubspot.com, Retrieved 6 June, 2019

- Rowley, Jennifer (2008-07-07). "Understanding digital content marketing". Journal of Marketing Management. 24 (5–6): 517–540. Doi:10.1362/026725708X325977. ISSN 0267-257X

- Integrated-digital-marketing-basics, content: socialmediatoday.com, Retrieved 7 July, 2019

- Lieb, Rebecca (2011-10-14). Content Marketing: Think Like a Publisher - How to Use Content to Market Online and in Social Media. Que Publishing. ISBN 9780789748379

- Seo-in-digital-marketing: educba.com, Retrieved 8 August, 2019

- Rowley, Jennifer (2008-07-07). "Understanding digital content marketing". Journal of Marketing Management. 24 (5–6): 517–540. Doi:10.1362/026725708X325977. ISSN 0267-257X

- White-hat-seo: wordstream.com, Retrieved 9 January, 2019

- "Re: Complaint Requesting Investigation of Various Internet Search Engine Companies for Paid Placement or (Pay per click)". Ftc.gov. June 22, 2002. Archived from the original on July 23, 2013. Retrieved 2007-06-09

Mobile Commerce

Mobile commerce, also called m-commerce, is an advancement of e-commerce and includes the different monetary transactions which are conducted through mobile devices. This chapter closely examines the key concepts of mobile commerce such as mobile ticketing, mobile banking and mobile marketing to provide an extensive understanding of the subject.

Mobile commerce popularly known as m-commerce is actually just a subset of e-commerce. The term itself was coined in 1997 by Kevin Duffy. It is essentially a way of carrying thousands and millions of retail shops in your pocket.

Very simply put M-commerce entails the e-commerce transactions done with a mobile phone. So, M-commerce is the use of mobile phones to conduct any type of business transaction. It takes the help of the e-commerce background and WAP technology.

The use of wireless technology (WAP) to conduct sales of goods, provide services, make payments and other financial transactions, the exchange of information etc. is the basis of mobile commerce.

M-commerce is actually a rapidly growing sector of e-commerce. Nearly 70% of the online transactions that occur in India happen from mobile phones. Globally it is a 700 billion dollar industry.

M-commerce is about exploiting new opportunities made available to us thanks to e-commerce. So it involves the advent of new technologies, services, business models and marketing strategies. It differentiates itself in many ways from e-commerce. This is because mobile phones have very different characteristics than desktop computers. And it opens so many windows of opportunities for businesses to exploit.

Applications

Other than the straightforward m-commerce transactions of buying and selling of goods and services, they have so many applications:

- Mobile Banking: Using a mobile website or application to perform all your banking functions. It is one step ahead of online banking and has become commonplace these days. For example, in Nigeria, the majority of banking transactions happen on mobile phones.

- Mobile Ticketing and Booking: Making bookings and receiving your tickets on the mobile. The digital ticket or boarding pass is sent directly to your phone after you make the payment from it. Even in India now IRTC and other services provide m-ticketing services.

- E-bills: This includes mobile vouchers, mobile coupons to be redeemed and even loyalty points or cards system.

- Auctions: Online auctions having now been developed to be made available via mobile phones as well.

- Stock Market Reports and even stock market trading over mobile applications.

Disadvantages

- The existing technology to set up an m-commerce business is very expensive. It has great start-up costs and many complications arise.

- In developing countries, the networks and service providers are not reliable. It is not most suitable for data transfer.

- Then there is the issue of security. There are many concerns about the safety of the customer's private information. And the possibility of a data leak is very daunting.

Advantages of Mobile Commerce

Ubiquity

It is the main advantage of mobile commerce (m-commerce). Users can get any information that they need, whenever they want regardless of their locations, via mobile devices that connected to the Internet. In mobile commerce applications, users may still be engaged in activities, such as meeting people or traveling while performing transactions or getting information. With this capability, mobile commerce (m-commerce) makes services or applications can meet consumer's need whenever and wherever it arises.

Reachability

The other advantage of mobile commerce is reachability. Through mobile devices, business entities may approach customers anywhere and anytime. On the other hand, with a mobile device, users can communicate with other people regardless of time and location. People will no longer be constrained by time or place in accessing e-commerce activities. Furthermore, users may limit their ability to approach some particular people and at some particular times.

Localization

The ability to know the physical location of the user at a particular time also increases the value of mobile commerce (m-commerce). With information of location, a lot of location-based applications can be provided. For instance, knowing the user's location, the mobile service can quickly notify him/her when his/her friends or colleagues are nearby. It also helps users have the direction to the nearest restaurant or automated teller machine (ATM).

Personalization

There is a huge amount of information, services and applications that currently available on the Internet, and the relevance of information users received is very important. Mobile devices are typically used by a sole individual. Thus, because different users of mobile devices often require different sets of services and applications, mobile commerce services and applications could be personalized to provide information or perform services appropriately to specific users.

Dissemination

Some wireless infrastructure supports the simultaneous delivery of data to all mobile users within a specified geographical area. This advantage of mobile commerce provides an effective means to disseminate information to a large number of consumers.

Convenience

It is very convenient for users to operate in the wireless computing environment. Mobile devices are more functional and convenience in use while their size remains the same or even getting smaller. Unlike traditional PCs, mobile devices can be carried easily, installed in various screen patterns, and mostly connected instantly. Moreover, mobile devices allow users to connect easily and quickly to the Internet, Intranet, other mobile devices, and online databases. Thus, the wireless device can achieve most of the convenience. In addition, by making services more convenient, the customer may actually become more loyal.

MOBILE TICKETING

Mobile ticketing is the process whereby customers can order, pay for, obtain and validate tickets using mobile phones, without the need of a physical ticket. A mobile ticket contains a unique ticket verification (QR code). Mobile tickets reduce the production and distribution costs connected with traditional paper-based ticketing channels and increase customer convenience by providing new and simple ways to purchase tickets. People will not worry about losing a ticket or realizing left tickets at home when arrive at the venue.

Mobile tickets should not be confused with E-tickets (electronic tickets) which are used by airlines since 1994, they can be sent by e-mail, printed and shown at the check-in desk at the airport to obtain a boarding pass. Many train and bus operators in Europe have created phone apps in which tickets can be bought and stored. These include but are not limited to SJ, DSB, NSB, DB and selected local transit authorities.

The first mobile ticketing deployment for a public transport operator in the UK was for Chiltern Railways in 2007. The first transit agency in the US to deploy mobile ticketing was in 2012 with Boston's MBTA and the first agency in Australia was in 2017 with Adelaide Metro.

Philips and Sony developed near field communication (NFC) in 2002. It is build on the same basis as common contactless smartcards. Philips published an early paper on NFC in 2004. In 2004, the NFC Forum was established. NFC incorporated in a mobile phone allows all kind of novel contactless applications, mobile ticketing being an important one of them. Mobile Tickets can be purchased via internet and will be downloaded in a few seconds to the mobile phone, be it in an sms with a 2-D barcode or to the connected NFC chip. In case of NFC at entrance the phone just has to be touched to the scanning device (in fact it makes contact within 10 cm). The GSM Association, GSMA, published a whitepaper on M-Ticketing in 2011. It describes extensively the use and advantages of M-ticketing, principally the use of NFC technology. They state that NFC is the best technology but "it is expected however that M-ticketing services using SMS and Bar Code implementations will be prevalent until the point that a critical mass of NFC enabled handsets is available."

Barcode and visual validation is still the accepted way to enable mobile ticketing with proven adoption thanks to the fact that tickets work across all smartphones.

MOBILE BANKING

Mobile banking is a service provided by a bank or other financial institution that allows its customers to conduct financial transactions remotely using a mobile device such as a smartphone or tablet. Unlike the related internet banking it uses software, usually called an app, provided by the financial institution for the purpose. Mobile banking is usually available on a 24-hour basis. Some financial institutions have restrictions on which accounts may be accessed through mobile banking, as well as a limit on the amount that can be transacted. Mobile banking is dependent on the availability of an internet or data connection to the mobile device.

Transactions through mobile banking depend on the features of the mobile banking app provided and typically includes obtaining account balances and lists of latest transactions, electronic bill payments, remote check deposits, P2P payments, and funds transfers between a customer's or another's accounts. Some apps also enable copies of statements to be downloaded and sometimes printed at the customer's premises. Using a mobile banking app increases ease of use, speed, flexibility and also improves security because it integrates with the user built-in mobile device security mechanisms.

From the bank's point of view, mobile banking reduces the cost of handling transactions by reducing the need for customers to visit a bank branch for non-cash withdrawal and deposit transactions. Mobile banking does not handle transactions involving cash, and a customer needs to visit an ATM or bank branch for cash withdrawals or deposits. Many apps now have a remote deposit option; using the device's camera to digitally transmit cheques to their financial institution.

Mobile banking differs from mobile payments, which involves the use of a mobile device to pay for goods or services either at the point of sale or remotely, analogously to the use of a debit or credit card to effect an EFTPOS payment.

In one academic model, mobile banking is defined as:

> "Mobile Banking refers to provision and availment of banking and financial services with the help of mobile telecommunication devices. The scope of offered services may include facilities to conduct bank and stock market transactions, to administer accounts and to access customised information."

According to this model mobile banking can be said to consist of three inter-related concepts:

- Mobile accounting,

- Mobile financial information services,

Most services in the categories designated accounting and brokerage are transaction-based. The non-transaction-based services of an informational nature are however essential for conducting transactions - for instance, balance inquiries might be needed before committing a money remittance. The accounting and brokerage services are therefore offered invariably in combination with information services. Information services, on the other hand, may be offered as an independent module.

Mobile banking may also be used to help in business situations as well as for financial situation.

Mobile Banking Services

Account Information

- Mini-statements and checking of account history.

- Alerts on account activity or passing of set thresholds.

- Monitoring of term deposits.

- Access to loan statements.

- Access to card statements.

- Mutual funds/equity statements.

- Insurance policy management.

Transaction

- Funds transfers between the customer's linked accounts.

- Paying third parties, including bill payments and third party fund transfers.

- Check Remote Deposit.

Investments

- Portfolio management services.

- Real-time stock.

Support

- Status of requests for credit, including mortgage approval, and insurance coverage.

- Check (cheque) book and card requests.

- Exchange of data messages and email, including complaint submission and tracking.

- ATM Location.

Content Services

- General information such as weather updates, news.

- Loyalty-related offers.

- Location-based services.

A report by the US Federal Reserve found that 21 percent of mobile phone owners had used mobile banking in the past 12 months. Based on a survey conducted by Forrester, mobile banking will be attractive mainly to the younger, more "tech-savvy" customer segment. A third of mobile phone users say that they may consider performing some kind of financial transaction through their mobile phone. But most of the users are interested in performing basic transactions such as querying for account balance and making bill.

Prospective Functionalities in Mobile Banking

Based on the 'International Review of Business Research Papers' from World business Institute, Australia, following are the key functional trends possible in world of Mobile Banking. With the advent of technology and increasing use of smartphone and tablet based devices, the use of Mobile Banking functionality would enable customer connect across entire customer life cycle much comprehensively than before.

Illustration of objective based functionality enrichment in Mobile Banking:

- Communication enrichment: Video Interaction with agents, advisors.

- Pervasive Transactions capabilities: Comprehensive "Mobile wallet".

- Customer Education: "Test drive" for demos of banking services.

- Connect with new customer segment: Connect with Gen Y – Gen Z using games and social network ambushed to surrogate bank's offerings.

- Content monetization: Micro level revenue themes such as music, e-book download.

- Vertical positioning: Positioning offerings over mobile banking specific industries.

- Horizontal positioning: Positioning offerings over mobile banking across all the industries.

- Personalization of corporate banking services: Personalization experience for multiple roles and hierarchies in corporate banking as against the vanilla based segment based enhancements in the current context.

- Build Brand: Built the bank's brand while enhancing the "Mobile real estate".

Key challenges in developing a sophisticated mobile banking application are:

Handset Accessibility

There are a large number of different mobile phone devices and it is a big challenge for banks to offer a mobile banking solution on any type of device. Some of these devices support Java ME and others support SIM Application Toolkit, a WAP browser, or only SMS.

Initial interoperability issues however have been localized, with countries like India using portals like "R-World" to enable the limitations of low end java based phones, while focus on areas such as South Africa have defaulted to the USSD as a basis of communication achievable with any phone.

The desire for interoperability is largely dependent on the banks themselves, where installed applications (Java based or native) provide better security, are easier to use and allow development of more complex capabilities similar to those of internet banking while SMS can provide the basics but becomes difficult to operate with more complex transactions.

There is a myth that there is a challenge of interoperability between mobile banking applications due to perceived lack of common technology standards for mobile banking. In practice it is too early in the service lifecycle for interoperability to be addressed within an individual country, as very few countries have more than one mobile banking service provider. In practice, banking interfaces are well defined and money movements between banks follow the ISo-8583 standard. As mobile banking matures, money movements between service providers will naturally adopt the same standards as in the banking world.

In January 2009, Mobile Marketing Association (MMA) Banking Sub-committee, chaired by CellTrust and VeriSign Inc., published the Mobile Banking Overview for financial institutions in which it discussed the advantages and disadvantages of Mobile Channel Platforms such as Short Message Services (SMS), Mobile Web, Mobile Client Applications, SMS with Mobile Web and Secure SMS.

Security

As with most internet-connected devices, as well as mobile-telephony devices, cyber-crime rates are escalating year-on-year. The types of cybercrimes which may affect mobile-banking might range from unauthorized use while the owner is using the mobile banking, to remote-hacking, or even jamming or interference via the internet or telephone network data streams. This is demonstrated by the malware called *SMSZombie.A*, which infected Chinese Android devices. It was embedded in wallpaper apps and installed itself so it can exploit the weaknesses of China Mobile SMS Payment system, stealing banks credit card numbers and information linked to financial transactions. One of the most advanced malwares discovered recently was the Trojan called *Bankbot*. It went past Google's protections in its Android app marketplace and targeted Wells Fargo, Chase, and Citibank customers on Android devices worldwide before its removal by Google in September 2017. This malicious app was activated when users opened a banking app, overlaying it so it can steal banking credentials. In the banking world, currency rates may change by the millisecond.

Security of financial transactions, being executed from some remote location and transmission of financial information over the air, are the most complicated challenges that need to be addressed jointly by mobile application developers, wireless network service providers and the banks' IT departments.

The following aspects need to be addressed to offer a secure infrastructure for financial transaction over wireless network:

1. Physical part of the hand-held device. If the bank is offering smart-card based security, the physical security of the device is more important.

2. Security of any thick-client application running on the device. In case the device is stolen, the hacker should require at least an ID/Password to access the application.

3. Authentication of the device with service provider before initiating a transaction. This would ensure that unauthorized devices are not connected to perform financial transactions.

4. User ID/Password authentication of bank's customer.

5. Encryption of the data being transmitted over the air.

6. Encryption of the data that will be stored in device for later/off-line analysis by the customer.

One-time password (OTPs) are the latest tool used by financial and banking service providers in the fight against cyber fraud. Instead of relying on traditional memorized passwords, OTPs are requested by consumers each time they want to perform transactions using the online or mobile banking interface. When the request is received the password is sent to the consumer's phone via SMS. The password is expired once it has been used or once its scheduled life-cycle has expired.

Because of the concerns made explicit above, it is extremely important that SMS gateway providers can provide a decent quality of service for banks and financial institutions in regards to SMS services. Therefore, the provision of service level agreements (SLAs) is a requirement for this industry; it is necessary to give the bank customer delivery guarantees of all messages, as well as measurements on the speed of delivery, throughput, etc. SLAs give the service parameters in which a messaging solution is guaranteed to perform.

Scalability and Reliability

Another challenge for the CIOs and CTOs of the banks is to scale-up the mobile banking infrastructure to handle exponential growth of the customer base. With mobile banking, the customer may be sitting in any part of the world (true anytime, anywhere banking) and hence banks need to ensure that the systems are up and running in a true 24 x 7 fashion. As customers will find mobile banking more and more useful, their expectations from the solution will increase. Banks unable to meet the performance and reliability expectations may lose customer confidence. There are systems such as Mobile Transaction Platform which allow quick and secure mobile enabling of various banking services. Recently in India there has been a phenomenal growth in the use of Mobile Banking applications, with leading banks adopting Mobile Transaction Platform and the Central Bank publishing guidelines for mobile banking operations.

Application Distribution

Due to the nature of the connectivity between bank and its customers, it would be impractical to expect customers to regularly visit banks or connect to a web site for regular upgrade of their mobile banking application. It will be expected that the mobile application itself check the upgrades and updates and download necessary patches (so called "Over The Air" updates). However, there could be many issues to implement this approach such as upgrade/synchronization of other dependent components.

Studies have shown that a huge concerning factor of having mobile banking more widely used, is a banking customer's unwillingness to adapt. Many consumers, whether they are misinformed or not, do not want to begin using mobile banking for several reasons. These can include the learning curve associated with new technology, having fears about possible security compromises, just simply not wanting to start using technology, etc.

Personalization

It would be expected from the mobile application to support personalization such as:

- Preferred Language.

- Date/Time format.

- Amount format.

- Default transactions.

- Standard Beneficiary list.

- Alerts.

Mobile Payment

Mobile payment (also referred to as mobile money, mobile money transfer, and mobile wallet) generally refer to payment services operated under financial regulation and performed from or via a mobile device. Instead of paying with cash, cheque, or credit cards, a consumer can use a mobile to pay for a wide range of services and digital or hard goods. Although the concept of using non-coin-based currency systems has a long history, it is only in the 21st century that the technology to support such systems has become widely available.

Mobile payment is being adopted all over the world in different ways. The first patent exclusively defined "Mobile Payment System" was filed in 2000.

In developing countries mobile payment solutions have been deployed as a means of extending financial services to the community known as the "unbanked" or "underbanked", which is estimated to be as much as 50% of the world's adult population, according to Financial Access' 2009 Report "Half the World is Unbanked". These payment networks are often used for micropayments. The use of mobile payments in developing countries has attracted public and private funding by organizations such as the Bill & Melinda Gates Foundation, United States Agency for International Development and Mercy Corps.

Mobile payments are becoming a key instrument for PSPs and other market participants, in order to achieve new growth opportunities, according to the European Payments Council (EPC). The EPC states that "new technology solutions provide a direct improvement to the operations efficiency, ultimately resulting in cost savings and in an increase in business volume".

Models

There are five primary models for mobile payments:

- Mobile wallets.

- Card-based payments.

- Carrier billing (Premium SMS or direct carrier billing).

- Contactless payments NFC (Near Field Communication).

- Direct transfers between payer and payee bank accounts in near real-time (bank-led model, intra/inter-bank transfers/payments that are both bank and mobile operator agnostic).

Mobile money outlet.

There can be combinations:

- Direct carrier/bank co-operation, emerging in Haiti.

- Both bank account and card, like Vipps and MobilePay (users with an account at the right bank can debit their account, while other users can debit their card).

Financial institutions and credit card companies as well as Internet companies such as Google and a number of mobile communication companies, such as mobile network operators and major telecommunications infrastructure such as w-HA from Orange and smartphone multinationals such as Ericsson and BlackBerry have implemented mobile payment solutions.

Mobile wallets

A mobile wallet is an app that contain your debit and credit card information so that users can pay for goods and services digitally by using their mobile devices. Notable mobile wallets include:

- Alipay.

- Android Pay.

- ApplePay.

- eWallet (Ilium Software).

- GooglePay.

- Gyft.

- Samsung Pay.

- Venmo.

- WeChat.

Generally, this is the process:

- First payment:

  ○ User registers, inputs their phone number, and the provider sends them an SMS with a PIN.

  ○ User enters the received PIN, authenticating the number.

  ○ User inputs their credit card info or another payment method if necessary (not necessary if the account has already been added) and validates payment.

- Subsequent payments:

  ○ The user re enters their PIN to authenticate and validates payment.

  ○ Requesting a PIN is known to lower the success rate (conversion) for payments. These systems can be integrated with directly or can be combined with operator and credit card payments through a unified mobile web payment platform.

Credit Card

A simple mobile web payment system can also include a credit card payment flow allowing a consumer to enter their card details to make purchases. This process is familiar but any entry of details on a mobile phone is known to reduce the success rate (conversion) of payments.

In addition, if the payment vendor can automatically and securely identify customers then card details can be recalled for future purchases turning credit card payments into simple single click-to-buy giving higher conversion rates for additional purchases.

Carrier Billing

The consumer uses the mobile billing option during checkout at an e-commerce site- such as an online gaming site — to make a payment. After two-factor authentication involving the consumer's mobile number and a PIN or One-Time-Password (often abbreviated as OTP), the consumer's mobile account is charged for the purchase. It is a true alternative payment method that does not require the use of credit/debit cards or pre-registration at an online payment solution such as PayPal, thus bypassing banks and credit card companies altogether. This type of mobile payment method, which is prevalent in Asia, provides the following benefits:

- Security – Two-factor authentication and a risk management engine prevents fraud.

- Convenience – No pre-registration and no new mobile software is required.

- Easy – It's just another option during the checkout process.

- Fast – Most transactions are completed in less than 10 seconds.

- Proven – 70% of all digital content purchased online in some parts of Asia uses the Direct Mobile Billing method.

SMS or USSD-based Transactional Payments

Premium SMS and Premium MMS

In the predominant model for SMS payments, the consumer sends a payment request via an SMS text message or an USSD to a short code and a premium charge is applied to their phone bill or their online wallet. The merchant involved is informed of the payment success and can then release the paid for goods.

Since a trusted physical delivery address has typically not been given, these goods are most frequently digital with the merchant replying using a Multimedia Messaging Service to deliver the purchased music, ringtones, wallpapers etc.

A Multimedia Messaging Service (MMS) can also deliver barcodes which can then be scanned for confirmation of payment by a merchant. This is used as an electronic ticket for access to cinemas and events or to collect hard goods.

Transactional payments by SMS have been popular in Asia and Europe and are now accompanied by other mobile payment methods, such as mobile web payments (WAP), mobile payment client (Java ME, Android) and Direct Mobile Billing.

Inhibiting factors of Premium SMS include:

- Poor reliability – Transactional premium SMS payments can easily fail as messages get lost.

- Slow speed – Sending messages can be slow and it can take hours for a merchant to get receipt of payment. Consumers do not want to be kept waiting more than a few seconds.

- Security – The SMS/USSD encryption ends in the radio interface, then the message is a plaintext.

- High cost – There are many high costs associated with this method of payment. The cost of setting up short codes and paying for the delivery of media via a Multimedia Messaging Service and the resulting customer support costs to account for the number of messages that get lost or are delayed.

- Low payout rates – Operators also see high costs in running and supporting transactional payments which results in payout rates to the merchant being as low as 30%. Usually around 50%.

- Low follow-on sales – Once the payment message has been sent and the goods received there is little else the consumer can do. It is difficult for them to remember where something was purchased or how to buy it again. This also makes it difficult to tell a friend.

Remote Payment by SMS and Credit Card Tokenization

Even as the volume of Premium SMS transactions have flattened, many cloud-based payment systems continue to use SMS for presentment, authorization, and authentication, while the payment itself is processed through existing payment networks such as credit and debit card networks. These solutions combine the ubiquity of the SMS channel, with the security and reliability of existing payment infrastructure. Since SMS lacks end-to-end encryption, such solutions employ a higher-level security strategies known as 'tokenization' and 'target removal' whereby payment occurs without transmitting any sensitive account details, username, password, or PIN.

To date, point-of-sales mobile payment solutions have not relied on SMS-based authentication as a payment mechanism, but remote payments such as bill payments, seat upgrades on flights, and membership or subscription renewals are commonplace.

In comparison to premium short code programs which often exist in isolation, relationship marketing and payment systems are often integrated with CRM, ERP, marketing-automation platforms, and reservation systems. Many of the problems inherent with premium SMS have been addressed by solution providers. Remembering keywords is not required since sessions are initiated by the enterprise to establish a transaction specific context. Reply messages are linked to the proper session and authenticated either synchronously through a very short expiry period (every reply is assumed to be to the last message sent) or by tracking session according to varying reply addresses and reply options.

Mobile Web Payments

The consumer uses web pages displayed or additional applications downloaded and installed on the mobile phone to make a payment. It uses WAP (Wireless

Application Protocol) as underlying technology and thus inherits all the advantages and disadvantages of WAP. Benefits include:

- Follow-on sales where the mobile web payment can lead back to a store or to other goods the consumer may like. These pages have a URL and can be book-marked making it easy to re-visit or share.

- High customer satisfaction from quick and predictable payments.

- Ease of use from a familiar set of online payment pages.

Mobile payment system.

However, unless the mobile account is directly charged through a mobile network operator, the use of a credit/debit card or pre-registration at online payment solution such as PayPal is still required just as in a desktop environment.

Mobile web payment methods are now being mandated by a number of mobile network operators.

Direct Operator Billing

Direct operator billing, also known as mobile content billing, WAP billing, and carrier billing, requires integration with the mobile network operator. It provides certain benefits:

- Mobile network operators already have a billing relationship with consumers, the payment will be added to their bill.

- Provides instantaneous payment.

- Protects payment details and consumer identity.

- Better conversion rates.

- Reduced customer support costs for merchants.

- Alternative monetization option in countries where credit card usage is low.

One of the drawbacks is that the payout rate will often be much lower than with other mobile payments options. Examples from a popular provider:

- 92% with PayPal

- 85 to 86% with Credit Card

- 45 to 91.7% with operator billing in the US, UK and some smaller European countries, but usually around 60%

More recently, Direct operator billing is being deployed in an in-app environment, where mobile application developers are taking advantage of the one-click payment option that Direct operator billing provides for monetising mobile applications. This is a logical alternative to credit card and Premium SMS billing.

In 2012, Ericsson and Western Union partnered to expand the direct operator billing market, making it possible for mobile operators to include Western Union Mobile Money Transfers as part of their mobile financial service offerings. Given the international reach of both companies, the partnership is meant to accelerate the interconnection between the m-commerce market and the existing financial world.

Contactless Near-field Communication

Near-field communication (NFC) is used mostly in paying for purchases made in physical stores or transportation services. A consumer using a special mobile phone equipped with a smartcard waves his/her phone near a reader module. Most transactions do not require authentication, but some require authentication using PIN, before transaction is completed. The payment could be deducted from a pre-paid account or charged to a mobile or bank account directly.

Mobile payment method via NFC faces significant challenges for wide and fast adoption, due to lack of supporting infrastructure, complex ecosystem of stakeholders, and standards. Some phone manufacturers and banks, however, are enthusiastic. Ericsson and Aconite are examples of businesses that make it possible for banks to create consumer mobile payment applications that take advantage of NFC technology.

NFC vendors in Japan are closely related to mass-transit networks, like the Mobile Suica used on the JR East rail network. Osaifu-Keitai system, used for Mobile Suica and many others including Edy and nanaco, has become the *de facto* standard method for mobile payments in Japan. Its core technology, Mobile FeliCa IC, is partially owned by Sony, NTT DoCoMo and JR East. Mobile FeliCa utilize Sony's FeliCa technology, which itself is the de facto standard for contactless smart cards in the country.

Other NFC vendors mostly in Europe use contactless payment over mobile phones to pay for on- and off-street parking in specially demarcated areas. Parking wardens may enforce the parkings by license plate, transponder tags or barcode stickers. First conceptualized in the 1990s, the technology has seen commercial use in this century in both Scandinavia and Estonia. End users benefit from the convenience of being able to pay for parking from the comfort of their car with their mobile phone, and parking operators are not obliged to invest in either existing or new street-based parking infrastructures. Parking wardens maintain order in these systems by license plate, transponder tags or barcode stickers or they read a digital display in the same way as they read a pay and display receipt.

Other vendors use a combination of both NFC and a barcode on the mobile device for mobile payment, because many mobile devices in the market do not yet support NFC.

Other Modes of Payment

QR Code Payments

QR Codes 2D barcode are square bar codes. QR codes have been in use since 1994. Originally used to track products in warehouses, QR codes were designed to replace traditional (1D bar codes). Traditional bar codes just represent numbers, which can be looked up in a database and translated into something meaningful. QR, or "Quick Response" bar codes were designed to contain the meaningful info right in the bar code.

QR Codes can be of two main categories:

- The QR Code is presented on the mobile device of the person paying and scanned by a POS or another mobile device of the payee.

- The QR Code is presented by the payee, in a static or one time generated fashion and it is scanned by the person executing the payment.

Mobile self-checkout allows for one to scan a QR code or barcode of a product inside a brick-and-mortar establishment in order to purchase the product on the spot. This theoretically eliminates reduces the incidence of long checkout lines, even at self-checkout kiosks.

Cloud-based Mobile Payments

Google, PayPal, GlobalPay and GoPago use a cloud-based approach to in-store mobile payment. The cloud based approach places the mobile payment provider in the middle of the transaction, which involves two separate steps. First, a cloud-linked payment method is selected and payment is authorized via NFC or an alternative method. During this step, the payment provider automatically covers the cost of the purchase with issuer linked funds. Second, in a separate transaction, the payment provider charges the purchaser's selected, cloud-linked account in a card-not-present environment to recoup its losses on the first transaction.

Audio Signal-based Payments

The audio channel of the mobile phone is another wireless interface that is used to make payments. Several companies have created technology to use the acoustic features of cell phones to support mobile payments and other applications that are not chip-based. The technologies Near sound data transfer (NSDT), Data Over Voice and NFC 2.0 produce audio signatures that the microphone of the cell phone can pick up to enable electronic transactions.

Bank Co-operation

In the T-Cash model, the mobile phone and the phone carrier is the front-end interface to the consumers. The consumer can purchase goods, transfer money to a peer, cash out, and cash in. A 'mini wallet' account can be opened as simply as entering *700# on the mobile phone, presumably by depositing money at a participating local merchant and the mobile phone number. Presumably, other transactions are similarly accomplished by entering special codes and the phone number of the other party on the consumer's mobile phone.

Bank Transfer Systems

Swish is the name of a system established in Sweden. It was established through a collaboration from major banks in 2012 and has been very successful, with 66 percent of the population as users in 2017. It is mainly used for peer-to-peer payments between private people, but is also used by church collect, street vendors and small businesses. A person's account is tied to his or her phone number and the connection between the phone number and the actual bank account number is registered in the internet bank. The electronic identification system mobile BankID, issued by several Swedish banks, is used to verify the payment. Users with a simple phone or without the app can still receive money if the phone number is registered in the internet bank. Like many other mobile payment system, its main obstacle is getting people to register and download the app, but it has managed to reach a critical mass and it has become part of everyday life for many Swedes.

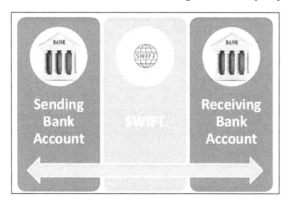

Swedish payments company Trustly also enables mobile bank transfers, but is used mainly for business-to-consumer transactions that occur solely online. If an e-tailer integrates with Trustly, its customers can pay directly from their bank account. As opposed to Swish, users don't need to register a Trustly account or download software to pay with it.

The Danish MobilePay and Norwegian Vipps are also popular in their countries. They use direct and instant bank transfers, but also for users not connected to a participating bank, credit card billing.

Mobile Payment Service Provider Model

There are four potential mobile payment models:

1. Operator-Centric Model: The mobile operator acts independently to deploy mobile payment service. The operator could provide an independent mobile wallet from the user mobile account (airtime). A large deployment of the Operator-Centric Model is severely challenged by the lack of connection to existing payment networks. Mobile network operator should handle the interfacing with the banking network to provide advanced mobile payment service in banked and under banked environment. Pilots using this model have been launched in emerging countries but they did not cover most of the mobile payment service use cases. Payments were limited to remittance and airtime top up.

2. Bank-Centric Model: A bank deploys mobile payment applications or devices to customers and ensures merchants have the required point-of-sale (POS) acceptance capability. Mobile network operator are used as a simple carrier, they bring their experience to provide Quality of service (QOS) assurance.

3. Collaboration Model: This model involves collaboration among banks, mobile operators and a trusted third party.

4. Peer-to-Peer Model: The mobile payment service provider acts independently from financial institutions and mobile network operators to provide mobile payment.

Advantages and disadvantages

Mobile money accounts are on the rise, and will only continue to skyrocket as technology continues to evolve. In truth, the market is saturated with hundreds of startups, while some banks, retailers and financial service agents are launching their own channels. It's the smartphone that drives this revolution, helped, in turn, by smartphone apps that allow users to store, send and receive money using their phone, lessening the need for physical banks all together.

Advantages of Mobile Money

Pervasive Mobile payment covers everything including utility bills, school fees, taxes, and international transfers from family and friends. You can pay your bills, transfer funds, check account balances, review your recent transaction, andblock your ATM card, etc., all through your smartphone. Everything that your bank does, mobile payment does just as well, and faster.

Cheap Mobile money transfer avoids the high interest and exchange rates of banks that are, particularly, steep in certain remote areas of the USA or Canada. Banks offer this service at extremely low to nil charge to customers making mobile money transfers very cost effective.

Safe Mobile payments are just as safe as bank transfers, since they're protected by local financial regulations such as the Consumer Financial Protection Bureau (CFPB) in the United States or the Department for International Development (DFID) in Britain. All transactions are protected by private PIN, while Mobile Money stores a record of each deal.

Accessible Going to a bank takes time and hassle. Mobile banking is available round the clock 24/7/365 and is there when you are unlike your bank.

Disadvantages of Mobile Money

Security While sending money via mobile money transfers is safe, it is still possible that users may receive fake messages called "Smishing" which ask for Bank details and because of this, many users fall victim to scam and theft.

Availability You need an app for mobile banking and certain apps may only be available only on certain high-end smartphones.

In addition to these drawbacks, it is also possible that your bank may start charging you more for the mobile banking services as well as the fact that mobile phones are limited in processing speeds, screen size and battery life, which may interfere with your payment transference.

More people around the world turn to mobile payments rather than to banks. It's cheaper, faster, safer and more accessible. On the other hand, you need a high-end smartphone to conduct the service, you may need to pay more in the long run and watch out for scams. Even with these drawbacks however, money transfer agencies still see mobile payment as the future for sending funds from one country to another.

MOBILE MARKETING

Mobile marketing is a multi-channel online marketing technique focused at reaching a specific audience on their smartphones, feature phones, tablets, or any other related devices through websites, E-mail, SMS and MMS, social media, or mobile applications. Mobile marketing can provide customers with time and location sensitive, personalized information that promotes goods, services, appointment reminders and ideas. In a more theoretical manner, academic Andreas Kaplan defines mobile marketing as "any marketing activity conducted through a ubiquitous network to which consumers are constantly connected using a personal mobile device".

SMS Marketing

Marketing through cellphones' SMS (Short Message Service) became increasingly popular in the early 2000s in Europe and some parts of Asia when businesses started to collect mobile phone numbers and send off wanted (or unwanted) content. On average, SMS messages have a 98% open rate, and are read within 3 minutes, making it highly effective at reaching recipients quickly.

Over the past few years SMS marketing has become a legitimate advertising channel in some parts of the world. This is because unlike email over the public internet, the carriers who police their own networks have set guidelines and best practices for the mobile media industry (including mobile advertising). The IAB (Interactive Advertising Bureau) and the Mobile Marketing Association (MMA), as well, have established guidelines and are evangelizing the use of the mobile channel for marketers. While this has been fruitful in developed regions such as North America, Western Europe and some other countries, mobile SPAM messages (SMS sent to mobile subscribers without a legitimate and explicit opt-in by the subscriber) remain an issue in many other parts of the world, partly due to the carriers selling their member databases to third parties. In India, however, government's efforts of creating National Do Not Call Registry have helped cellphone users to stop SMS advertisements by sending a simple SMS or calling 1909.

Mobile marketing approaches through SMS has expanded rapidly in Europe and Asia as a new channel to reach the consumer. SMS initially received negative media coverage in many parts of Europe for being a new form of spam as some advertisers purchased lists and sent unsolicited content to consumer's phones; however, as guidelines are put in place by the mobile operators, SMS has become the most popular branch of the Mobile Marketing industry with several 100 million advertising SMS sent out every month in Europe alone. This is thanks impart to SMS messages being hardware agnostic—they can be delivered to practically any mobile phone, smartphone or feature phone and accessed without a Wi-Fi or mobile data connection. This is important to note since there are over 5 billion unique mobile phone subscribers worldwide in 2017, which is about 66% of the world population.

SMS marketing has both inbound and outbound marketing strategies. Inbound marketing focuses on lead generation, and outbound marketing focuses on sending messages for sales, promotions, contests, donations, television program voting, appointment and event reminders.

There are 5 key components to SMS marketing: sender ID, message size, content structure, spam compliance, and message delivery.

Sender ID

A sender ID is the name or number that identifies who the sender is. For commercial purposes, virtual numbers, short codes, and custom names are most commonly used and can be leased through bulk SMS providers.

Shared Virtual Numbers

As the name implies, shared virtual numbers are shared by many different senders. They're usually free, but they can't receive SMS replies, and the number changes from time to time without notice or consent. Senders may have different shared virtual numbers on different days, which may make it confusing or untrustworthy for recipients depending on the context. For example, shared virtual numbers may be suitable for 2 factor authentication text messages, as recipients are often expecting these text messages, which are often triggered by actions that the recipients make. But for text messages that the recipient isn't expecting, like a sales promotion, a dedicated virtual number may be preferred.

Dedicated Virtual Numbers

To avoid sharing numbers with other senders, and for brand recognition and number consistency, leasing a dedicated virtual number, which are also known as a long code or long number (international number format, e.g. +44 7624 805000 or US number format, e.g. 757 772 8555), is a viable option. Unlike a shared number, it can receive SMS replies. Senders can choose from a list of available dedicated virtual numbers from a bulk SMS provider. Prices for dedicated virtual numbers can vary. Some numbers, often called Gold numbers, are more easy to recognise, and therefore more expensive to lease. Senders may also get creative and choose a vanity number. These numbers spell out a word using the keypad, like +1-(123)-ANUMBER.

Short Codes

Short codes offer very similar features to a dedicated virtual number, but are short mobile numbers that are usually 5-6 digits. Their length and availability are different in each and every country. These are usually more expensive and are commonly used by enterprises and governmental organisations. For mass messaging, short codes are preferred over a dedicated virtual number because of their higher throughput, and are great for time-sensitive campaigns and emergencies.

In Europe, the first cross-carrier SMS shortcode campaign was run by Txtbomb in 2001 for an Island Records release. In North America it was the Labatt Brewing Company in 2002. Over the past few years mobile short codes have been increasingly popular as a new channel to communicate to the mobile consumer. Brands have begun to treat the mobile short code as a mobile domain name allowing the consumer to text message the brand at an event, in store and off any traditional media.

Custom Sender ID

A custom sender ID, also known as an alphanumeric sender ID, enables users to set a business name as the sender ID for one way organisation-to-consumer messages. This is only supported in certain countries and are up to 11 characters long, and support uppercase and lowercase ASCII letters and digits 0-9. Senders aren't allowed to use digits only as this would mimic a shortcode or virtual number that they don't have access to. Reputable bulk SMS providers will check customer sender IDs beforehand to make sure senders are not misusing or abusing them.

Message Size

The message size will then determine the number of SMS messages that are sent, which then determines the amount of money spent on marketing a product or service. Not all characters in a message are the same size.

Character Count	Character Type
1	Standard GSM character
1	Space
1	Line Break
2	Escape characters (e.g. ^ € { } [ ] ~)

A single SMS message has a maximum size of 1120 bits. This is important because there are two types of character encodings, GSM and Unicode. Latin-based languages like English are GSM based encoding, which are 7 bits per character. This is where text messages typically get their 160 character per SMS limit. Long messages that exceed this limit are concatenated. They are split into smaller messages, which are recombined by the receiving phone.

Concatenated messages can only fit 153 characters instead of 160. For example, a 177 character message is sent as 2 messages. The first is sent with 153 characters and the second with 24 characters. The process of SMS concatenation can happen up to 4 times for most bulk SMS providers, which allows senders a maximum 612 character message per campaign.

Non-Latin based languages, like Chinese, and also emojis use a different encoding process called Unicode or Unicode Transformation Format (UTF-8). It is meant to encompass all characters for efficiency but has a caveat. Each unicode character is 16 bits in size, which takes more information to send, therefore limiting SMS messages to 70 characters. Messages that are larger than 70 characters are also concatenated. These messages can fit 67 characters, and can be concatenated up to 4 times for a maximum of 268 characters.

Number of SMS	Maximum GSM characters	Maximum Unicode characters
1 regular	160	70
2 concatenated	306	134
3 concatenated	459	201
4 concatenated	612	268

Content Structure

Special elements that can be placed inside a text message include:

- UTF-8 Characters: Send SMS in different languages, special characters, or emojis.

- Keywords: Use keywords to trigger an automated response.

- Links: Track campaigns easily by using shortened URLs to custom landing pages.

- Interactive Elements: Pictures, animations, audio, or video.

Texting is simple, however when it comes to SMS marketing there are many different content structures that can be implemented. Popular message types include sale alerts, reminders, keywords, and multimedia messaging services (MMS).

SMS Sales Alerts

Sale alerts are the most basic form of SMS marketing. They are generally used for clearance, flash sales, and special promotions. Typical messages include coupon codes, and information like expiration dates, products, and website links for additional information.

SMS Reminders

Reminders are commonly used to in appointment-based industries or for recurring events. Some senders choose to ask their recipients to respond to the reminder text with an SMS keyword to confirm their appointment. This can really help improve the sender's workflow and reduce missed appointments, leading to improved productivity and revenue.

SMS Keywords

This allows people to text a custom keyword to a dedicated virtual number or shortcode. Through custom keywords, users can opt-in to a service with minimal effort. Once a keyword is triggered, an autoresponder can be set to guide the user to the next step. They can also activate different functions, which include entering a contest, forwarding to an email or mobile number, group chat, and sending an auto response.

Spam Compliance

Similar to email, SMS has anti-spam laws which differ from country to country. As a general rule, it's important to obtain the recipient's permission before sending any text message, especially an SMS marketing type of message. Permission can be obtained in a myriad of ways, including allowing prospects or customers to: tick a permission checkbox on a website, filling in a form, or getting a verbal agreement.

In most countries, SMS senders need to identify themselves as their business name inside their initial text message. Identification can be placed in either the sender ID or within the message body copy. Spam prevention laws may also apply to SMS marketing messages, which must include a method to opt-out of messages.

One key criterion for provisioning is that the consumer opts into the service. The mobile operators demand a double opt in from the consumer and the ability for the consumer to opt out of the service at any time by sending the word STOP via SMS. These guidelines are established in the CTIA Playbook and the MMA Consumer Best Practices Guidelines which are followed by all mobile marketers in the United States. In Canada, opt in will be mandatory once the Fighting Internet and Wireless Spam Act comes in force in mid-2012.

Message Delivery

At the most simple level, SMS infrastructure is made up of special servers that talk to each other, using a software called Short Message Service Centre (SMSC) that use a special protocol called Short Message Peer to Peer (SMPP).

Through the SMPP connections, bulk SMS providers (also known as SMS Gateways) like the ones mentioned above can send text messages and process SMS replies and delivery receipts.

When a user sends messages through a bulk SMS provider, it gets delivered to the recipient's carrier via an ON-NET connection or the International SS7 Network.

SS7 Network

Operators around the world are connected by a network known as Signaling System number 7. It's used to exchange information related to phone calls, number translations, prepaid billing systems, and is the backbone of SMS. SS7 is what carriers around the world use to talk to each other.

ON-NET Routing

ON-NET routing is the most popular form of messaging globally. It's the most reliable and preferable way for telecommunications/carriers to receive messages, as the messages from the bulk SMS provider is sent to them directly. For senders that need consistency and reliability, seeking a provider that uses ON-NET routing should be the preferred option.

Grey Routing

Grey Routing is a term given to messages that are sent to carriers (often offshore) that have low cost interconnect agreements with other carriers. Instead of sending the messages directly to the intended carrier, some bulk SMS providers send it to an offshore carrier, which will relay the message to the intended carrier. At the cost of consistency and reliability, this roundabout way is cheaper, and these routes can disappear without notice and are slower. Many carriers don't like this type of routing, and will often block them with filters set up in their SMSCs.

Hybrid Routing

Some bulk SMS providers have the option to combine more reliable grey routing on lower value carriers with their ON-NET offerings. If the routes are managed well, then messages can be delivered reliably. Hybrid routing is more common for SMS marketing messages, where timeliness and reliable delivery is less of an issue.

Africa

Country	Number of Mobile Phones	Popular SMS Providers
Nigeria	167,371,945	Express Bulk SMS, SMS Portal Nigeria, Bulk SMS Nigeria
South Africa	59,474,500	SMS Portal, CM.com, Clickatell
Algeria	33,000,000	Innovative Txt, Broad Net SMS, My Cool SMS

Asia

Country	Number of Mobile Phones	Popular SMS Providers
China	1,321,930,000	Bysoft, EzTexting, Web2Asia
India	1,162,470,432	SMS Gateway Hub, SMS Gateway Center, Txt Local, Tubelight Communications
Indonesia	236,800,000	Thai Bulk SMS, One Way SMS, Bulk SMS
Iran	78,600,000	Medianasms

Australia/Oceania

Country	Number of Mobile Phones	Popular SMS Providers
Australia	20,570,000	ClickSend, Burst SMS, Message Media, SMS Central
New Zealand	4,761,000	Texta, Burst SMS, ClickSend

North America

Country	Number of Mobile Phones	Popular SMS Providers
United States of America	327,577,529	Twilio, Message Bird, Tatango
Mexico	101,339,000	Nextel, Active Campaign, Expert Texting
Canada	31,210,628	Simply Cast, Modis Club, Clickatell

Europe

Country	Number of Mobile Phones	Popular SMS Providers
Germany	107,000,000	Txt Nation, Message Mobile, Burst SMS
Italy	88,580,000	Vola, E-BC, KDEV SMS
United Kingdom	83,100,000	Text Local, Voodoo SMS, Burst SMS

South America

Country	Number of Mobile Phones	Popular SMS Providers
Brazil	284,200,000	Clickatell, Bulk SMS, Txt Nation
Argentina	56,725,200	Innovative Txt, Intis Telecom, Via Nett
Colombia	57,900,472	SMS Gateway, Clickatell, Bulk SMS

MMS

MMS mobile marketing can contain a timed slideshow of images, text, audio and video. This mobile content is delivered via MMS (Multimedia Message Service). Nearly all new phones produced with a color screen are capable of sending and receiving standard MMS message. Brands are able to both send (mobile terminated) and receive (mobile originated) rich content through MMS A2P (application-to-person) mobile networks to mobile subscribers. In some networks, brands are also able to sponsor messages that are sent P2P (person-to-person).

A typical MMS message based on the GSM encoding can have up to 1500 characters, whereas one based on Unicode can have up to 500 characters. Messages that are longer than the limit are truncated and not concatenated like an SMS.

Good examples of mobile-originated MMS marketing campaigns are Motorola's on-going campaigns at House of Blues venues, where the brand allows the consumer to send their mobile photos to the LED board in real-time as well as blog their images online.

Push Notifications

Push notifications were first introduced to smartphones by Apple with the Push Notification Service in 2009. For Android devices, Google developed Android Cloud to Messaging or C2DM in 2010. Google replaced this service with Google Cloud Messaging in 2013. Commonly referred to as GCM, Google Cloud Messaging served as C2DM's successor, making improvements to authentication and delivery, new API endpoints and messaging parameters, and the removal of limitations on API send-rates and message sizes. It is a message that pops up on a mobile device. It is the delivery of information from a software application to a computing device without any request from the client or the user. They look like SMS notifications but they are reached only the users who installed the app. The specifications vary for iOS and android users. SMS and push notifications can be part of a well-developed inbound mobile marketing strategy.

According to mobile marketing company Leanplum, Android sees open rates twice as high as those on iOS. Android sees open rates of 3.48 percent for push notification, versus iOS which has open rates of 1.77 percent.

App-based Marketing

With the strong growth in the use of smartphones, app usage has also greatly increased. The annual number of mobile app downloads over the last few years has exponentially grown, with hundreds of billions of downloads in 2018, and the number of downloads expecting to climb by 2022. Therefore, mobile marketers have increasingly taken advantage of smartphone apps as a marketing resource. Marketers aim to optimize the visibility of an app in a store, which will maximize the number of downloads. This practice is called App Store Optimization (ASO).

There is a lot of competition in this field as well. However, just like other services, it is not easy anymore to rule the mobile application market. Most companies have acknowledged the potential of Mobile Apps to increase the interaction between a company and its target customers. With the fast progress and growth of the smartphone market, high-quality Mobile app development is essential to obtain a strong position in a mobile app store.

Here are several models for APP marketing:

1. Content embedded mode: For the most part at present, the downloading APP from APP store is free, for APP development enterprise, need a way to flow to liquidate, implantable advertising and APP combines content marketing and game characters to seamlessly integrating user experience, so as to improve advertising hits. With these free downloading apps, developers use in-app purchases or subscription to profit.

2. Advertising model advertisement implantation mode is a common marketing mode in most APP applications. Through Banner ads, consumer announcements, or in-screen advertising, users will jump to the specified page and display the advertising content when users click. This model is more intuitive, and can attract users' attention quickly.

3. User participation mode is mainly applied to website transplantation and brand APP. The company publishes its own brand APP to the APP store for users to download, so that users can intuitively understand the enterprise or product information better. As a practical tool, this APP brings great convenience to users'

life. User reference mode enables users to have a more intimate experience, so that users can understand the product, enhance the brand image of the enterprise, and seize the user's heart.

4. The shopping website embedded mode is the traditional Internet electric business offering platforms in the mobile APP, which is convenient for users to browse commodity information anytime and anywhere, order to purchase and order tracking. This model has promoted the transformation of traditional e-commerce enterprises from shopping to mobile Internet channels, which is a necessary way to use mobile APP for online and offline interactive development, such as Amazon, eBay and so on. The above several patterns for the more popular marketing methods, as for the details while are not mentioned too much, but the hope can help you to APP marketing have a preliminary understanding, and on the road more walk more far in the marketing.

In-game Mobile Marketing

There are essentially three major trends in mobile gaming right now: interactive real-time 3D games, massive multi-player games and social networking games. This means a trend towards more complex and more sophisticated, richer game play. On the other side, there are the so-called casual games, i.e. games that are very simple and very easy to play. Most mobile games today are such casual games and this will probably stay so for quite a while to come.

Brands are now delivering promotional messages within mobile games or sponsoring entire games to drive consumer engagement. This is known as mobile advergaming or ad-funded mobile game.

In in-game mobile marketing, advertisers pay to have their name or products featured in the mobile games. For instance, racing games can feature real cars made by Ford or Chevy. Advertisers have been both creative and aggressive in their attempts to integrate ads organically in the mobile games.

Although investment in mobile marketing strategies like advergaming is slightly more expensive than what is intended for a mobile app, a good strategy can make the brand derive a substantial revenue. Games that use advergaming make the users remember better the brand involved. This memorization increases virality of the content so that the users tend to recommend them to their friends and acquaintances, and share them via social networks.

One form of in-game mobile advertising is what allows players to actually play. As a new and effective form of advertising, it allows consumers to try out the content before they actually install it. This type of marketing can also really attract the attention of users like casual players. These advertising blur the lines between game and advertising, and provide players with a richer experience that allows them to spend their precious time interacting with advertising.

This kind of advertisement is not only interesting, but also brings some benefits to marketers. As this kind of in-gaming mobile marketing can create more effective conversion rates because they are interactive and have faster conversion speeds than general advertising. Moreover, games can also offer a stronger lifetime value. They measure the quality of the consumer in advance to provide some more in-depth experience. So this type of advertising can be more effective in improving user stickiness than advertising channels such as stories and video.

Bluetooth

Bluetooth technology is a wireless short range digital communication that allows devices to communicate without the now superced RS-232 cables.

Proximity Systems

Mobile marketing via proximity systems, or proximity marketing, relies on GSM 03.41 which defines the Short Message Service Cell Broadcast. SMS-CB allows messages (such as advertising or public information) to be broadcast to all mobile users in a specified geographical area. In the Philippines, GSM-based proximity broadcast systems are used by select Government Agencies for information dissemination on Government-run community-based programs to take advantage of its reach and popularity (Philippines has the world's highest traffic of SMS). It is also used for commercial service known as Proxima SMS. Bluewater, a super-regional shopping centre in the UK, has a GSM based system supplied by NTL to help its GSM coverage for calls, it also allows each customer with a mobile phone to be tracked though the centre which shops they go into and for how long. The system enables special offer texts to be sent to the phone. For example, a retailer could send a mobile text message to those customers in their database who have opted-in, who happen to be walking in a mall. That message could say "Save 50% in the next 5 minutes only when you purchase from our store." Snacks company, Mondelez International, makers of Cadbury and Oreo products has committed to exploring proximity-based messaging citing significant gains in point-of-purchase influence.

Location-based Services

Location-based services (LBS) are offered by some cell phone networks as a way to send custom advertising and other information to cell-phone subscribers based on their current location. The cell-phone service provider gets the location from a GPS chip built into the phone, or using radiolocation and trilateration based on the signal-strength of the closest cell-phone towers (for phones without GPS features). In the United Kingdom, which launched location-based services in 2003, networks do not use trilateration; LBS uses a single base station, with a "radius" of inaccuracy, to determine a phone's location.

Some location-based services work without GPS tracking technique, instead transmitting content between devices peer-to-peer.

There are various methods for companies to utilize a device's location.

1. Store locators: Utilizing the location-based feedback, the nearest store location can be found rapidly by retail clients.

2. Proximity-based marketing: Companies can deliver advertisements merely to individuals in the same geographical location.

    Location-based services send advertisements prospective customers of the area who may truly take action on the information.

3. Travel information: Location-based services can provide actual time information for the smartphones, such as traffic condition and weather forecast, then the customers can make the plan.

4. Roadside assistance:In the event of sudden traffic accidents, the roadside assistance company can develop an app to track the customer's real-time location without navigation.

Ringless Voicemail

The advancement of mobile technologies has allowed the ability to leave a voice mail message on a mobile phone without ringing the line. The technology was pioneered by VoAPP, which used the technology in conjunction with live operators as a debt collection service. The FCC has ruled that the technology is compliant with all regulations. CPL expanded on the existing technology to allow for a completely automated process including the replacement of live operators with pre recorded messages.

User-controlled Media

Mobile marketing differs from most other forms of marketing communication in that it is often user (consumer) initiated (mobile originated, or MO) message, and requires the express consent of the consumer to receive future communications. A call delivered from a server (business) to a user (consumer) is called a mobile terminated (MT) message. This infrastructure points to a trend set by mobile marketing of consumer controlled marketing communications.

Due to the demands for more user controlled media, mobile messaging infrastructure providers have responded by developing architectures that offer applications to operators with more freedom for the users, as opposed to the network-controlled media. Along with these advances to user-controlled Mobile Messaging 2.0, blog events throughout the world have been implemented in order to launch popularity in the latest advances in mobile technology. In June 2007, Airwide Solutions became the official sponsor for the

Mobile Messaging 2.0 blog that provides the opinions of many through the discussion of mobility with freedom. GPS plays an important role in location-based marketing.

Privacy Concerns

Mobile advertising has become more and more popular. However, some mobile advertising is sent without a required permission from the consumer causing privacy violations. It should be understood that irrespective of how well advertising messages are designed and how many additional possibilities they provide, if consumers do not have confidence that their privacy will be protected, this will hinder their widespread deployment. But if the messages originate from a source where the user is enrolled in a relationship/loyalty program, privacy is not considered violated and even interruptions can generate goodwill.

The privacy issue became even more salient as it was before with the arrival of mobile data networks. A number of important new concerns emerged mainly stemming from the fact that mobile devices are intimately personal and are always with the user, and four major concerns can be identified: mobile spam, personal identification, location information and wireless security. Aggregate presence of mobile phone users could be tracked in a privacy-preserving fashion.

Classification

Kaplan categorizes mobile marketing along the degree of consumer knowledge and the trigger of communication into four groups: strangers, groupies, victims, and patrons. Consumer knowledge can be high or low and according to its degree organizations can customize their messages to each individual user, similar to the idea of one-to-one marketing. Regarding the trigger of communication, Kaplan differentiates between push communication, initiated by the organization, and pull communication, initiated by the consumer. Within the first group (low knowledge/push), organizations broadcast a general message to a large number of mobile users. Given that the organization cannot know which customers have ultimately been reached by the message, this group is referred to as "strangers". Within the second group (low knowledge/ pull), customers opt to receive information but do not identify themselves when doing so. The organizations therefore does not know which specific clients it is dealing with exactly, which is why this cohort is called "groupies". In the third group (high knowledge/push) referred to as "victims", organizations know their customers and can send them messages and information without first asking permission. The last group (high knowledge/pull), the "patrons" covers situations where customers actively give permission to be contacted and provide personal information about themselves, which allows for one-to-one communication without running the risk of annoying them.

Importance of Mobile Marketing

Today, a large fraction of population access internet through mobile rather than laptop or desktop. Mobile's portability feature enables a user to get in touch with world through internet from anywhere and anytime. Increasing number of internet and mobile user drags a revolutionary trend in marketing sector called Mobile marketing.

1. Availability of Quick Services Anytime: People want good, easy and quick services. They are looking for a service provider which can fulfill their requirements anytime, anywhere, and can be easily reached. A company can contact a user via mobile marketing techniques. A customer can also send feedback easily.

2. Mobile has become an undetachable part of life: Mobile is a necessary part of daily life. It can easily carried to anywhere and that's why becomes a favorite device for e-shopping in leisure time.

3. Mobile is not only used for e-shopping but also used in physical store: A physical store also uses mobile services for providing services and advertising. Many store will save your number to notify you about special products and discounts offers.

4. SMS Marketing: SMS and MMS marketing bring a tremendous change in marketing. Now users are getting offers and discounts or get notified for sale via sms or mms.

5. Mobile search index becomes primary contents for ranking: Google is going to make search index based on mobile search ranking rather than desktop search ranking. So your website search ranking will be based on mobile searching rather than desktop searching.

6. Importance of Mobile advertisement: Advertising on mobile sites or directly to mobile seems more effective in marketing.

Mobile Marketing Strategies

These days, most of the people are investing time on internet via smart phones. They start and end their days with mobile. In today's time when mobile is the first thing needed after waking up in the morning and last thing used before going to bed. It means your websites has been visited mostly via mobile in comparison of desktop. So you should follow a strategy in order to expand and enhance your business based on mobile marketing.

Now marketing strategies should be changed to attract mobile users via internet. This change forced people to follow mobile marketing strategy. Business should have an important place for mobile marketing otherwise it will definitely affect your business. You can improve your business by adopting trendy techniques of mobile marketing and advertising.

1. SMS marketing: It is true that a SMS is checked by a user in less time. So, SMS

is a perfect way to contact a customer for their requirement and for advertisement.

2. MMS marketing: Text, video, audio, and image slideshow can be delivered via MMS to users for advertise your business or products. Mobile marketing helps you to understand nature of your customer. You can verify about service requirements of a user and you can help them via MMS.

3. Push notification: It is a flash text to notify users to advertise products and services. It is easily visible to user instead of SMS.

4. App-based marketing: Mobile platform based App of an ecommerce website can be effectively used in a business promotion. You just have to maintain search ranking of app in a store to make it visible.

5. In-game mobile marketing: Marketers used to provide promoting messages within games. This is called mobile advergaming or ad-funded mobile game.

6. QR codes: QR code is an alternative of URL typing. One can go to a page by scanning a 2D image instead of typing a URL.

7. Bluetooth: Some marketers use hotspot to deliver Content Marketing. It is a permission based and a radio-based technology and free of cost. It is an effective way of advertising products. Greatly effective, in case user has activated DND for such advertisements. It works on fact that whenever a customer will comes in range with activated Bluetooth, starts getting notification and ads.

8. Proximity service: Proximity systems or marketing based on GSM also called SMS-CB (Short message Service-Cell Broadcast. This will help in broadcast of messages to all users in a specific geographical area.

9. Location-based services: Location based services are specially conducted through cell phone networks. It is used to send advertise or other messages to user based on location.

10. Voice mail: Marketers can send a voice SMS or a prerecorded message without making any ring for advertising their business.

MOBILE ADVERTISING

Mobile advertising is a form of advertising via mobile (wireless) phones or other mobile devices. It is a subset of mobile marketing.

It is estimated that mobile app-installed ads accounted for 30% of all mobile advertising revenue in 2014, and will top $4.6bn in 2016, and over $6.8bn by the end of 2019. Other ways mobile advertising can be purchased include working with a

Mobile Demand Side Platform, in which ad impressions are bought in real-time on an Ad exchange.

Some see mobile advertising as closely related to online or internet advertising, though its reach is far greater — currently, most mobile advertising is targeted at mobile phones, that came at an estimated global total of $4.6bn as of 2009. Notably computers, including desktops and laptops, are currently estimated at 1.1 billion globally. Moreover, mobile advertising includes SMS and MMS advertising units in addition to the advertisement types served and processed via online channels.

It is probable that advertisers and media industry will increasingly take account of a bigger and fast-growing mobile market, though it remains at around 1% of global advertising spend. Mobile media is evolving rapidly and while mobile phones will continue to be the mainstay, it is not clear whether mobile phones based on cellular backhaul or smartphones based on WiFi hot spot or WiMAX hot zone will also strengthen. However, such is the emergence of this form of advertising, that there is now a dedicated global awards ceremony organised every year by Visiongain.

According to the research firm, the global mobile advertising market that was estimated to €1 billion in 2008. Furthermore, Berg Insight forecasts the global mobile advertising market to grow at a compound annual growth rate of 43 percent to €8.7 billion in 2014.

Types of Mobile Ads

1. Click-to-download ads: The user will be directed to the Appstore or Google Play.

2. Click-to-call ads: The user will call to a phone number after clicking the button.

3. Click-to-message ads: The user will be directed to an SMS application to message the advertiser.

4. Image text and banner ads: A click opens your browser and re-directs you to a page.

5. Push notification.

Mobile Rich Media

There are limitations to rich media on mobile because all of the coding must be done in HTML5, since iOS does not support flash.

Handsets Display and Corresponding Ad Images

There are hundreds of handsets in the market and they differ by screen size and supported technologies (e.g. MMS, WAP 2.0). For color images, formats such as PNG, JPEG, GIF and BMP are typically supported, along with the monochrome WBMP format. The following gives an overview of various handset screen sizes and a recommended image size for each type.

Handset	Approx Handset Screen Size (px W x H)	Example Handsets	Ad Unit	Ad Size (pixels)
X-Large	320 x 320	Palm Treo 700P, Nokia E70	X-Large	300 x 50
Large	240 x 320	Samsung MM-A900, LG VX-8500 Chocolate, Sony Ericsson W910i	Large	216 x 36
Medium	176 x 208	Motorola RAZR, LG VX-8000, Motorola ROKR E1	Medium	168 x 28
Small	128 x 160	Motorola V195	Small	120 x 20

Mobile as Media

This unobtrusive three-way communications caught the attention of media industry and advertisers as well as cellphone makers and telecom operators. Usually, Text SMS became a new media – called the "third mass media channel" by several media and mobile experts – and even more, it is a no-way mobile media, as supposed to neither imobile or any other media like radios, newspapers and TV. Besides, the immediacy of responsiveness in this two-way media is a new territory found for media industry and advertisers, who are eager to measure up market response immediately. Additionally, the possibility of fast delivery of the messages and the ubiquity of the technology (it does not require any additional functionality from the mobile phone, all devices available today are capable of receiving SMS), make it ideal for time- and location-sensitive advertising, such as customer loyalty offers (shopping centers, large brand stores), SMS promotions of events, etc. To leverage this strength of SMS advertising, timely and reliable delivery of messages is paramount, which is guaranteed by some SMS gateway providers.

Mobile media has begun to draw more significant attention from the media advertising industry since the mid 2000-2001-s, based on a view that mobile media was to change the way advertisements were made, and that mobile devices can form a new media sector. Despite this, revenues are still a small fraction of the advertising industry as a whole but are most certainly on the rise. Informa reported that mobile advertising in 2007 was worth $2.2 billion, which is less than 0.5% of the approximately $450 billion global advertising industry.

Types of mobile advertising are expected to change rapidly or immediately as the case may be. In other words, mobile technology will come up with a strong push for identifying newer and unheard-of mobile multimedia, with the result that subsequent media migration will greatly stimulate a consumer behavioral shift and establish a paradigm shift in mobile advertising. A major media migration is on, as desktop Internet evolves into mobile Internet. One typical case in point is Nielsen's buyout of Telephia.

The rapid change in the technology used by mobile advertisers can also have adverse effect to the number of consumers being reached by the mobile advertisements, Telephia. due to technical limitations of their mobile devices. Because of that, campaigns that aim to achieve wide response or are targeting lower income groups might be better of relying on older, more widespread mobile media advertising technologies, such as SMS or any other mode of communication.

Viral Marketing

As mobile is an interactive mass media similar to the internet, advertisers are eager to utilize and make use of viral marketing methods, by which one recipient of an advertisement on mobile, will forward that to a friend. This allows users to become part of the advertising experience. At the bare minimum mobile ads with viral abilities can become powerful interactive campaigns. At the extreme, they can become engagement marketing experiences. A key element of mobile marketing campaigns is the most influential member of any target audience or community, which is called the alpha user.

Privacy Concern

Advocates have raised the issue of privacy. Targeted mobile marketing requires customization of ad content to reach interested and relevant customers. To customize such behavioral personal data, user profiling, data mining and other behavior watch tools are employed, and privacy advocates warn that this may cause privacy infringement.

Some mobile carriers offer free or cheaper rate plans in exchange for SMS or other mobile ads. However, mobile TV and mobile search may override this privacy concern, as soon as they are implemented on a full-blown basis. In a naive way to override privacy concern, however, a user's prior consent needs to be obtained through membership to join or user account to set up. Both mobile TV and mobile search may supersede the way of getting users' prior consent through membership or user account because users are free to choose mobile TV channels or mobile search services on a voluntary basis.

Interactivity

Mobile devices aim to outgrow the domain of voice-intensive cellphones and to enter a new world of multimedia mobile devices, like laptops, PDA phones and smartphones. Unlike the conventional one-way media like TV, radio and newspaper, web media has enabled two-way traffic, thereby introducing a new phase of interactive advertising, regardless of whether static or mobile. This user-centric approach was noted at the 96th annual conference of Association of National Advertisers in 2006, which described "a need to replace decades worth of top-down marketing tactics with bottom-up, grass-roots approaches". Many use 2D bar codes to make offline print material more interactive with their mobile device. This has been proven to be successful in Japan, UK, Philippines and has been catching on in Northern America.

Mobile Device Issues

Coincidentally, however, mobile devices are encountering technological bottlenecks in terms of battery life, formats, and safety issues.

In a broad sense, mobile devices are categorically broken down into portable and stationary equipment. Technically, mobile devices are categorized as below:

- Handheld (portable).

- Laptop, including ultraportable (portable).

- Dashtop, including GPS navigation, satellite radio, and WiMAX-enabled dashtop mobile payment platforms (fixed on dashboards).

The battery life and safety issues will perhaps combine to eventually push mobile equipment's inroads into vehicle dashtops. However, satellite-based GPS navigation and satellite radio may already hit a snag because of their part-time usage and technological hierarchy. Put differently, people want more functions than GPS navigation and satellite radios. The trend indicates an ongoing convergence into all-in-one dashtop mobile devices incorporating GPS navigators, satellite radios, MP3 players, mobile TV, mobile Internet, MVDER (vehicle black box), driving safety monitors, smartphones and even video games.

MOBILE PROCUREMENT

Mobile procurement is mobile business software that helps organizations streamline their procurement process from a mobile device. Features of mobile procurement software include mobile purchase order creation, on-demand notifications, and real-time analytics. What makes mobile procurement successful is the ability to leverage software-side servers to move data along. The key benefit for organizations using mobile procurement systems is the ability to track business operations using any ordinary mobile device.

Mobile procurement software is generally represented in the form of custom applications provided as an add-on feature of a larger enterprise resource planning software solution. As such, if the goal of a mobile procurement system should be to complement existing information systems, mobile procurement software should typically involve the needs of procurement professionals before implementation. Assuring that necessary features are prioritized over having many features is key to successful user adoption.

It also simplifies order management processes by removing the confusion and disorder often seen with paper-based procurement. Mobile procurement provides a clearer view of the steps behind procurement.

Mobile Enterprise Applications

Mobile enterprise application software is the use of office software applications on a mobile platform in a way that adapts to different devices and networks. Many organizations use these applications to increase employee productivity and streamline business operations.

The first common mobile enterprise application was the implementation of email. Now, 53% of emails are opened on a mobile device, a 45% increase in three years. The next wave of popular mobile enterprise application software was the advent of the CRM software. This allows salespeople to stay up-to-date with the business and manage customer relationships crucial to success from anywhere.

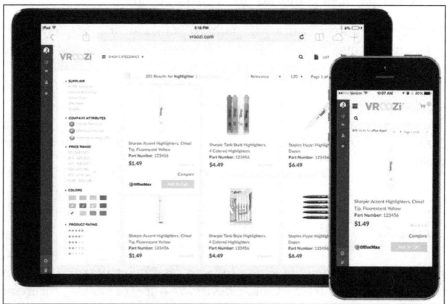

Mobile procurement platform renders the same marketplace
console in perfect optimization for all devices.

Another enterprise software application being leveraged on a mobile platform is procurement. This trend is led by the consumer shopping experience. Over 36% of online sales on Black Friday in 2015 came from mobile shopping, according to IBM. As more shoppers are migrating to mobile applications, procurement departments need to keep up with user preferences. This mobile platform provides capabilities to complete the procurement process from start to finish. This includes searching for items and services, comparing vendors and prices, submitting purchase requests, approving requests, electronic signing, purchase orders and invoicing. Being able to accomplish this all in one place from any device significantly streamlines business procurement and operations.

Users leverage mobile procurement for various reasons, and the tool can benefit businesses in many ways.

User Convenience: The clear advantage of using mobile procurement is the ability to use it anywhere from any device. This eliminates interruptions in the process or the need to complete a request from a single device. Users can search, compare and request items from anywhere. Suppliers can receive and sign purchase orders electronically. Checking inventory levels of physical locations provides a strong utility for mobile procurement.

Save Time: Mobile procurement saves time by reducing approval cycle time. A manager can make approvals from anywhere, not just his office. Users can request things they need when they need it, instead of after the fact, breaking corporate policy. Procurement now fills idle time rather than being a major item on a to-do list. This keeps employees and business moving forward. A fast procurement turnaround increases outcomes.

Visibility: Full visibility of suppliers and information helps businesses make informed decisions for better results and quicker processes. User analytics also help companies shop smarter in the long run.

Native Apps vs. HTML5

Mobile interaction now exceeds desktop Web interaction by 9%. Now that mobile is the dominant form of online activity, mobile procurement is simply a natural step into today's digital landscape. Mobile procurement platforms can be approached in two ways: native apps or Web apps using HTML5.

Native Apps: A native app is a mobile application developed specifically for use on mobile devices, launched directly from the home screen. In the United States, use of mobile apps greatly exceeds use of mobile Web browsing, but that trend is not worldwide.

Using a native app requires development for all operating systems and brands. A fully operational native app needs to be designed for iOS, Android, Microsoft, all their various generations, and at different resolutions and orientations. For total success of an app, users will expect it to work on everything from a high-resolution tablet down to an Apple Watch.

The other factor to consider with native apps is the way they access backend data. This is often more complex than a simple push to read data that takes place on a Web browser. Apps are developed, depending on their purpose and functionality, to access other applications such as the camera or local storage.

Native apps can be the preferred use of mobile procurement in environments with either no IT access or highly secure networks. Financial institutions value privacy and security when considering mobile tools operating in their network. Oil and gas environments are often remote and require apps that can work with limited Internet access.

A downside to mobile apps is the memory they occupy on a device. Because of this, many businesses will steer away from apps that require a great deal of storage.

Web Apps and HTML5: A Web app is run by a browser and is really a responsive Web site. Responsive sites change and adapt to any digital environment, including operating system, screen size and orientation. This has several advantages for mobile procurement platforms.

Responsive design can adjust to any browser on any device. The design is such that images, text, and user experience adjust based on the size and resolution of the platform. Adaptive web design is based on predetermined parameters for each platform. Both are ideal for any business that plans on interacting with customers on any type of mobile device.

HTML, JavaScript and CSS3 seamlessly integrate backend systems with browsers and user interfaces. This creates an easy-to-use experience for all users on any device. Although some designs are scaled down, which can limit functionality, responsive and adaptive web design is easily accessible for any customer. And functionality is all about priority. If a scaled down site still performs the necessary functions, users will still find the advantages of increased turnarounds and time saving.

The widespread availability of Wi-Fi increases the availability of HTML5 sites, reducing concerns about accessibility. With Wi-Fi everywhere, mobile procurement can happen in any place on a responsive site.

Elegantly designed responsive and adaptive sites are the ideal solution for mobile procurement because of the simplicity of creating and implementing one. If a user's experience is smooth and consistent, they will have no problem accessing a mobile procurement platform from any device. With the advancement of tools and technology it is currently possible to provide a native feel and minimal native feature set to your mobile products. Examples would be AngularJS, which allows for rapid web app development while preserving quality.

MOBILE TRADING

Mobile trading refers to the use of wireless technology in securities trading. Mobile trading allows investors to access trading platforms from their telephones rather than being confined to traditional trading methods via computer. Such technology allows easier access for smart phone users to actively manage their portfolios even when they are away from a desktop/laptop.

How Mobile Trading Works

While mobile devices, such as Android phones and iPhones, have always allowed users to check the performance of the stock market, mobile trading apps provide access to online trading platforms, which can be utilized to execute trades instantly from anywhere. Every major brokerage has an Android app or iPhone app or both, to allow their customers to trade directly from their mobile devices.

Mobile trading has allowed individuals to become traders and investors, not only from the comfort of their own homes, but from anywhere in the world with an internet connection. This means that people can trade from work or even on vacation in faraway lands. With mobile trading-only apps, such as Robinhood and its commission-free trading, mobile seems to be the most convenient and indeed cheapest way for most people to trade.

Major Mobile Trading Apps

TD Ameritrade

As one of the first companies to pioneer online trading from desktops, TD Ameritrade now offers a variety of mobile apps for trading and investing, that can be tailored to specific trading or investing styles and needs.

The basic TD Ameritrade Mobile app offers a similar experience to what a trader might have on their desktop stock trading setup, customized for mobile. Meanwhile, the TD Ameritrade Mobile Trader app, is even more powerful-unusually so. The TD Trader app allows an investor to customize their screens as interactive and modular dashboards. From your dashboard you can obtain company research and analyst reports, deposit and withdraw funds, set alerts, and even find educational content. TD Trader is best-suited for active or more sophisticated market participants, as it is chock full of interactive charts and technical indicators to help you stay up-to-date with the market while on the go.

Robinhood

Robinhood started as a mobile-only app before it launched its website. Robinhood is best known for offering completely free stock trades. While Robinhood won't let you trade assets such as mutual funds or options, it is an excellent choice if your portfolio is made up of stocks and ETFs. Recently, the company added support for trading Bitcoin as well. The app is focused on providing easy tracking of stocks you own and on your watch-list. While Robinhood trades are free, more sophisticated users can upgrade to Robinhood Gold account, which allows for margin trading and extended hours trading.

Acorns

Acorns is a roboadvisor that targets new investors or those who just want to set it and forget it. The app will construct optimized indexed portfolios using ETFs across several asset classes that are suited to your own risk tolerance and time horizon. If you link your bank account or credit card to the app, Acorns will furthermore track your spending and round-up purchases to the nearest dollar.

References

- "The World's first WAP Bank is Norwegian". Itavisen.no. 24 September 1999. Archived from the original on 4 May 2011. Retrieved 18 October 2010

- M-commerce, emerging-trends-in-business, business-environment, guides: toppr.com, Retrieved 13 May, 2019

- Das, Kedar; Deep, Kusum; Pant, Millie; Bansal, Jagdish; Nagar, Atulya (2014). Proceedings of Fourth International Conference on Soft Computing for Problem Solving: socpros 2014, Volume 2. Heidelberg: Springer. P. 377. ISBN 9788132222194

- Advantages-of-mobile-commerce: simicart.com, Retrieved 14 June, 2019

- Banerjee, Syagnik (Sy) and Rishika, Rishika,(2015) The Art of Mistiming: How Interruptions Make Mobile Coupon Campaigns Effective, Journal of Direct, Data and Digital Marketing Practice, December

- Lee, Gunwoong; Raghu, T. S. (7 December 2014). "Determinants of Mobile Apps' Success: Evidence from the App Store Market" (PDF). Journal of Management Information Systems. 31 (2): 133–170. Doi:10.2753/MIS0742-1222310206

- Importance-of-mobile-marketing: technians.com, Retrieved 15 July, 2019

- "Global Mobile Internet Usage Overtakes Desktop for the First Time". Techpp. 24 July 2015. Retrieved 20 November 2015

Electronic Payment Systems

An electronic payment system or e-payment system is a way of conducting transactions or paying for goods and services through an electronic medium. Some of these electronic payment systems include digital wallet, e-commerce credit card payment system, etc. All these types of electronic payment systems have been carefully analyzed in this chapter.

Electronic Payment is a financial exchange that takes place online between buyers and sellers. The content of this exchange is usually some form of digital financial instrument (such as encrypted credit card numbers, electronic cheques or digital cash) that is backed by a bank or an intermediary, or by a legal tender. The various factors that have lead the financial institutions to make use of electronic payments are:

- Decreasing technology cost: The technology used in the networks is decreasing day by day, which is evident from the fact that computers are now dirt-cheap and Internet is becoming free almost everywhere in the world.

- Reduced operational and processing cost: Due to reduced technology cost the processing cost of various commerce activities becomes very less. A very simple reason to prove this is the fact that in electronic transactions we save both paper and time.

- Increasing online commerce: The above two factors have lead many institutions to go online and many others are following them.

We began E-commerce with EDI, this was primarily for large business houses not for the common man. Many new technologies, innovations have lead to use of E-commerce for the common man also.

- Affecting the consumers: Credit cards, Debit Cards, ATMs (Automated Teller Machines), Stored value cards, E-banking.

- Enabling online commerce: Digital Cash, E-cash, Smart cards (or Electronic Purse) and encrypted Credit cards.

- Affecting Companies: The payment mechanisms that a bank provides to a company have changed drastically. The company can now directly deposit money into its employee's bank account. These transfers are done through Automated Transfer Houses.

There are also many problems with the traditional payment systems that are leading to its fade out. Some of them are enumerated below:

- Lack of Convenience: Traditional payment systems require the consumer to either send paper cheques by snail-mail or require him/her to physically come over and sign papers before performing a transaction. This may lead to annoying circumstances sometimes.

- Lack of Security: This is because the consumer has to send all confidential data on a paper, which is not encrypted, that too by post where it may be read by anyone.

- Lack of Coverage: When we talk in terms of current businesses, they span many countries or states. These business houses need faster transactions everywhere. This is not possible without the bank having branch near all of the companies offices. This statement is self-explanatory.

- Lack of Eligibility: Not all potential buyers may have a bank account.

- Lack of support for micro-transactions: Many transactions done on the Internet are of very low cost though they involve data flow between two entities in two countries. The same if done on paper may not be feasible at all.

We will now focus attention on the various ways available to pay online these methods of payment are still new even when seen as a technology. Each has its own benefits and shortcomings:

- Electronic Tokens: An electronic token is a digital analog of various forms of payment backed by a bank or financial institution. There are two types of tokens:

  ○ Real Time: (or Pre-paid tokens): These are exchanged between buyer and seller, their users pre-pay for tokens that serve as currency. Transactions are settled with the exchange of these tokens. Examples of these are Digi-Cash, Debit Cards, Electronic purse etc.

  ○ Post Paid Tokens: They are used with fund transfer instructions between the buyer and seller. Examples – Electronic cheques, Credit card data etc.

- Electronic or Digital Cash: This combines computerized convenience with security and privacy that improve upon paper cash. Cash is still the dominant form of payment as: The consumer still mistrusts the banks. The non-cash transactions are inefficiently cleared. In addition, due to negative real interests rates on bank deposits. Now we will enumerate some qualities of cash:

  ○ Cash is a legal tender i.e. payee is obligatory to take it.

  ○ It is negotiable i.e. can be given or traded to someone else.

- ◦ It is a bearer instrument i.e. possession is proof of ownership.

- ◦ It can be held & used by anyone, even those without a bank certificate.

- ◦ It places no risk on part of acceptor.

The following are the limitations of Debit and Credit Cards:

- They are identification cards owned by the issuer & restricted to one user i.e. cannot be given away.

- They are not legal tender

- Their usage requires an account relationship and authorization system.

Properties of digital cash:

- Must have a monetary value: It must be backed by cash (currency), bank authorized credit or a bank certified cashier's check.

- Must be interoperable or exchangeable as payment for other digital cash, paper cash, goods or services, lines of credit, bank notes or obligations, electronic benefit transfers and the like.

- Must be storable and retrievable: Cash could be stored on a remote computer's memory, in smart cards, or on other easily transported standard or special purpose devices. Remote storage or retrieval would allow users to exchange digital cash from home or office or while traveling.

- Should not be easy to copy or tamper with while it is being exchanged. This is achieved by using the following technologies, these are nothing but new and very efficient versions of the old art of cryptography.

  - ◦ Digital cash is based on cryptographic systems called "Digital Signatures" similar to the signatures used by banks on paper cheques to authenticate a customer.

  - ◦ Purchase of digital cash from an online currency server (or bank) involves 2 steps:

    - ▫ Establishment of an account in this step we are given a unique digital number which also becomes our digital signature. As it is a number known only to the customer and the bank, forgery, which may be done in paper cheques becomes very difficult.

    - ▫ Maintenance of sufficient money in the account is required to back any purchase.

Electronic Cheques

The electronic cheques are modeled on paper checks, except that they are initiated electronically. They use digital signatures for signing and endorsing and require the use of digital certificates to authenticate the payer, the payer's bank and bank account. They are delivered either by direct transmission using telephone lines or by public networks such as the Internet.

Benefits of electronic Cheques:

- Well suited for clearing micro payments. Conventional cryptography of e-cheques makes them easier to process than systems based on public key cryptography (like digital cash).

- They can serve corporate markets. Firms can use them in more cost-effective manner.

- They create float and the availability of float is an important requirement of Commerce.

E-banking

Banking as a business can be divided into five broad types:

- Retail.

- Domestic wholesale.

- International Wholesale.

- Investment.

- Trust.

Of all these types, retail and investment banking are most affected by online technological innovations and are the ones that stand to profit most from e-commerce.

Role of e-commerce in banking is multifaceted impacted by:

- Changes in technology.

- Rapid deregularization of many parts of finance.

- Emergence of new banking institutions.

- Basic economic restructuring.

E-Banking offers an inexpensive alternative to branching to expand a bank's customer base, and many banks are using e-banking to increase services to their customers.

Many banks have started websites on the Internet and many plan to offer banking services over the Internet.

Smart Cards and other forms of electronic cash could be the key to consumer acceptance of home banking, eventually allowing banks to reduce the number of their physical branches.

Four major categories of home banking are:

- Proprietary bank dial-up services: A home banking service in combination with a Computer and Modem lets the bank become and electronic gateway to consumer's accounts, enabling them to transfer funds or pay bills directly to creditor's accounts.

- Off-the-shelf home finance Software: This category is a key player in making relationships between current customers and helping banks gain new customers. Example: Microsoft's Money and Bank of America's MECA Software.

- Online Service Based Banking: This category allows banks to setup retail branches or subscriber based online services such as Prodigy, CompuServe and America Online.

- WWW Based Banking: This allows banks to bypass subscriber based online services and reach the customer's browser directly through worldwide web. Advantage of this model is its flexibility to adapt to new online transaction processing models facilitated by e-commerce and elimination of the constricting intermediary.

E-commerce and Retailing

Retailing is expected to change with the rapid development of new online sales and distribution channels that literally can be used from anywhere, anytime – from work, school, a hotel, car or airplane. As an example of the Electronic retailing we can see Amazon which sells books online and Dell computers who sell computers online. These retailers started as small players in a market, which did not trust them. However, they have become major players after taking over some small retailers.

Almost every retailer is now re-evaluating every aspect of its operation from customer service to advertising, merchandising to store design and logistics to order fulfillment and further more reacting to the pressure of retailers, suppliers are assessing technology based solutions to drive down costs and become more efficient producers of goods.

Online channels are impacting traditional retail business models with online retailing constraints of time and space disappear.

Electronic Retailing

Today electronic retailing is still far from being a competitive threat to more traditional store retailing but it is becoming increasingly attractive as technology and application improve and retailers gain experience.

Some traditional retail outlets:

- Shopping malls and departmental stores.

- Super Centers.

- Factory outlets.

- Warehouses.

- Mail order and catalogue shopping.

Electronic Retailing Channels are:

- Television Retailing: The T.V. retail marketing and programming are divided into segments that are televised live, with a show host who presents the merchandise and conveys information relating to the product including price, quality, features and benefits.

  Success of T.V. shopping is the result of effective utilization of electronic media for capturing the power and influence of celebrity and the magic of showmanship and bringing them to bear on a sale.

- CD-ROM Based Shopping has the following advantages:

  ◦ A CD-ROM catalogue has multimedia capability and can enable a merchant to add sound, photographs an a full motion video to a product presentation.

  ◦ It can be interactive enabling the customer to select which category to view.

  ◦ Relatively inexpensive to produce and distribute.

It has the following disadvantages:

- Not all possible customers may have a CD-ROM drive or software to see it.

- It is a static device to catalogue a company's products, but the list or style of the products a company makes may vary from time to time.

E-commerce Phases

- Marketing: Marketing is not a new term, to sell anything companies have to market it. But to use the Internet, as a medium of marketing is new as the bandwidth is still limited so no commercials can be shown as on T.V. Internet marketing has a different approach. We market things on the net by showing small banner ads that everyone who surfs the net is familiar. Also web sites like Amazon pay other web sites if someone from their web site comes to Amazon's web site by clicking on a banner ad or a link. The whole business on the web is *sticky* the term refers to the fact that the customer has to be sold a product and also the web site should be so attractive that the customer keeps coming back to it for further buying. This is done by sending attractive offer mails and referrals.

- Customer/Visitor: Here we have to make distinction between the type of commerce web site. There actually exist three broad types of commerce web sites:

  - B2C: These web sites provide business to consumer. These are micro-payment based web sites. They have to attractive and should be able to show the products properly.

  - B2B: These are web sites that provide business to the business, that is their function is similar to the stock exchanges, i.e. they are meeting points for a buyer and a seller. These do not focus on content but rather on service. Functions of such web sites are online order processing, tender filling, tracking of orders etc.

  - Auction Sites: These are sites that let you auction or sell something online it may be an old motorcycle or bed or books.

  - Web Site Visit: Once a user visits a web site the site begins tracking him/her, by presenting him/her with products based on his/her preference. Some means of doing this are cookies, registration forms, surveys etc.

- Product Browsing: A user will typically browse through departments and then various products; he/she may be attracted by sowing blinking new offers and other discounts.

- Shopping Basket: Shopping basket is a term taken straight from regular shopping, as in a store the user adds the items of need to a basket the online store also implement a shopping basket, in which we can keep on adding items o our need.

- Checkout: Once we have added all items we need to the basket the web site lists all the items that we intend to purchase, we also have to fill in all the billing related information here. We enter the credit card numbers here. Other things such as gift-wrapping etc. are also specified here.

  - Tax & Shipping: Once it has been decided where the product has to go and who is going to pay for it, we now decide on various taxex and shipping routes the product may take. These become very challenging especially in international orderings as countries have different taxes and shipping rates.

- Payment: This is the most important part of the purchasing online. The user is presented with a list of all the items purchased, and a total of the payments he has to make then he has to decide on the mode of payment whether by credit card or cash on delivery etc.

- Receipt: Once an order has been placed and confirmed, we may want to place a copy of the order with the user. This may be done either by snail mail or e-mail.

- Process Order: At this stage the consumer leaves the picture, we now begin to check the credit card number and other data. This may be done online or offline, then the product is made and prepared for shipping to the customer.

- Fulfill Order: Once the order has been processed it has to be fulfilled duly. Even though 90% of the transactions are online but the product has to reach the consumer physically and in well shape.

- Ship Order: Once we have processed the order fully it is ready to be sent to the consumer it is then shipped to the consumer.

The tools that go into the making of a web site depend on the platform or OS being used to develop the store:

- Windows NT platform:

  ○ Database support – A must, either in form of Access or SQL Server.

  ○ ASP support – This is the technology from Microsoft that will enable dynamic content on the web site.

  ○ MTS support – Every transaction should pass the ACID test (i.e. it should be Atomic Consistent Isolated and Durable) MTS has built in transaction objects that can be used.

  ○ Site Server – Has a rich set of tools to build a site, these help to engage a customer.

  ○ Commerce Server – This has a rich set of tools that can help in commerce transactions.

- Unix/Linux platforms:

  ○ MySQL support – This is the database supported by sites on this platform.

  ○ Perl – Is the scripting language that enables dynamic content on these web sites.

- JAVA: Java is a platform independent package, so JAVA has Java Server Pages for scripting and can interact with most of the databases with the use of some third party addons etc.

E-COMMERCE CREDIT CARD PAYMENT SYSTEM

Electronic commerce, commonly known as e-commerce or eCommerce, or e-business consists of the buying and selling of products or services over electronic systems such as the Internet and other computer networks. The amount of trade conducted electronically has grown extraordinarily with widespread Internet usage. The use of commerce is conducted in this way, spurring and drawing on innovations in electronic funds transfer, supply chain management, Internet marketing, online transaction processing, electronic data interchange (EDI), inventory management systems, and automated data collection systems. Modern electronic commerce typically uses the World Wide Web at least at some point in the transaction's lifecycle, although it can encompass a wider range of technologies such as e-mail as well.

A large percentage of electronic commerce is conducted entirely electronically for virtual items such as access to premium content on a website, but most electronic commerce involves the transportation of physical items in some way. Online retailers are sometimes known as e-tailers and online retail is sometimes known as e-tail. Almost all big retailers have electronic commerce presence on the World Wide Web.

This flow of ecommerce payment system can be better understood from the flow of the system below.

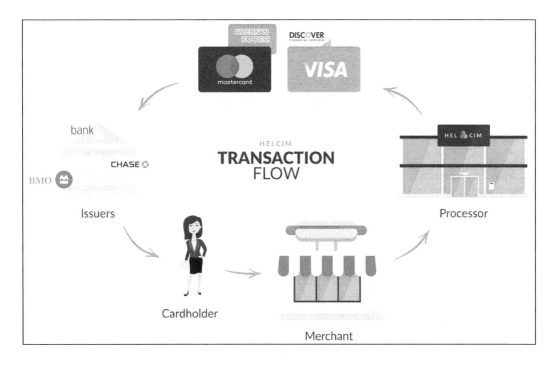

Online Credit Card (VISA) Transaction Process.

Electronic commerce that is conducted between businesses is referred to as business-to-business or B2B. B2B can be open to all interested parties (e.g. commodity market) or limited to specific, pre-qualified participants (private electronic market). Electronic commerce that is conducted between businesses and consumers, on the other hand, is referred to as business-to-consumer or B2C. This is the type of electronic commerce conducted by companies such as Amazon.com. Online shopping is a form of electronic commerce where the buyer is connected directly online to the seller's computer usually via the Internet. There is no specific intermediary service. The sale and purchase transaction is completed electronically and interactively in real-time, such as when buying a new book. If an intermediary is present, then the sale and purchase transaction is called consumer-to-consumer, such as an online auction conducted.

This payment system has been widely accepted by consumers and merchants throughout the world, and is by far the most popular method of payments especially in the retail markets. Some of the most important advantages over the traditional modes of payment are: privacy, integrity, compatibility, good transaction efficiency, acceptability, convenience, mobility, low financial risk and anonymity.

DIGITAL WALLET

A digital wallet also known as "e-wallet" refers to an electronic device or online service that allows an individual to make electronic transactions. This can include purchasing items on-line with a computer or using a smartphone to purchase something at a store. Money can be deposited in the digital wallet prior to any transactions or in other cases, an individual's bank account can be linked to the digital wallet. Users might also have their driver's license, health card, loyalty card(s) and other ID documents stored within the wallet. The credentials can be passed to a merchant's terminal wirelessly via near field communication (NFC). Increasingly, digital wallets are being made not just for basic financial transactions but to also authenticate the holder's credentials. For example, a digital wallet could verify the age of the buyer to the store while purchasing alcohol. The system has already gained popularity in Japan, where digital wallets are known as "wallet mobiles". A cryptocurrency wallet is a digital wallet where private keys are stored for cryptocurrencies like bitcoin.

Technology

A digital wallet has both a software and information component. Secure and fair electronic payment systems are important issue. The software provides security and encryption for the personal information and for the actual transaction. Typically, digital wallets are stored on the client side and are easily self-maintained and fully compatible with most e-commerce websites. A server-side digital wallet, also known as a thin wallet, is one that an organization creates for and about you and maintains on its servers. Server-side digital wallets are gaining popularity among major retailers due to the security, efficiency, and added utility it provides to the end-user, which increases their satisfaction of their overall purchase. The information component is basically a database of user-input information. This information consists of your shipping address, billing address, payment methods (including credit card numbers, expiry dates, and security numbers), and other information.

Digital wallets are composed of both digital wallet devices and digital wallet systems. There are dedicated digital wallet devices such as the biometric wallet by Dunhill, a physical device that holds cash and cards along with a Bluetooth mobile connection. Presently there are further explorations for smartphones with NFC digital wallet capabilities, such as the Samsung Galaxy series and the Google Nexus smartphones utilizing Google's Android operating system and Apple's iPhone 6 and iPhone 6 Plus utilizing Apple Pay. Others include Samsung Pay, Android Pay, as well as payment services like PayPal and Venmo.

Digital wallet systems enable the widespread use of digital wallet transactions among various retail vendors in the form of mobile payments systems and digital wallet applications. The M-PESA mobile payments system and microfinancing service has widespread use in Kenya and Tanzania, while the MasterCard PayPass application has been adopted by a number of vendors in the U.S. and worldwide.

Digital wallets are being used more frequently among Asian countries as well. One in every five consumers in Asia are now using a digital wallet, representing a twofold increase from two years ago. A MasterCard mobile shopping survey among 8500 adults, aged 18–64 across 14 markets, showed that 45% of users in China, 36.7% of users in India and 23.3% of users in Singapore are the biggest adopters of digital wallets. The survey was conducted between October and December 2015. Further analysis showed that 48.5% of consumers in these regions made purchases using smartphones.

Payments for Goods and Services Purchased Online

A client-side digital wallet requires minimal setup and is relatively easy to use. Once the software is installed, the user begins by entering all the pertinent information. The digital wallet is now set up. At the purchase or check-out page of an e-commerce site, the digital wallet software has the ability to automatically enter the user information in the online form. By default, most digital wallets prompt when the software recognizes a form in which it can fill out; if one chooses to fill out the form automatically, the user will be prompted for a password. This keeps unauthorized users away from viewing personal information stored on a particular computer.

ECML

Digital wallets are designed to be accurate when transferring data to retail checkout forms; however, if a particular e-commerce site has a peculiar checkout system, the digital wallet may fail to properly recognize the form's fields. This problem has been eliminated by sites and wallet software that use Electronic Commerce Modeling Language (ECML) technology. Electronic Commerce Modeling Language is a protocol that dictates how online retailers structure and set up their checkout forms.

Security

Consumers are not required to fill out order forms on each site when they purchase an item because the information has already been stored and is automatically updated and entered into the order fields across merchant sites when using a digital wallet. Consumers also benefit when using digital wallets because their information is encrypted or protected by a private software code; merchants benefit by receiving protection against fraud.

Digital wallets are available to consumers free of charge, and they're fairly easy to obtain. For example, when a consumer makes a purchase at a merchant site that's set up to handle server-side digital wallets, they type their name, payment and shipping information into the merchant's own form. At the end of the purchase, the consumer is asked to sign up for a wallet of their choice by entering a user name and password for future purchases. Users can also acquire wallets at a wallet vendor's site.

Although a wallet is free for consumers, vendors charge merchants for wallets. Some wallet vendors make arrangements for merchants to pay them a percentage of every successful purchase directed through their wallets. In other cases, digital wallet vendors process the transactions between cardholders and participating merchants and charge merchants a flat fee.

Advantages for E-commerce Sites

Upwards of 25% of online shoppers abandon their order due to frustration in filling in forms. The digital wallet combats this problem by giving users the option to transfer their information securely and accurately. This simplified approach to completing transactions results in better usability and ultimately more utility for the customer.

Digital Wallets can also increase the security of the transaction since the wallet typically does not pass payment card details to the website (a unique transaction identifier or token is shared instead). Increasingly this approach is a feature of online payment gateways, especially if the payment gateway offers a "hosted payment page" integration approach.

ONLINE BANKING EPAYMENTS

Online Banking ePayments (OBeP) is a type of payments network, developed by the banking industry in conjunction with technology providers. It is specifically designed to address the unique requirements of payments made via the Internet.

Key aspects of OBeP that distinguish it from other online payments systems are:

1. The consumer is authenticated in real-time by the consumer financial institution's online banking infrastructure.

2. The availability of funds is validated in real-time by the consumer's financial institution.

3. The consumer's financial institution provides guarantee of payment to the merchant.

4. Payment is made as a credit transfer (push payment) from the consumer's financial institution to the merchant, as opposed to a debit transfer (pull payment).

5. Payment is made directly from the consumer's account rather than through a third-party account.

Nearly half of the bills paid in the US during 2013 were done via electronic bill payment. Also, during 2014, nearly 48% of all online shopping in North America were made with a credit card. Globally, online payments are expected to exceed 3 trillion Euros (approximately US $3.2 trillion) in the next 5 years.

Privacy and Security Features

OBeP systems protect consumer personal information by not requiring the disclosure of account numbers or other sensitive personal data to online merchants or other third parties. During the checkout process, the merchant redirects the consumer to their financial institution's online banking site where they login and authorize charges. After charges are authorized, the financial institution redirects the consumer back to the merchant site. All network communications are protected using industry standard encryption. Additionally, communications with the OBeP network take place on a virtual private network, not over the public Internet.

In order to be positive that your identity, information and other personal features are truly secure, the following cautions should be taken: Make sure a secure browser is being used. Read all privacy policies provided. Many individuals simply skip over such important information that could spell out potential risks. If a risk seems unnecessary and odd, it would be safer to skip this payment rather than take the risk with one's hard earned money. Keep all personal information private. If phone numbers, social security numbers or other private, important information is asked for one should be cautious. Banking information is important information as it is, asking for unnecessary personal information should be a red flag of suspicious behavior. Selecting businesses that are trustworthy is key. Most companies will email a customer with a transaction receipt upon payment. Keeping a record of these is important in order to have proof of purchase or payment. Lastly, checking bank statements regularly is crucial in keeping up-to-date with transactions.

Costs

Costs associated with fraud, estimated at 1.2% of sales by online retailers in 2009, are reported to be dramatically reduced with OBeP, because the issuer bank is responsible for the authentication of the credit transaction and provides guaranteed funds to the merchant.

Because the merchant is not responsible for storing and protecting confidential consumer information, OBeP systems also reduce costs associated with mitigating fraud, fraud screening, and PCI audits.

Transaction fees on Online Banking ePayments vary by network, but are often fixed, and lower than the average 1.9% merchant fees associated with credit card transactions – especially for larger purchases.

Other Benefits

For Consumers

- The use of cash-like payment encourages responsible consumerism.
- It does not require set-up or registration with a third-party payments entity.
- It presents familiar interface to facilitate online payment.
- The awareness of funds availability.

For Merchants

- It improved sales conversion/reduced abandoned carts.
- The real time authorization of guaranteed ACH payment (good funds).
- The offering preferred payment methods may drive repeat transactions.

For Financial Institutions

- It recapture revenue being lost to alternative payment providers.
- It encourages consumers to move to online banking, replacing more costly branch and telephone alternatives.

Potential Downfalls

The idea of online payments and transactions has led numerous individuals, corporations and groups to be hesitant. Sharing of personal information to such a vast entity, such as the internet, can lead to potential problems. Remaining cautious and careful with what information is shared and to whom it is shared with is key in remaining safe and secure when using ePayments.

- Identity theft is prevalent with online transactions.

- No face-to-face interaction for help, questions, issues.

- Website issues can hinder the ability to make payments in a timely manner.

- Passwords - Sometimes remembering a password can be difficult and with something as important as an ePayment website, it is crucial this information is not lost or forgotten.

Types and Implementations

- Multi-Bank – Requires that a merchant have a single connection to the OBeP network in order to accept payment from any participating financial institution.

- Mono-Bank – Requires that a merchant have a separate connection to each participating financial institution.

- A third category, also known as "overlay payment solutions" provide a similar consumer experience to Online Banking ePayments, but violate a key tenet of the OBeP definition by requiring the consumer to share their online banking credentials with a third party.

- A fourth category requires that a merchant have a single connection to an alternative payment provider. This alternative payment provider has connections to multiple online banks. This does not require the consumer to share their online banking credentials, but still offers the same advantages to the merchants as "overlay payment solutions".

MICROPAYMENT

A micropayment is a financial transaction involving a very small sum of money and usually one that occurs online. A number of micropayment systems were proposed and developed in the mid-to-late 1990s, all of which were ultimately unsuccessful. A second generation of micropayment systems emerged in the 2010s.

While micropayments were originally envisioned to involve very small sums of money, practical systems to allow transactions of less than US$1 have seen little success. One problem that has prevented the emergence of micropayment systems is a need to keep costs for individual transactions low, which is impractical when transacting such small sums even if the transaction fee is just a few cents.

The term was coined by Ted Nelson, long before the invention of the World Wide Web. Initially this was conceived as a way to pay the various copyright holders of a compound work. Micropayments, on the Web, were initially devised as a way of allowing the sale of online content and as a way to pay for very low cost network services. They were envisioned to involve small fractions of a cent, as little as US $0.0001 to a few cents. Micropayments would enable people to sell content on the Internet and would be an alternative to advertising revenue. During the late 1990s, there was a movement to create microtransaction standards, and the World Wide Web Consortium (W3C) worked on incorporating micropayments into HTML even going as far as to suggest the embedding of payment-request information in HTTP error codes. The W3C has since stopped its efforts in this area, and micropayments have not become a widely used method of selling content over the Internet.

Early Research and Systems

In the late 1990s, established companies like IBM and Compaq had microtransaction divisions, and research on micropayments and micropayment standards was performed at Carnegie Mellon and by the World Wide Web Consortium.

IBM Micro Payments

IBM's Micro Payments was established 1999, and were it to have become operational would have "allowed vendors and merchants to sell content, information, and services over the Internet for amounts as low as one cent".

iPIN

An early attempt at making micropayments work, iPIN was a 1998 venture-capital-funded startup that provided services that allowed purchasers to add incremental micropayment charges to their existing bill for Internet services. Debuting in 1999, its service was never widely adopted.

Millicent

Millicent, originally a project of Digital Equipment Corporation, was a micropayment system that was to support transactions from as small as 1/10 of a cent up to $5.00. It grew out of The Millicent Protocol for Inexpensive Electronic Commerce, which was presented at the 1995 World Wide Web Conference in Boston, but the project became associated with Compaq after that company purchased Digital Equipment Corporation. The payment system employed symmetric cryptography.

NetBill

The NetBill electronic commerce project at Carnegie Mellon university researched distributed transaction processing systems and developed protocols and software to support payment for goods and services over the Internet. It featured pre-paid accounts from which micropayment charges could be drawn. NetBill was initially absorbed by CyberCash in 1997 and ultimately taken over by PayPal.

Online Gaming

The term micropayment or microtransaction is sometimes attributed to the sale of virtual goods in online games, most commonly involving an in-game currency or service bought with real world money and only available within the online game.

Recent Systems

Current systems either allow many micropayments but charge the user's phone bill one lump sum or use funded wallets.

Flattr

Flattr is a micropayment system (more specifically, a microdonation system) which launched in August 2010. Actual bank transactions and overhead costs are involved only on funds withdrawn from the recipient's accounts.

Jamatto

Jamatto is a micropayments and microsubscriptions system that allows websites and publishers to accept payments as small as 1c by modifying just their HTML source code Jamatto is in use by newspapers across three continents.

M-Coin

A service provided by TIMWE, M-Coin allows users to make micropayments on the Internet. The user's phone bill is then charged by the mobile network operator.

Pay Pal

PayPal MicroPayments is a micropayment system that charges payments to user's PayPal account and allows transactions of less than US$12 to take place. As of 2013, the service is offered in selected currencies only. The PayPal charge for a micropayment from a U.S. account is a flat five cents per transaction plus five percent of the transaction (as compared with PayPal's normal 2.9% and 30 cents for larger sums).

Swish

Swish is a payment system between bank accounts in Sweden. It is designed for small instant transactions between people, instead of using cash, but is also used by small businesses such as sports clubs that don't want to deal with the cost of a credit card reader. A cell phone number is used as a unique user identifier, and must have been registered at a Swedish bank. A smartphone app is used to send money, but any cell phone can be used as a receiver. The lowest permitted payment is 1 SEK (around €0.11) and the highest is 10,000 (around €1,100), although 150,000 SEK can be transferred if the transaction is preregistered in the internet bank. The fee is generally zero for private people, but when the receiver is a organisation e.g. sports club or company, there is fee of 2 SEK, which is considered significant if a sports club sells coffee and cookies at an event. Swish has become popular, with 50% of the Swedish population registered as users in 2016.

Similar apps with zero fee for small instant private transactions, Vipps and MobilePay have become popular in Norway and Denmark.

Blendle

Blendle is an online news platform that aggregates articles from a variety of newspapers and magazines and sells them on a pay-per-article basis, leading Nieman Lab to describe it as a "micropayments-for-news pioneer". It operates in the Netherlands, Germany and the US. In 2019, five years after its launch, it announced that it would change its business model away from micropayments to premium subscriptions. Nieman Lab commented that "micropayments keep not panning out".

Obsolete Systems

Zong

Zong mobile payments was a micropayment system that charged payments to users' mobile phone bills. The company was acquired by eBay and integrated with PayPal in 2011.

GOOGLE WALLET

Google Wallet is a mobile payment system that acts as a virtual wallet, allowing users to make payments and transfer money straight from their phones. The service is free for users and can store credit, debit, gift and loyalty card information. Available to anyone with a newer Android or Apple smartphone, Google Wallet gives users another fast way to make payments at ecommerce stores that accept it.

Mobile payments are a relatively new strategy that has the potential to greatly benefit online sales. Currently, mobile devices account for just under 50 percent of ecommerce traffic, but when it comes time for users to purchase items online, nearly 77 percent of users do so exclusively on a personal computer instead. Customers avoid making actual purchases on mobile devices because of concerns about security and the inherent difficulty of entering bank card information using a touch screen interface.

Electronic wallets look to sidestep these concerns by streamlining the mobile payment process via a secure service. Customers simply click to buy something and all of their payment info is already entered into the wallet. The fast checkout works both in-app and on participating mobile sites.

Google Wallet also gives merchants the ability to highlight special offers or discounts from their websites or emails directly to the shopper via the app. Customers can also add any gift card balances to their virtual wallets, which helps drive additional sales.

How it Works

Google Wallet is what is known as a server-side wallet, which means that all of a user's information is stored remotely on Google's system, rather than on the user's device. Transactions take place between Google's servers and the merchant's existing payment processor.

It acts somewhat like a gift card: users place a set amount of money into the wallet they can then spend as desired. As far as the user's bank is concerned, the transaction is identical to any other debit or credit, only the transactions go exclusively through Google rather than the merchant's point of sale. Assuming the merchant's point of sale is configured to accept Google Wallet, transactions work the same as any other accepted payment method.

While support for the mobile app is still sketchy, Google Wallet offers a physical card as well that can be used anyplace that accepts debit MasterCard.

How does Google Wallet Stack up to other options

Google Wallet's main competitor is Apple, although other companies such as Samsung and PayPal have their own digital payment systems as well (Samsung Pay and PayPal Wallet, respectively). While the products may have a few differences when it comes to the user, they offer similar features from the perspective of an online store owner. Both want to make it as easy as possible to facilitate transactions.

- Neither charge fees.

- Liability rules are the same as regular card transactions.

- Both can support rewards programs.

- Both make the purchasing process much faster.

- Both utilize NFC (near field communications) for in-store purchases.

The main difference between the two initiatives is the companies behind them. Google pioneered NFC technology years ago, which allowed users to pay with a mobile device at a point of sale using a secure, short-range signal. However, the technology was not widely adopted at the time, which put Google on the back foot, giving Apple an opening to push their Apple Pay model.

Apple, having an established and loyal user base, was able to roll out its system a great deal more effectively, coupling it with specific technology offerings, such as the Apple Watch. Seeing an opportunity to partner with the high-prestige Apple brand, retailers and banks have been a great deal more eager to adopt the technology now.

Google, however, is retooling its wallet to take advantage of their more flexible and open system. Unlike Apple, Google is allowing other developers access to its API in hopes that other companies will create innovative new ways to use the technology. With 80 percent of global market share for the Android platform, payment processors and merchants have good reason to support Google's initiatives.

When compared with other virtual wallets, Google Wallet and Apple Pay stand above most for online transactions. The focus of many other virtual wallets is in-store purchases. Most of them, like Samsung Pay, can only process offline purchases and PayPal Wallet is not widely supported.

What Ecommerce Merchants Need to Know

Google Wallet is becoming more popular, which means more people are going to expect it at their favorite stores. Ecommerce business owners should consider offering digital wallets such as Google Wallet, which provide shoppers with more payment options. While there are several other options out there, Google Wallet and Apple Pay are most likely going to be the big players in the future. Both services keep adding more features in the hopes that their virtual wallets will catch on quicker. For instance, Google's open API will allow financial institutions to integrate their mobile banking apps with Google Wallet, thereby giving their customers direct access to new rewards programs.

Google Wallet was initially released in 2011, and Apple Pay has only been in existence since 2014, so the mobile wallet industry is still in its infancy. Both companies are jockeying for position in a fragmented marketplace. Consumers, meanwhile, are hesitant to adopt either wholeheartedly. Yet, as mobile commerce is integrated into everyday life, their role in purchasing is inevitable.

The reason virtual wallet adoption is still fairly low is because debit and credit cards have almost universal acceptance with merchants and customers. For this reason, Google and Apple are both racing to discover some innovation to give virtual wallets a clear and distinct advantage which bank cards cannot offer. Neither one has yet found that tipping point.

Limitations of Google Wallet

Google is discontinuing the processing of payments for certain digital goods such as e-books, subscriptions, online games and music. They are, however, hoping to expand Google Wallet's influence on ecommerce with increased support for physical goods merchants.

Google Wallet isn't yet the best payment option for ecommerce; but as time goes on, it is likely to become a viable and even essential financial service.

E-Commerce Softwares

E-commerce software refers to the tool which is used to manage the diverse activities in an online store, facilitating the management of inventory, adding or removing products and calculating taxes. This chapter closely examines the key concepts of popular e-commerce software such as Drupal Commerce, NopCommerce and PrestaShop to provide an extensive understanding of the subject.

Ecommerce software is the engine behind the scenes of an online store, making it possible to easily manage inventory, add or remove products, calculate taxes, and everything else required to manage a website and fulfill orders.

Ecommerce software simplifies intricate processes in a friendly user interface that enables people non-technical backgrounds to oversee an entire ecommerce operation. Despite the ease of use that ecommerce software brings to an online business, it is a multifaceted and complex machine.

Types of Ecommerce Software

Ecommerce software comes in two basic flavors, with many varieties of each:

- On-Premise: Installed and managed on-site by developers who facilitate manual updates, fix problems and do general troubleshooting. Traditionally, merchants went with on-premise solutions due to the increased flexibility from hosted solutions.

- SaaS: Software as a Service (or "hosted") solutions are much more hands-off from a technical standpoint. The only development requirements are for additional design and custom features — all updates, patches, and newly-released features are done automatically or with one-click integrations. Hosted ecommerce software has evolved to the point where the customization and flexibility, previously exclusive to on-premise, is robust, making it more than sufficient for most online retailers. Ecommerce stores using SaaS software can be launched in 1/3 of the time and at a much lower cost than on-premise solutions.

Purpose of Ecommerce Software

The purpose of ecommerce software is to put everything you need to run your store in one place. While the platform itself doesn't fulfill every task, integrations with leading providers make it possible to seamlessly run a business without jockeying between different services. Accounting software, ERP, 3PL, social media — such as Facebook, Twitter and Pinterest — and much more can be linked to ecommerce software so data sharing is not manual.

Ecommerce Software

- Simplifies marketing: Built-in SEO and easy optimization allow online stores to rank higher in organic search engines such as Google for increased discovery and lower customer acquisition costs.

- Automates shipping and taxes: Printing shipping labels, calculating sales taxes based on customer location, and sending notification emails to customers.

- Manage products: From SKUs and variations (size, color, quantity) to product names and images, ecommerce software allows an online store manager to get a high-level view or drill down to the specifics without any technical knowledge required.

- Customer & order management: Managing an order from inception to delivery is crucial to the success of any business. Ecommerce software lets you filter by customer, check order status, and make changes on the fly. Integrations with email platforms such as Mailchimp provide another medium for managing customer communications.

- Enhance overall user experience: If customers can't find what they need — and fast — then ecommerce software hasn't done it's job. Hosted solutions offer service-level agreements to guarantee uptime, and simple website management with analytic insights help you find optimization opportunities.

Brick-and-mortar Businesses Moving Online

Physical storefronts are not an alternative to online businesses: in fact, they can enhance each other. An online presence greatly expands a business' reach and brand awareness, opening up sales to the entire web (as opposed to nearby customers only). Ecommerce is estimated to comprise 10% of the economy in 2015, with predicted growth of 44% by 2019. Many physical stores are adopting ecommerce due to the the ability to reach more people and expand their brand across all channels. They can now display, solicit and ship their products or services to the end-user, or the customer who bought what they're selling.

Working Procedure of Ecommerce Software

Selling on the internet via your website entails a series of steps and processes that e-commerce software takes care of. What is e-commerce but a system to streamline those steps. How does e-commerce software work? It usually goes like this:

- A shopper visits your website which displays products and categories that are loaded in/stored in the website database.

- The customer uses a shopping cart to add items and creates an account with all information saved in the database.

- Once the customer is in the checkout stage, the website normally goes into secure mode displaying a lock symbol and using an SSL certificate.

- While in checkout the website may utilize third-party software or services to provide the customer with delivery options, shipping rates, and expected delivery date.

- When the customer enters the credit card number, the information is sent to a payment processor or payment gateway such as PayPal.

- The customer order is now completed and all sensitive information is stored with the payment processor (not with the e-commerce website).

- You can have the payment deposited in your merchant account (a service usually provided by a payment gateway) or transferred to your bank account.

The steps above, from order to payment processing, can take just minutes to complete giving you and your customer/shopper utmost efficiency and convenience. E-commerce software makes all of the above happen worry-free and hassle-free. Which is why you need a fully capable e-commerce platform to make your online store or website operate in the most flawless and responsive manner.

Shopify: One unified platform to run your online business with ease.

Take note that for your e-commerce site to run successfully, some other components would have to come into play. These include:

- Web Hosting Service: These companies and service providers offer Web servers to host your website and all the elements and apps that go with it. This is a vital component because having a good online store that is always open, accessible, loads quickly, and is able to handle high traffic depends on a reliable and dependable Web host.

- Product Catalog: The product catalog is what your customers view and learn about the products you're selling. Similar to a printed catalog, your online catalog is made up of products, pages and information you present to your customers. They must be designed to attract, appeal and entice your customers, and reflect your brand, company or theme of your store.

- Shopping Cart: This is what your customers will use to place their orders where they can add the products they want to purchase, provide information about shipping and payment preferences, and submit the order. The shopping cart component may spell the difference between a completed or abandoned sale. It must thus work optimally and smoothly.

- Merchant Interface: This is the tool you use to manage your online store as well as set up and use all other tools and apps that you may need. The interface must be robust, flexible, customizable while straight forward to operate.

- Payment Processing: The backbone of an online store is accepting payment. Simply put, without this component customers can't place in their orders. There are several online payment services, payment gateway, and merchant account providers that integrate with e-commerce platforms to ensure safe, secure, accurate, and efficient payment processing.

- Order Fulfillment and Shipping: There are many order fulfillment, third party logistics, and shipping services that provide next-day, second-day, and ground shipping that you can offer your customers giving them many options which they can avail for prompt and fast delivery. These services removes the "heavy lifting" from you so can focus on your selling.

E-commerce software ties all of the above components and services to give you one integrated solution to manage and run you online store from end-to-end.

Advantages of E-commerce Software

- Quickly start your online business: Most e-commerce software comes with easy to use online store builders with pre-built templates and an assortment of themes to help you build your store quickly. We're talking here of minutes, not hours, if you're familiar with drag-and-drop functions where you just put your store elements into place, add product images, put in descriptions and prices, set up your shopping cart, and you're basically good to go.

- Your store is always open: One of the biggest business advantages of using e-commerce software is that it keeps your online store open 24 hours a day,

7 days a week. Your business hours are not limited by physical location or the working schedule of your staff. Since everything is automated, you are not required to continually monitor your online store through your dashboard.

- You can sell to anyone, anywhere: In relation to the above which allows you to sell anytime, you can sell to everyone from any location in the world. You have a global market for your products, unhindered by time, geography and boundaries. You harness the internet's connectivity to sell to anyone wherever they may be.

- You save time, money and resources: When you calculate your expenses, you will find that it costs you less operating an online store than running a brick-and-mortar store where you'll have to rent expensive space in a prime location, employ sales staff, and pay for utilities, among others. Paying monthly for an affordable e-commerce platform that takes care of your online store reduce expenses and maximize profits.

- You can sell as many products: Unlike a traditional retail outlet which has limited storage space to fit all your products, an online store has no physical space to constrict the number of products that you can carry, display and sell. Since more people are shopping online nowadays, this allows you to sell more, offering products organized in catalogue web pages that can easily be searched and viewed by customers. This also results in shorter selling cycles, providing you maximum returns at minimum investment.

- Easy online payment and shipping: E-commerce software and shopping cart platforms are equipped to process online payments, either as a built-in feature or integrated with a payment gateway service, allowing for safe and secured online transactions. The software can also be connected seamlessly with 3PL or order fulfillment service providers that can offer your customers with their preferred delivery and shipping options.

- Built-in marketing tools: Many e-commerce software are loaded with powerful marketing tools and SEO features to help your store rank higher in search engine results and attract potential customers. There are also built-in analytics and statistical tools that can provide you with real-time analytical data, helping you to come up with targeted marketing campaigns, special deals and offers, as well as make improvements in your product mix or promotion.

- You can provide quality online customer service: E-commerce software gives you the means to provide your customers the best online shopping experience – from easy product selection, order, and checkout, to convenient online payment, shipping and delivery – everything is designed through automation to make it as simple as possible for customers to buy at your store, and get the best service they expect.

We can go on with several other benefits or advantages, but the above are enough to firm up your understanding and appreciation of the many positive things and the competitive edge that e-commerce software can bring to your online business.

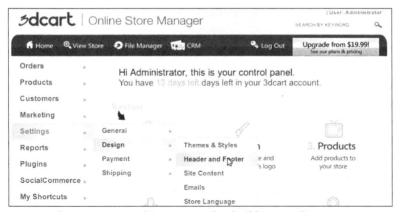

3dcart: Has everything you need to build your online store.

Key Features of E-commerce Software

To be able to realize its purpose, e-commerce software is designed with a wide range of features and functions that streamline and support the many aspects involved in online selling. Here are the common features of ecommerce software:

- Automation: The checkout process including accurate computation of pricing, taxes, shipping rates, and handling costs are automated to give customers an immediate idea of how much they'll be paying on items they select for purchase.

- Website builder: If you don't have an existing website, e-commerce software can help you build one from the ground up. It provides design templates for you to quickly create a professional-looking website and storefront based on your preferences without the need to hire commercial designers.

- Central database: You get a centralized location for easy storing, access and retrieval of product information, customer data, accounting transactions, product listings, browsing histories, and payment and shipping status.

- Search function: Sophisticated search functions make it simple for shoppers to find the items or products they're looking for. E-commerce platforms are capable of listing, categorizing, and updating new products together with descriptions, pictures, and feature lists.

- Integration: Most e-commerce solutions are able to integrate with various business apps and third-party platforms and services to allow you to handle various tasks – accounting, email marketing, order fulfillment, and payment processing – within a single system.

- Marketing tools: You can use your e-commerce software to enhance your website's marketing, promotion, and branding. You can utilize an array of tools to come up with targeted campaigns, SEO optimization strategies, and branding/image reinforcement.

- Analytics and reporting: E-commerce software can help you to analyze and identify trends and patterns that affect customer buying habits, providing you insights and stats on customer demographics, keywords, and clickstreams. You'll get to know what is working or not, and craft strategies to improve revenues.

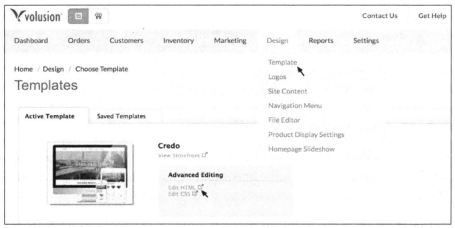

Volusion: All-in-one e-commerce software, store builder, and marketing hub.

VIRTUEMART

VirtueMart (formerly known as mambo-phpShop) is an open-source e-commerce solution designed as an extension of the Mambo or Joomla! content management systems (CMS). VirtueMart is written in PHP and requires the MySQL database environment for storage. It is best suited for low to medium level traffic web-sites.

VirtueMart began as offshoot of the stand-alone phpShop e-commerce web application. Originally dubbed mambo-phpShop it became the first substantial native e-commerce component for the Mambo CMS system. After the community forked Mambo into Joomla, the developer re-branded mambo-phpShop as VirtueMart, officially supporting the newer Joomla CMS. While current implementations may still function with Mambo CMS, and older editions of mambo-phpShop are still available to download, they are no longer actively supported.

Originally developed by Sören Eberhardt-Biermann, in September 2009 a new team began developing VirtueMart 2. The new version was released in December 2011. In October 2012, the developer team declared end of life for VirtueMart 1.1 and since then VirtueMart 2 is no longer maintaining Joomla 1.5 compatibility.

Features

VirtueMart supports an unlimited number of products and categories, with products assignable to multiple categories. Until version 3, it permitted the sale of downloadable products. That functionality is now mostly supported by separate, subscription plugins. It offers a catalog mode where the shopping cart features are turned off. VirtueMart supports multiple prices for a single product, based around shopper groups or a quantity range, and permits the use of a variety of different payment gateways.

Because VirtueMart is an open-source e-commerce solution all the application code is openly visible in PHP. This allows PHP developers to view, update or customize the operation of the shopping cart. In addition VirtueMart itself offers simplified templates (called 'fly pages' in VirtueMart) structure that allows various shopping and cart page(s) to be edited as standard HTML and CSS.

Notably new to VirtueMart 1.1.0 was the inclusion of the ability quickly to change themes for category, product, checkout and cart pages. The cart is also integrated with Rapid 3.0, which enables transaction data to be sent directly from the customer's browser to the payment gateway without passing through the merchant's systems. Virtuemart is supported by an iPhone app by iVMStore.

Usage

VirtueMart has been adopted by over 269,000 online retailers. For the week of Sep 23rd 2013, Quantcast data collated by BuiltWith Trends indicated that VirtueMart ran on 1.47% of the top 10K sites, 3.25% of the top 100K sites, and 6.02% of the top million sites.

BATAVI

Batavi is an open-source webshop under the GNU General Public License. The development of Batavi started in 2007 inspired by a preliminary osCommerce 3.0 version, a version that seemed to be never finished by the osCommerce team. In Batavi, an Object oriented design model is adopted, and on a functional level XML-EDI integration with the systems of suppliers is a lead theme, as most merchants don't run 'standalone' webshops. This distinguishes Batavi also from other webshops like PrestaShop, Zen Cart and Magento.

Batavi is developed on LAMP (software bundle), especially PHP and MySQL, and adopts a three layer model in which design objects, code and the database are strictly separated. From a designer perspective, this creates the advantage of easy manipulation of template objects, without the need of adapting code.

Key Features: 1.0 Version

- Fully flexible template system, including pages/boxes groups layout and page access limitation.

- Full content management including menus, texts, mails, pages etc.

- Robust architecture to process vast numbers of products, visitors, customers and orders.

- Customer/group specific pricing, payment or shipping modules.

- Related products for cross and upselling.

- Unlimited product segmentation to present products.

- Product price rules for pricing vast numbers of products.

- Product group price rules to make selecting products easier for pricing purposes.

- Fully automated integration with product content providers: Open icecat interface available.

- Interface for multi warehouse and multi supplier (including stock and purchase prices) support.

- Possibilities to filter certain UNSPSC during import.

- Integration possibilities for Google Analytics.

- Integration possibilities with a number of payment providers (PayPal, iDeal, MrCash).

- Advanced batch price list import and order export & status feedback facilities (e.g. interfaces to ICEimport/ICEorder).

- A big group of modules like: Product Tax Modules, Realtime modules, Order total modules, GeoIP modules, Coupons etc.

- Automatic Brand pages.

- Standard Open Catalog Interface to Open icecat XML.

DRUPAL COMMERCE

Drupal Commerce is open-source eCommerce software that augments the content management system Drupal. Within the context of a Drupal-based site, Drupal Commerce presents products for purchase; walks customers through the checkout process;

keeps track of invoices, receipts, orders, and payments; facilitates shipping and payment; and performs other functions needed by online merchants.

Drupal Commerce was created by Commerce Guys under the leadership of Ryan Szrama. It was originally born as a rearchitecture project of Ubercart, and was called "Ubercore" until January 14, 2010, when Mr. Szrama renamed it "Drupal Commerce". Version 1.0 was released on August 23, 2011.

Drupal Commerce has had steady growth since its introduction. Over 53,000 active sites use it, including U.K. postal service Royal Mail, international language school Eurocentres, McDonald's (France), and hundreds of consumer brands. The Drupal Commerce market has also supported publication of several instructional books and video courses.

Extending Drupal Commerce

Like Drupal itself, Drupal Commerce can be extended through the use of modules that add functionality and themes that define visual presentation. There are more than 300 Drupal Commerce-specific modules available for free in such categories as payment gateways, shipping service providers, and administrative and development tools.

NOPCOMMERCE

The nopCommerce is an open-source E-commerce solution based on Microsoft's ASP.NET Core framework and MS SQL Server 2012 (or higher) backend database. It provides a catalog frontend and an administration tool backend, allowing shopping cart creation. It is available under the nopCommerce Public License V3 and officially launched in October 2008 for small to medium-sized businesses.

nopCommerce development started in 2008 by Andrei Mazulnitsyn in Yaroslavl, Russia. In 2009, Nop Solutions was founded and expanded to a company of two, with offices in Yaroslavl, Russia. Later that year, Microsoft recognized nopCommerce as significant and included it with Microsoft's Web platform Installer.

The first versions introduced basic functionality such as order processing, attributes, plugins, discounts, tier pricing, news, blogs, private messages, forums, tax and shipping support. In June 2010, a new data access layer was introduced in version 1.70. Version 2.00 launched nopCommerce as an ASP.NET MVC based solution. Later in 2011 nopCommerce moved to ASP.NET MVC 4. Versions 3.00 and 3.10 were extended to include multi-store and multi-vendor features and to simplify the product logic. In versions 3.50, 3.60 and 3.70 a modern and responsive template were included. Version 3.80 was released with a brand new and responsive admin area with basic and advanced views and with the capability to run in web farms. Version 3.90 contains significant improvements in marketing and content management functionality, in performance optimization, and in the admin area UI and UX. In version 4.00 nopCommerce was moved to ASP.NET Core 2.0. Starting from version 4.20, the platform provides support of UNIX-based systems. The version release cycle is 7-8 months.

Usage

As of May 2019, a report says that 36,435 websites have used nopCommerce. The installation package was downloaded more than 2.5 million times. It is used by such brands as Volvo, Puma, Reebok, DHC skincare, Columbia, Medindia, and Speedo.

Business Model

The nopCommerce can be downloaded, installed and used free of charge. The community forum provides free support. There is an optional fee for white-labeling, premium support services, and partnership program. Until 2014, the documentation was downloaded on a paid basis and now is available free of charge.

Community

The nopCommerce has an active community of users and developers, which provides assistance to other users; contributes with code, plugins and other extensions; and helps with planning the roadmap. It has 107 solution partners in 37 countries providing custom development, graphic theme creation, and other services. As of January 2019, the stackoverflow.com has more than 1,000 questions tagged "nopCommerce". Current marketplace offers more than thousand plug-ins and themes. As of December 2015, the program had been translated to 30 languages.

On 30 October 2015, the first conference of the nopCommerce community #NopDevDays took place in Amsterdam, Netherlands, attracting more than 65 delegates from 14 countries. The nopCommerce Days was the second conference in Amsterdam in October 2016, which hosted 160 attendees from 30 countries and was a 2-day event with 19 presentations and 4 workshops. The third nopCommerce Days conference was held in November 2017 in New York, and the fourth in November 2018 in Las Vegas. In 2016 nopCommerce community started organizing webinars and meetups around the world.

PRESTASHOP

PrestaShop is a freemium, open source e-commerce solution. The software is published under the Open Software License (OSL). It is written in the PHP programming language with support for the MySQL database management system. PrestaShop is currently used by 250,000 shops worldwide and is available in 60 different languages.

PrestaShop started in 2005 as a student project within the EPITECH IT School in Paris, France. Originally named phpOpenStore, the software was first available in two languages: English and French. Three months after its launch the project was translated in thirteen languages. The company, PrestaShop SA, was founded in 2007 by Igor Schlumberger and Bruno Lévêque.

Between May 2010 and April 2012, PrestaShop grew from 17 employees to more than a hundred, with the establishment of secondary headquarters in Miami. As of April 2016, PrestaShop has over 120 employees and offices in 6 countries.

In March 2014, PrestaShop SA secured $9.3M in Series B Funding to continue its global expansion efforts.

In January 2015, the company launched PrestaShop Cloud, a free self-hosted version of its software, but at least since 2016 is no longer available.

According to technology tracking website, the market share of PrestaShop for open-source e-commerce websites is 9%. According to W3Techs, PrestaShop is used by 0.5% of all websites.

Business Model

As an open-source organization, PrestaShop is faced with the challenge of generating revenues. By leveraging the size and international scope of its open-source community, the company established two main sources of revenue:

- PrestaShop Addons, a marketplace through which merchants purchase custom addons and themes for their stores.

- Strategic partnerships with e-commerce industry leaders such as PayPal or Google.

Features

PrestaShop has more than three hundred built-in features for managing product listing, payments, shipping, manufacturers and suppliers. PrestaShop uses a web template system which allows users to customize store themes and add new features through add-on modules. The PrestaShop Addons marketplace provides a platform for third-party developers to sell themes and modules to merchants.

Themes

PrestaShop provides a basic responsive theme by default. Users can install or develop their own themes which change the display of the website without altering its content.

Modules

Add-on modules extend the software's built-in functionalities. Users may install modules directly within the software administration panel or develop their own.

MAGENTO

Magento is an ecommerce platform built on open source technology which provides online merchants with a flexible shopping cart system, as well as control over the look, content and functionality of their online store. Magento offers powerful marketing, search engine optimization, and catalog-management tools.

Magento's ability to scale allows shops with only a few products and simple needs to easily expand to tens of thousands of products and complex custom behavior without changing platforms. It offers a variety of plug-ins and themes which can easily enhance a customer's experience. There are a lot of aspects to the online store which need to be configured, and how well that is accomplished is often dependent on business acumen. When it comes to custom functionality, however, that is where more complex programming is required.

Magento is designed to be utilized as an application by someone who isn't a developer. The Magento community is extremely large and very helpful. However, at some point the average person is going to hit a wall.

There are a number of reasons why developers are called upon to adjust a Magento website. It is a very robust system even at its most basic. Once you begin to integrate with other systems, or introduce tens of thousands of products, businesses often need the assistance of experienced developers.

Experienced developers will also tell you that speed is of the essence in ecommerce. No one wants to have to wait for systems to reload when you're doing a lot of online shopping. With such a robust list of features native to the application, strains can be put on your server.

Benefits of using Magento

- Easy to install and add additional layouts and plug-ins.

- Open source technology that offers flexible, scalable ecommerce solutions.

- Effective and cost sensitive program.

- Allows for various discounts and promotions during check-out.

- Provides more than 50 payment gateways.

WOOCOMMERCE

WooCommerce is an open-source e-commerce plugin for WordPress. It is designed for small to large-sized online merchants using WordPress. Launched on September 27, 2011, the plugin quickly became popular for its simplicity to install and customize and free base product.

WooCommerce was first developed by WordPress theme developer WooThemes, who hired Mike Jolley and James Koster, developers at Jigowatt, to work on a fork of Jigoshop that became WooCommerce. In August 2014, WooCommerce powered 381,187 sites (or 17.77% of e-commerce sites online).

In November 2014, the first WooConf, a conference focusing on eCommerce using WooCommerce was held in San Francisco, California. It attracted 300 attendees.

Usage

WooCommerce is used by a number of high-traffic websites such as Small Press Expo. For the 3rd week of September 2015, Trends indicated that WooCommerce ran on 30% of e-commerce sites and millions of active installs. Ecommerce is rapidly growing worldwide and WooCommerce has over 39 million downloads as a plugin and is currently active on more than three million websites and is the most popular eCommerce platform in 2018. WooCommerce has approximately 4% of the top million HTML pages. In 2015, statistics show that the percentage of online stores that utilize WooCommerce through Wordpress.org's plugin is more than 30% of all stores. The current 2019 market share for WooCommerce is 22% of the top 1 million sites using eCommerce technologies.

Since Automattic's acquisition WooCommerce has kept gaining market share, and has now become one of the leading E-commerce platforms on the Internet.

Themes

With many Woocommerce-ready themes sold on third party websites it makes it difficult to exactly estimate how many themes can be associated with this Wordpress plugin, but here are some Woocommerce stats for the bigger theme providers.

- There are 1,135 Woocommerce themes on ThemeForest.

- The Wordpress.org theme directory has 548 WooCommerce themes.

- Mojo Themes has 240 WooCommerce themes.

Extensions

WooCommerce has attracted significant popularity because the base product, in addition to many extensions and plugins, is free and open-source. In 2018, WooCommerce has near 330 extensions and over 1,000 plugins. In addition, there are thousands of paid add-ons for fixed prices. Many Premium Themes now offer capability with Woo-Commerce as well as plugins that make a theme framework compatible.

Notable WooCommerce extensions include:

- WooCommerce Bookings: Which allows users to sell blocks of time as appointments.

- WooCommerce Memberships: which allows the user to restrict access to certain parts of their Wordpress website, and sell access to these parts of the website.

SOFTWARE AS A SERVICE

More businesses are turning to Software-as-a-Service (SaaS) apps and systems to run their operations like Office 365, Salesforce, Box, and Google Apps. Retailers can also benefit from using SaaS eCommerce platforms to better manage their own processes.

Using a SaaS eCommerce platform instead of open source or on-premise software can seem overwhelming for any size business. It feels like an even more daunting decision if you're planning on switching platforms. And since SaaS platforms are relatively new to the market, there are still a lot of questions about them and how they compare to legacy software.

SaaS is a word that's thrown around a lot lately. There are all types of SaaS platforms that fulfill different business functions. SaaS eCommerce platforms are just a small piece of the SaaS industry.

SaaS stands for Software-as-a-Service. It's a software licensing and delivery model in which software is licensed to a user and accessed via the internet. SaaS eCommerce platforms then are cloud-based systems that are accessed on any web browser.

One of the biggest advantages of SaaS platforms is that the software isn't installed on-premise or maintained by the user themselves. Instead, your eCommerce system runs on the SaaS provider's hosted servers. Your 3rd-party provider then is responsible for the security, performance, and maintenance of the application on their servers.

Typically, SaaS applications are licensed on a subscription basis. Users pay a monthly fee based on level of service and number of users. This licensing model is usually a cost-effective way for merchants to have real-time access to their eCommerce platform whenever and wherever there's an internet connection.

Popular examples of SaaS eCommerce providers are Shopify, BigCommerce, and Volusion. All of these platforms have seen significant growth in total users over the past few years, especially Shopify.

SaaS vs. Open Source vs. On-premise Platforms

When merchants are comparing eCommerce platform options, you're most likely choosing between SaaS, open source or on-premise. There are some stark differences between these types of platforms.

SaaS eCommerce platforms, are licensed to users. The 3rd-party vendor hosts and maintains the cloud servers used to run the software. Merchants access the software via an internet browser and pay a monthly subscription to use the software. They provide most of the functionality you need out-of-the-box. It's really 1-stop shop for all your webstore needs.

When comparing SaaS vs on-premise or open source eCommerce platforms like Magento, Prestashop, and WooCommerce, the difference is that you are responsible for maintaining all aspects of your software like security patches, software updates, and hosting services. For most merchants, especially SMB's, this can be expensive. You'll have to juggle a handful of vendors to take care of these areas for you and have less predictable maintenance costs. You'll exclusively work with a provider to host your webstore and take care of performance, PCI compliance and installing firewalls. Then, you'll work with a web developer or agency to work on your storefront design, security patches and software updates. This can be overwhelming to find and manage different vendors and drain resources over time. Most of the time, eCommerce business owner don't want to manage these messy technical decisions and just want to focus on growing their business.

Merchants turn to platforms like Magento because they are open source, meaning that their software code is available to anyone. Freedom make changes and edit the software code gives merchants unlimited customization and flexibility. While these platforms are usually free to download, you'll either need an IT team in house or work with a partner to use the platform effectively in the long run.

Advantages of SaaS E-commerce Platforms

There are many reasons while more merchants are turning to SaaS platforms to run their e-commerce business, especially SMBs.

Out-of-the-box Solution

SaaS eCommerce platforms are out-of-the-box solutions. Most platforms have a handful of basic shopping cart functionality built into the platform already. Merchants can take advantage of prebuilt, customizable themes, basic product information management, marketing capabilities, and other needed functionality.

Because of these features, new merchants can set up and run an online store very quickly. SaaS projects don't take several months to complete. You don't need your own IT team or extensive developer knowledge to run your business. Merchants can leverage intuitive, user-friendly interfaces.

Maintenance

The biggest advantage of SaaS eCommerce platforms is that the provider hosts and maintains the software. You don't need to search and find a hosting provider to work with. Instead, they're also responsible for uptime, performance speed, software bug fixes, software updates, and anything else of the sort. Your provider is constantly watching and monitoring the performance of your store. SaaS providers are usually known for their helpful and quick support teams.

Security and PCI Compliance

If you want to sell online, then you must be PCI compliant so you can safeguard your customers' payment information. eCommerce SaaS providers ensure that you meet PCI compliance standards. It's their responsibility to stay up to date with any patches or bug fixes that affect your security.

For many retailers, this is an important advantage. Your customers can trust you with their sensitive information. With the amount of data hacks there are today, it's more important than ever to have their trust.

Scalability

Growing retailers need their eCommerce platform to scale along with them. It should be easy to take on more customers, process more orders, and add more complex functionality when needed.

SaaS eCommerce platforms tend to be more flexible than other platforms. Additional functionality can be added with new apps. You can add new sales channels when you're ready. You can increase your bandwidth on servers to deal with increased traffic, this is especially important when running flash sales.

Also, growing your business doesn't have to mean incurring high new expenses. Your platform doesn't have to be rebuilt every time you change business processes. It can be as easy as just moving up a payment tier when adding new users or features.

Cost

Overall, SaaS eCommerce systems can be more affordable. There's minimum up-front costs to get started. You won't have crazy expenses for development work since you're not building your platform from scratch. You don't always have to work with a partner to create a complete, custom design for your webstore. With so much functionality already built into the platform, you don't have to spend as much on add-ons.

Another area where merchants save costs is maintenance. You aren't responsible for ongoing maintenance of your webstore. You don't have to pay partners to work on patches or bug fixes in the software.

Easy Integration

While your eCommerce system is the foundation of your business, it's not always the only system you use to run all your operations. Often, it's even recommended that you don't run your entire business from your eCommerce platform. After all, the software is just a shopping cart.

Whether you need integration right away or later, SaaS eCommerce platforms are usually easier to integrate with an ERP, POS, 3PL, or any other financial software. Most SaaS platforms have powerful APIs that make integration easier with predictable projects because there isn't as much customization.

Instead, merchants should be able to use any number of best systems for their ERP, POS, 3PL and eCommerce systems. Then, integrate those systems so you can sync inventory, orders, customers, items, and shipping/tracking data, thus automating your business processes.

Cloud-based, SaaS platforms often make that happen the easiest.

Disadvantages of SaaS E-commerce Platforms

While SaaS platforms have many benefits, they're not always the right platform choice for every business.

Lack of Customization

SaaS platforms leverage prebuilt templates and built in functionality. While these features make their platforms easy to use and quick to get started with, they can also limit you. In some cases, SaaS eCommerce platforms lack the ability for extreme customization.

Unlike open source, most SaaS eCommerce platforms don't give you access to the software's code. So, you cannot make changes to it. What you get, is what you get. If you need very unique functionality, then a SaaS platform might not be able to make that happen.

Handling Complexity

Advanced customization is usually needed to handle very complex business processes. You could have advanced logistic needs because you work with multiple distributors and warehouses. Selling across dozens of marketplaces, multiple eCommerce, and selling internationally also complicate your selling processes.

A simpler, out-of-the-box SaaS platform is not going to fulfill all your needs. You'll need to customize your platform and use integration to connect all your systems and processes. In this case, most merchants rely on their own custom-built platform.

Supporting B2B Needs

Whether a platform is SaaS or not, most eCommerce systems fall short for B2B sellers. While although B2B is beginning to look more like B2C, B2B requirements are different. There are requirements for things like customer-specific pricing, discounts by quantities, wholesale pricing, and different payment terms that just aren't needed for B2C sellers. Not all eCommerce systems have solutions for these requirements. Or if they do, they don't do it well.

Ideal SaaS eCommerce Platform Users

Looking at both the advantages and disadvantages of SaaS eCommerce platforms should give you a better idea if it's the right choice for your business.

VOLUSION

Volusion provides a fully cloud-based ecommerce platform.

Features

One of the reasons Volusion is so popular among store owners is the fact that it has many features built directly into the dashboard. In other words, you don't need to purchase costly add-ons through a separate app store. For example, Volusion provides everything from variant pricing to rich text product descriptions. The built-in SEO is pretty easy to understand, and the integrations with places like Amazon Marketplace and eBay are far more intuitive than Shopify and BigCommerce.

With the live and abandoned carts feature, store owners can quickly gain an overview of which clients are currently completing an order, as well as which clients have abandoned their cart. Volusion encourages you to send emails to the customers who have abandoned their carts, however unlike other platforms that offer this as an automatic process, you need to send these emails manually, and if you have a lot of customers then this can quickly become a rather time-consuming process. However, the new one-page checkout is tested and shown to decrease the number of abandoned carts in your store.

If you are away from your computer, then you can monitor your store on the go. This is thanks to their native iOS and Android apps that allow you to check incoming orders as well as keep tabs on inventory levels.

Growing your business is a big part of Volusion, seeing as how it provides simple social management along with awesome tools for selling on places like Instagram, Pinterest, and Facebook. Some of these integrations and social tools are provided in the actual platform, but some of the time you have to install a Volusion app to get the functionality. Regardless, there are plenty of solutions for you to extend your website.

One excellent feature is the option to process phone orders directly from the dashboard. In other words, if you have a contact number listed on your site, then customers can call you and place their order in person. All you need to do is open the console and enter the required information. While Shopify offers something similar with their POS solution, they don't offer processing of phone orders directly from within the admin panel.

Mobile capability is a strong suit from Volusion, from responsive templates to mobile-optimized checkout modules. This means that shoppers and store owners alike can easily navigate Volusion stores from any device.

Volusion used to have some more unique features, but it's done a great job of honing in on the ones that matter most to merchants. With that approach, you can see that the user experience has improved, and beginners are more likely to find Volusion approachable.

Some other nice built-in features include:

- A rewards program.
- Coupons.
- Newsletters.
- Affiliates.
- Gift certificates.
- Purchase orders.
- Advanced shipping.

For instance, customer reviews are now standard on all Volusion sites. There's also a Zapier integration for creating your own combinations (Zaps) with your email, or sites like Facebook and Slack.

Volusion: Ease of Use

It is simple to navigate. Volusion used to only have a few "get started" guides, but all of that has changed. Not only do you receive some awesome support videos in the dashboard, but the primary steps for building your site are highlighted in the main area. For example, you can click on buttons for choosing a design, uploading a logo and adding products.

Most other competitors such as BigCommerce and Shopify have a setup wizard; so Volusion is on-par with those now.

Furthermore, you constantly have an eye on the status of your website. Volusion offers several reports right on the dashboard. This way you can see if sales are going well and if anything needs to be changed. Other than that, you have direct access to buttons for orders, customers, inventory, marketing, design, reports and settings.

To make it easier for users, Volusion has recently launched a helpful video series that walks users through key areas of the setup for their new Volusion stores.

Version 2 of Volusion has added quite a few elements that make it easier for the user to get set up and selling online. The first benefit is the streamlined onboarding, where you're presented with a process for rapidly selecting themes, adding products, and launching your online store.

Dropshipping with Volusion

With the popularity of dropshipping, Volusion has responded to the call with a complete dropshipping integration system. The dropshipping app is completely free and lets you search for products to sell in a wide range of categories. Also, the product selection seems to be quite large, meaning that you can decide on the type of store you want to run, or make a network of shops. It lets you make changes to your site on the fly, without having to rely on only your computer. Along with enhanced image features and the ability to purchase your postage directly through Volusion, this Version 2 release is sure to be a big one for both users who craved more from the Volusion user interface, and the company itself.

References

- Geller, Tom (November 17, 2011). Create Your First Online Store with Drupal Commerce. Lynda. com. Retrieved 10 June 2014

- What-ecommerce-software, ecommerce-answers: bigcommerce.com.au, Retrieved 10 February, 2019

- Carter, Richard (June 2013). Building E-commerce Sites with Drupal Commerce Cookbook. Packt Publishing. P. 206. ISBN 9781782161226. Retrieved 10 June 2014

- E-commerce-software-analysis-features-benefits-pricing: financesonline.com, Retrieved 11 March, 2019

- "Woocommerce Stats 2018: How Many Websites Use woocommerce?". Barn2 Media. 2018-02-13. Retrieved 2018-09-15

- The-ultimate-volusion-ecommerce-review, ecommerce-reviews: ecommerce-platforms.com, Retrieved 11 March, 2019

- Saas-ecommerce-platforms: nchannel.com, Retrieved 12 April, 2019

PERMISSIONS

All chapters in this book are published with permission under the Creative Commons Attribution Share Alike License or equivalent. Every chapter published in this book has been scrutinized by our experts. Their significance has been extensively debated. The topics covered herein carry significant information for a comprehensive understanding. They may even be implemented as practical applications or may be referred to as a beginning point for further studies.

We would like to thank the editorial team for lending their expertise to make the book truly unique. They have played a crucial role in the development of this book. Without their invaluable contributions this book wouldn't have been possible. They have made vital efforts to compile up to date information on the varied aspects of this subject to make this book a valuable addition to the collection of many professionals and students.

This book was conceptualized with the vision of imparting up-to-date and integrated information in this field. To ensure the same, a matchless editorial board was set up. Every individual on the board went through rigorous rounds of assessment to prove their worth. After which they invested a large part of their time researching and compiling the most relevant data for our readers.

The editorial board has been involved in producing this book since its inception. They have spent rigorous hours researching and exploring the diverse topics which have resulted in the successful publishing of this book. They have passed on their knowledge of decades through this book. To expedite this challenging task, the publisher supported the team at every step. A small team of assistant editors was also appointed to further simplify the editing procedure and attain best results for the readers.

Apart from the editorial board, the designing team has also invested a significant amount of their time in understanding the subject and creating the most relevant covers. They scrutinized every image to scout for the most suitable representation of the subject and create an appropriate cover for the book.

The publishing team has been an ardent support to the editorial, designing and production team. Their endless efforts to recruit the best for this project, has resulted in the accomplishment of this book. They are a veteran in the field of academics and their pool of knowledge is as vast as their experience in printing. Their expertise and guidance has proved useful at every step. Their uncompromising quality standards have made this book an exceptional effort. Their encouragement from time to time has been an inspiration for everyone.

The publisher and the editorial board hope that this book will prove to be a valuable piece of knowledge for students, practitioners and scholars across the globe.

INDEX

CPSIA information can be obtained
at www.ICGtesting.com
Printed in the USA
BVHW012333250820
587325BV00003B/54

9 781641 723640